LOOKING OUT FOR ME

A Spiritual Journey from Paranoia to Acceptance

Alastair Gamble

Cherish
EDITIONS

First published in Great Britain 2023 by Cherish Editions

Cherish Editions is a trading style of Shaw Callaghan Ltd & Shaw Callaghan 23 USA, INC.

The Foundation Centre

Navigation House, 48 Millgate, Newark

Nottinghamshire NG24 4TS UK

www.triggerhub.org

British Library Cataloguing in Publication Data

A CIP catalogue record for this book is available upon request from the British Library

ISBN: 978-1-915680-59-4

This book is also available in the following eBook formats:

ePUB: 978-1-915680-60-0

Cover design by More Visual

Typeset by Lapiz Digital Services

Some names and identifying details have been changed to protect the anonymity of certain individuals.

TABLE OF CONTENTS

FOREWORD

In my early days of truth seeking at university in the early 90's, I pushed my mental capacities beyond what was healthy for me and succumbed to wilfulness in my meditation practice, which alienated me from my emotions. This sapped my life force and left me feeling like a zombie. By the end of the first term of my second year as an architecture student, the weight of my restrictive vegetarian diet, lack of sleep and intensive studying all combined to send my mind into freefall. Even though I was hospitalized, I later recovered to continue my studies and complete my first architectural degree. With this, I managed to secure employment in Glasgow for my sandwich year from '96 to '97.

After another partial psychotic and manic episode, while working at an architectural firm in Glasgow, I went on to successfully achieve my second degree in architecture in 2000. I was then fully employed in the architectural field for the next fourteen years, being stationed in several private practices, as well as at the University of Warwick as the in-house architect. I always kept my condition secret with my employers. Interestingly, they never suspected that I had a mental condition, as I was able to manage my stress levels to an appropriate degree and was always living healthily. I never displayed any symptoms that might have suggested otherwise.

My passion for spiritual matters took a hiatus from 1997 to 2003. Believing it had contributed to my mental breakdowns, I decided, for my own wellbeing, to sever all contact with Buddhism and meditation. When I resumed my spiritual practice in 2003, I trod very tentatively, never pushing my meditation, study or work too hard in an attempt to keep my mental state contained.

Since my episode in 2014, I have written and published this book, but I have also been working as a painter artist in Leamington Spa. The three main themes I work with are architecture, interiors and nature in all its guises. I have been able to exhibit at galleries in Leamington Spa and have had a solo exhibition in a coffee house and a pop-up exhibition in Buckinghamshire. I have sold many paintings and you can view a range of my work on my website: www.agtg-art.com

I appreciate the sense of autonomy and creativity that writing a book and painting give me, which an office set-up rarely did – even one designing architecture. Admittedly, to begin with, in 2014, I inherited some money, which gave me the ability to choose where to channel my energies. Since the inheritance came to an end, I have been relying on the generosity of my parents, who support me with a monthly allowance, thereby giving me the continued freedom to explore my creative options.

I have added to my vocation as an artist by joining a local charity art gallery, where I act as curator and still steward every month. A delightful equilibrium has been achieved in my life; by balancing my gallery commitments with the ability to meditate daily, being able to nurture close and deep friendships with people who share my values and aspirations, taking daily walks in the town and country, and reading current affairs, human interest stories, spiritual and meditation books, and works of fiction. Along with my passion for immersing myself in literature, I love viewing educational clips on YouTube, listening to podcasts and savouring a wide range of music. I also appreciate watching TV shows and films on streaming services.

I hope you, the reader, will be sufficiently enthralled and illuminated by the story of paranoia, mania, Buddhist teachings, hope, courage, honesty, tenderness, romance and at times humour that you are about to begin, as I was inspired by documenting this eventful period of my life.

Alastair Gamble, November 2022

To see a world in a grain of sand,
And a heaven in a wildflower –
Hold infinity in the palm of your hand,
And eternity in an hour.

– William Blake

CHAPTER 1

JEDI KNIGHT

It was Friday, 14 March 2014. I decided to get up very early and go into work before anyone turned up. My architectural office, which I had only been with for a month and a half, was situated in a large village called Knowle. I noticed as I entered the office that a lone umbrella, with what seemed to me like a particularly sharp-tipped end, was resting ominously by the office entrance door. I had never noticed this menacing looking everyday object before. Igniting sweaty palms and forehead, I had the definite belief that someone in the office was intent on seeing me dead.

Within the last week, I had been mulling over why Ben, a handsome man, had started to work at the office not long before my employment commenced there. Ben had a powerful physique and a long-standing relationship with one of the martial arts. He had recently been doing a lot of training in that field. I was sure he could do a lot of damage to someone, if he was threatened or instructed to do so. He had confided in me that he had almost killed someone when working as a bouncer in Birmingham, after that individual had said he specifically wanted a fight with him. A train of thought started to run through my head that he had been recruited by MI5 to kill me off.

This led me to ponder why the authorities saw me as such a threat. I realized that my views were a little hostile towards the Western world's over-emphasis on materialism and consumption, and how both were seen as a path of progress. This Western culture's ideology, which had now become a global way of thinking, was based primarily on greed and the delusion that real happiness and peace can be found in external objects and things, rather than internally developing the workings of the mind and the heart.

I believed that the authorities could see I was a very capable individual, who had all the nascent hallmarks of an inspiring and gifted leader. What also occurred to me was that I had released a video on YouTube, about half a year previously, in which I had made a very bold and radical statement. I had suggested that once I had transformed myself spiritually, I would then transform the world out of compassion for all beings. These ideas circled like vultures around fresh carcasses. They started acquiring a new validity and power.

Once my computer was on and ready to use, I spontaneously looked up anything to do with Superman, to provide myself with some heroic inspiration for what was becoming a burgeoning febrile imagination. With my heart thumping as I realized the enormous danger I might be in, I clicked on a trailer for the most recent Superman film. It started with stirring classical music that immediately hooked my emotions. There followed a scene with several noteworthy military officials, all assembled in a very large hall in a secretive location. They sat in a large oval seating configuration, accompanied by a multitude of video display units. They all seemed to concur on the fundamental point that Superman posed a real threat to democracy and their notion of peace in this world. According to them, his march of progress had to be curtailed or else, in their collective view, there could be an Armageddon. Then came some clips of Superman performing various heroic acts and trying to save humanity as much as he could from the evil forces around him. These were just snapshot images, but they were enough to get me sucked into this tremendous vision. I felt I was in a similar position. A sizeable portion of the population would forever regard me with suspicion and caution.

I looked at the clock: it was nearly 8:30am. I knew I had to leave as soon as possible, before meeting my boss or any of my other work colleagues that morning, otherwise my plan to abandon ship might have been scuppered. I thought I heard a car rolling up in the forecourt. My heart started to pummel faster in my ribcage. *It could, however, be the other company's employer next to our office,* I said to myself as an act of mollification. I just required a little luck to be on my side, but my nerves would not recede from their delicate state. Five minutes later, I was out the door. Luckily for me, the car in question had indeed been the one belonging to the neighbouring office.

As I strode purposefully along the high street to my car, parked at the other end of Knowle, I felt a little exhilarated yet apprehensive of this new departure opening in my life. However, a sense of liberation from the shackles of office life was slowly but gradually lifting my spirits to new heights. Experiencing a light breeze on my face, I appreciated the dappled light beneath the trees. Feeling now wonderfully alive, things appeared fresh. My nerves were beginning to find a natural equilibrium, and my heartbeat was also slowing down steadily. Fortune and luck were on my side, as I passed nobody familiar to me on the street.

On my way back home, I did not predominantly drive at a reckless speed, as I was prone to do in the previous few weeks. Every now and then, while listening to a few passionate rock tunes, I accelerated with racing driver pretensions, tempered with an awareness of other motorists and pedestrians around me.

While on my drive back home, I received a call from my father asking me how I was. In the back of my mind, I was desperately hoping that my father would not ask the question about whether I was going to work because I seriously believed that I would find it too difficult to lie. I momentarily prayed that because I had answered the call in my car, it would not raise any suspicions or concerns with him. Fortunately, the call was a practical one, and we discontinued our conversation quickly.

I then felt more empowered by the Superman trailer I had watched in the office that morning. A thought had formed that I should make an immediate trip to the centre of London, where all the significant powers in politics and culture converged. For this brief foray into the thriving metropolis, I would dress up in the most flamboyant attire that I had in my possession. About a year and a half earlier, I had bought some purple trousers at a well-known department store. I had, on several occasions afterwards, paraded around town in them. I knew they were striking to people, as purple was not a colour that men were normally comfortable wearing in public. I secretly felt that it caught the admiration of quite a few female passers-by. After making this purchase, I felt that a waistcoat would also be a good accessory. This article of clothing had been, in part, inspired by the sartorial presentation of Russell Brand, a well-known comedian turned political and spiritual activist, who I admired because of his audacity and some of the views he espoused.

I had found a wonderfully eccentric light-blue suede waistcoat in House of Fraser, a large department store in the centre of Leamington. This store was becoming my choice for any fashionable clothing. Although it was a very expensive garment, I knew I had to have it; otherwise, I would regret it for a long time. When I bought it, I was aware of how perfectly it would go with my purple trousers and a stylish white shirt.

Finally, there were the shoes. I realized that this item would either complete the visual spectacle or mar the beauty of the colourful ensemble. I found that expensive shoes from exclusive brands in my collection were very uncomfortable, as I had quite slender and flat feet. I had always appreciated the practical attributes of Clarks, one of the more traditional high-street brands. Some of the shoes in this store were becoming ever trendier in appearance. On one occasion, a couple of months before this day in March, I had visited one of these stores with the intention to buy some light-brown shoes. I spotted some sleek lightly tanned shoes with a lightweight but robust undersole. They had a wonderful quality in that, when worn with most long trousers in my possession, the laces would not be visible, but a large expanse of the front of the shoe with a rounded pointy front would be delightfully on show.

Upon arrival at my flat, I wasted no time in undressing from my somewhat boring office attire to put on my exuberant garb. I felt very safe and protected in my basement flat. Firstly, I had some kind and courteous neighbours, whom I found friendly and amenable. The road on which the flat was situated was especially quiet at night. It normally had very little passing traffic on it. The students who lived there in term time were generally not a bother to me. The station was conveniently only a five-minute walk away but was far enough that I would rarely hear the trains shuttling across the tracks. I left my flat about ten minutes after I had arrived and changed, and then I boarded the train.

As the train was pulling into Marylebone Station, I had gotten up out of my seat before any of the other passengers had done so. I felt emboldened to be setting a precedent for others to follow my lead. Once through the Underground ticket barriers, I went straight for the Bakerloo line.

Something curious happened to me while standing in the Tube. I encountered a short man dressed in a smart suit. His snappy attire looked incongruous with his unshaven face – at least, to me it did. He came over to part of the carriage where I was standing and started alternating between staring and looking away. As a few more people entered the carriage at the Baker Street stop, I overheard him say in a relatively loud voice to another gentleman in a suit who had just got on, "Someone needs to take out that cab driver. It's got to be only a matter of time." I felt that this seemingly malignant wish was directed at me, having interpreted the reference to a "cab driver" as something to do with the psychopath from the well-known film *Taxi Driver*. I thought that the short man was basing his assumption about me on what he had seen on satellite television. After an initial jab to my guts from this incident, the notion began to fester, but I also felt certain that I would not be beaten. I was sure it would be only a matter of time before I was able to conquer many of my fears and transform them into a demeanour of calmness and stillness.

Disembarking at Tottenham Court Road Tube station, I ascended the staircase leading to the busy junction of Oxford Street and Tottenham Court Road. As I arrived at the top of the stairs, I stopped for a good half-minute. I slowly surveyed all around me in a 360-degree arc. As everyone seemed to be in a hurry to get places, I tried to slow all my physical processes down to counter the general hustle and bustle. Then, I was on my way to the British Museum.

Earlier that day, while driving back from work, I had formed a plan to go to the British Museum. I wanted to go to a part of London with which I was familiar. On a few other occasions, accompanied by a couple of friends I had known at university, I had gone to the museum not only to get a flavour of the various exhibits on display, but also to appreciate the blend of both historic and contemporary architecture that the museum had for some time adapted into. There was one section that I was drawn to, and that was the Buddhist statuary.

On approaching the gates to the museum, I walked slowly and deliberately up to the monumentally sized colonnade at the museum entrance. I then wasted no time in delaying my view of the Buddhist art, within the vast and beautiful splendour of this magnificent institution. It had been a while since I had last paid a visit here. I could not remember in which part of the building the statuary was situated. Somehow, I was mysteriously drawn to the correct part of the museum, without having to study a map of the area. It was as if I was linked to the Buddhas by a gossamer thread, as if there was a magical force emanating from the room, tapping into my subconscious and delicately but assuredly pulling me in. My more sombre mood was now lifting to reveal a joy and relish.

Amongst the sculptures on view, there were some Hindu depictions of their gods, but at this juncture I had no time for the Hindu art. I focussed primarily on the statues I had set my sights on. One figure really caught my eye. There was a slender but strong quality in its physique, combined with a refinement and beauty of the Buddha's expression, which grabbed my attention most. It was the figure Avalokiteshvara – the Lord of compassion, a mythical, enlightened being.

Finding a stone seat directly opposite, I sat down and gazed lovingly at its beauty. For what seemed like ten minutes, I was rapt in the overall exquisiteness of this frozen, triumphant display, and I basked in a momentary peace. I knew that by the very action of remaining totally absorbed in this spectacle, I was causing heads to turn. I could not be sure of this, but I got an intuitive sense that this might be the reality.

After my deep reverie in and entrancement by the Buddha figure, I rose from my seat. I sauntered around the rest of the Buddhist exhibits in the space. None of the others quite seized my attention as much. I then ventured out of the ornate, high-ceilinged room to the main concourse area at the hub of the building, with its high-tech glass vaulted canopy. I knew this was a design by the celebrated star-architect, Norman Foster. At the time of its build, it was a stupendous engineering feat. I always marvelled at how some constructions managed to be built at all, with their complexity and their death-defying motionless acrobatics. These amazing edifices were all predominantly a team effort, but the public would always associate the construction or building with the lead architect only. It was, however, so much more than that one individual, but people were always prone to label and categorize. It seemed to me that life was always simpler if people and objects could be pinpointed and defined, to obviate the need to delve deep into the complexity and wonder of things and beings.

I glided across the light-buff coloured stone flooring towards the exit. I then spotted an inviting stone seating near the exit to the museum. I nestled myself between a mother with her young baby boy and a medium-sized group of young girls, speaking what sounded like Italian – undoubtedly on a school trip! From this commanding vantage point, I slowly took in the people around me. I had a niggling sense that some of the people in this vast internal space were not genuine. It seemed to me that the middle-aged man on his own about five meters to the right of me looked suspicious. He kept discreetly darting glances in my direction, but I still noticed them. A few minutes later, that individual greeted another man of a similar age, with what I felt was like a fake greeting. The smiles and what I could hear of their verbal exchange just did not seem authentic.

I then observed a couple of older, distinguished-looking gentlemen in the middle of the concourse, talking to each other. There was also something unnatural about their interaction, as they seemed intent to mill about in the same spot. Every now and then, they would shoot me furtive looks. I felt their deception to be palpable. As I sat on the slab, my body progressively tightened with fear. This was compounded by my belief that I was secretly known by so many people.

Although I had a deep, primal fear that was now gripping me, I reflected on what the Buddha had suggested in tackling that emotion. The Buddha said that one should just sit with the fear and try not to run from it. One should, however, continue with what one is currently doing – be it sitting, lying down, standing, or walking. The fear would eventually pass and be transformed into a calmness, stillness and joy. I possessed an underlying resilience in the face of this nameless dread. The Buddha's experience and wisdom provided me with a bone-deep solace.

While I scanned the concourse area, I also noticed a woman directly opposite of me, who struck me as being a highly competent type of worker. It was not so much what she was wearing – namely, a mustard-yellow shirt, untucked from her formal grey suit trousers – but her imperious look that led me to believe that she possessed superior intelligence. She was looking around the space, until she clapped eyes on me. She looked at me with a serious and concerned expression etched on her face. This woman, I was convinced, was also part of the secret service underworld.

The party of schoolgirls, who had been speaking Italian in quiet tones, eventually left, vacating their seats. This left my right side exposed. I took this as a natural cue for me to exit the museum. The fear was still very much present. My nerves were really being put to the test, but I knew I just had to be patient, and all would be well.

As I descended the grand staircase and made a slow path towards the main gates, I decided to pause yet again. I rested against the stone walls that lined the grass lawn at the front of the grounds, along the museum's main outdoor thoroughfare. I waited in this location for a short while. I was intent on taking my time to loiter. Once I felt comfortable, I went straight for a Starbucks, conveniently situated opposite the main gates of the museum.

Once I had ordered a flat white, I parked myself on a stool at one end of the countertop, by the plate glass window that overlooked the hurly-burly of traffic and people. There were hordes of beings in this part of London. It was hardly surprising, considering it was a Friday. Although terror was still pulsing through me, I was progressively feeling more together and composed. I knew I just needed to sit with it for longer, until it would eventually transform.

I realized that with all the Buddhist teachings that I had taken in over the last 21 years, the fruits of my spiritual labour were now beginning to blossom in this momentous period. I knew I was categorically following in the heroic footsteps of the Buddha, trodden some 2,500 years ago. What the Buddha ultimately achieved, I was sure, I would also realize.

I sat motionless on the barstool. I let the frenetic activity wash over my psyche. Next to me, I could hear two well-spoken and seemingly well-educated men. One looked like the boss, and the other appeared to be a junior colleague. I guessed the younger man to be in his thirties. He had a shock of ginger hair. He was trying to pitch some elaborate idea to the older gentleman. Not taking much notice of the content of their conversation, I spied, in the corner of my eye, the older gentleman swivelling his head towards me anxiously. It mildly amused me that they might also be spies, trying to get a handle on this enigmatic figure.

My gaze was also drawn to a group of girls giggling intermittently, sat at a metal table just outside from where I was parked. They were cradling their coffee cups with both hands, trying to eke out as much warmth as possible. There was a moment when I caught the eye of the blonde girl amongst the group. She was wearing a hip black leather jacket. I beamed her a warm smile. In that brief instant, my fear transformed fully into a deep stillness in what I could only describe as a blissful, expansive state of awareness. She looked away quickly with a quiver of embarrassment, but she reasserted the confident manner she'd had just moments before.

As I gazed out again, my attention was now drawn to a man and woman couple walking very slowly by. The man fascinated me. He was of a tall build, with a warm, brown complexion and grey stubble on his face. Initially estimating his age to be in his mid-forties, I then thought that he could have been a young-looking 50-something man. His attire was of a military persuasion, this being a khaki-coloured but very faded overcoat. He reminded me of a distinguished actor. A wire was dangling down from an earpiece, nestled tightly in his left ear. This suggested to me that he was someone who needed to be in continual contact with the intelligence services. The man looked directly at me. He then quickly – but naturally and effortlessly – turned his attention to the woman to the side of him. With a short, sharp jolt to my innards, this look of his immediately resurrected the fear. The man's speed had slowed right down, as did his female colleague's. They were currently inching forwards, right in my direction.

They suddenly stopped in their tracks, just a little beyond the coffee house. They angled their bodies towards the museum. His overall appearance and demeanour seemed to suggest that he was American, due to his overt self-assurance and composure. Were they working closely with the British government? He, along with others, would take any necessary preventative action against me, as I was at the centre of their vortex of paranoia.

I tilted my head back and poured the last remnants of the coffee down my gullet. The time was right to leave. Standing about a meter outside the store, I paused to check both directions. The man and his accomplice had disappeared. I did not register anything peculiar about the people hurriedly making their way past me, or the groups milling about at the entrance to the museum.

I put my hood up on my Paddington Bear-style duffel coat, which, as one of my friends had remarked, made me look like a Jedi Knight when the hood was up. This idea appealed to my sci-fi and cosmic interests and leanings. I made a point of not looking over my shoulder, but instead directed my focus straight ahead, at whatever was in my immediate field of vision. The dread was now lingering, after having seen the military man. That experience began to possess the whole of my psyche once more. I decided to play with the idea that the universe is just *flow* repeatedly, while walking slowly and mindfully back to Oxford Circus Tube station. The words that sweetly and gently resounded in my ear were *"just flow"*, which began to relax me into a more profound peace.

During my walk back to Oxford Circus Tube station, I saw some construction workers suddenly stop building. As I motioned past them, they expressed a deep curiosity in this thin, shadowy figure. I could also sense quite a few were keeping at my pace behind me. *Were any of them special agents? Could some of them be carrying weapons with silencers to discreetly put away this human challenge to their cherished ideals of power, status and wealth?* As well as the two words that I played as a continuous loop in my mind – *just flow* – I also reflected on how I had utter faith in the gods and their protection of me. They used their higher power, namely their magic, to help those beings who strive for goodness and purity.

As I joined Oxford Street from one of the narrower side streets, the sheer number of people swelled to a level beyond congested. I was conscious of how slow the walk had now become. I could hear someone behind me talking in an agitated voice on his mobile phone. Keeping my attention glued to the people in front, either going my way or passing me by, the fear was gradually transmuting again. My heart was calming down and expanding outwards. I felt as if it was accentuating the slow and deliberate nature of my physical movements, lending me an air of mystery.

Once back at Marylebone Rail station, I boarded the train. I was sitting on the aisle side of a two-seater bench, calmly pondering the earlier events of the day. An idea I'd had before began to raise its head again: I saw myself like the character Truman from the film *The Truman Show*. This felt totally plausible. Over the last day or so, it had become even more probable, due to many people's inquisitive reactions to me as they passed me on the streets, a trend I had begun to notice more and more in the weeks leading up to my London trip. Plus, I relied on my intuition, reason and keen intellect, and I used all three to deduce that this was the case.

On the journey back, the train came to a complete stop. It was announced that the train staff were busily trying to remove timber debris that had accidentally fallen on the railway lines, thus blocking the locomotive's path. This announcement seemed very strange to me. I felt that it confirmed the influence of the gods on my life's trajectory. I started to think that they were in some way softening the blow of what was awaiting me at my destination. Knowing I could not be sure about this notion that, in most people's minds, would be incredulous, it seemed to me that these branches hadn't fallen accidentally. As I sat there very still and composed, I was aware of the very quiet, hushed tones behind me, coming from a young couple in their mid-to-late twenties. I could feel their quiet yet curious observance of my movements boring into the side of me. I resisted the urge to turn around and sneak a peek. I sat in the seat not moving a muscle and felt paradoxically both energized and calm.

As we came to a halt at the Leamington station platform, I alighted with a little trepidation. This manifested as a more unsteady gait with heightened senses. *What would be awaiting me on the route back to my flat? Had the incident on my train journey in some way disrupted the secret service's original plans?* As I arrived back at my flat's outer entrance, I opened my low, black metal gate. I paused to look if anyone had been following me from the station. With a mixture of surprise and relief, I observed that no one had been trailing me.

Closing the front door, I turned the key in the lock. I took a few seconds to pause, breathe and relax. Inwardly, I reassured myself by saying, "I am now safe." I then let out an involuntary sigh.

CHAPTER 2

THE OFFICE

It was a Monday morning, several weeks before I made my abrupt exit from the office. I found it a strain to shift myself from the comforts of my warm duvet to go to work. I had eked out as much time in bed as was feasibly possible, but I was so enjoying being cocooned in its dreamy embrace.

I was a very professional employee. I quite often presented myself with what I would describe as boring attire from the waist up. This happened because of my reluctance to iron shirts. If I could get away with it, I would wear non-ironed shirts that had no deliberate creases but were, however, plainer. Not unlike others in the world, I suffered from a modicum of vanity. I would never dare parade in an office, or in a town, with a stylish cotton shirt that was un-ironed.

I would normally have respect for my colleagues, wherever I worked. I had a strong feeling of empathy with many of those I encountered. This was brought about mainly through my Buddhist practice, but also my very balanced upbringing and rounded education at Rugby School, a prestigious boarding school in the heart of Warwickshire. This was then contrasted by time subsequently spent at the University of Dundee, a down-to-earth yet successful university in Scotland.

It was a bright and cold morning in the middle of February. Only half a month ago, I had left the Estates Office at the University of Warwick to work in an architect's office again. At the university I had been more heavily involved in project management, which had become a source of general unease and discomfort. I felt there were greater demands being placed on me as project manager and as an architect, due to being put on a higher pay grade, in line with managers. The weight of responsibility did take its toll on my mental well-being. At the time, I thought I required a fresh outlook. A world that was more familiar to me – namely, one working in a dedicated architectural office.

I had a secret that I disclosed to very few people and was only willing to share with those friends who were very close to me. This linked to a couple of experiences in my early university life.

***

The first was at the start of my second academic year at university, where my mind went into meltdown. This was after several months of intense, wilful application in my Buddhist meditation, where I experienced alienation from my emotions. I gave up my bed to an additional lodger, due to reasons of unhelpful yet selfless generosity, so I was sleep deprived. This occurred in the last two weeks before my breakdown. My bed arrangements, which I had willingly volunteered, consisted of a sleeping bag on my bedroom floor. It did not help that I was also studying architecture and working late into the night to complete assignments. Lastly, I was subsisting on a restricted vegetarian diet, without much in the way of a varied range of vegetables or eating much protein. All these factors combined and caused a very serious mental breakdown. I felt the need to eliminate myself from the planet; I also experienced mania and partial psychosis, which meant not seeing things clearly or rationally

The second partial breakdown came while I was working my sandwich year – between my two degrees – in a firm called Parr Partnership, based in Glasgow. This time, before it got too serious, I had the wherewithal and insight to know that I needed help and support. Fortunately, I was living with my parents at the time. This happened to be a good safety net. Both my parents could see something was out of sorts with me. As swiftly as possible, I removed myself from the architectural firm, despite only having been there for a mere four months.

At the time of the first episode, I had been diagnosed with schizophrenia, and I was prescribed Largactil, or chlorpromazine. After a year of being on the drug, I managed to come off it slowly and gradually. After experiencing my second breakdown, I had developed the awareness to know when I needed treatment, or when the drug was not having the desired effect. Trying one type of drug after my second breakdown with no success, I was then put on a drug called Depixol, or flupentixol decanoate. This became the medication that kept me healthy and stable.

The latter course of medication consisted of an injection administered fortnightly at a local doctor's surgery. It was a small dose. I had been on a 30mg dosage up until the end of 2008. This was when I had begun to suffer a greater degree of mild paranoia, primarily brought on by greater stress at work. Agreeing with the doctor – and feeling a firm but gentle pressure from my parents – I had my dosage increased slightly. I noticed that the glue-like drug consistently had a stabilizing effect on my well-being. One of the side effects was that I felt noticeably more tired after the fourth or fifth day. After a temporary two-to-three-day lull, I would slowly start to recover my energy levels – without ever exhibiting any accompanying psychosis.

One of the overriding symptoms I noticed, when I went without the drug for a period of extended time, was an increase in my heartbeat. I also felt something was up with my medication when my sleep patterns were affected detrimentally. However, in my long period of being on this medication, I had successfully achieved two degrees, held down a series of architectural jobs, and then passed my Part 3 Architecture Diploma, which allowed me to call myself an architect. This was, by all accounts, no mean feat. My father had so often praised me for my achievements, being in awe of my commitment and dedication to work and further education at the time, despite my condition.

Depixol was the wonder drug that worked every time, to stabilize the chemical imbalance in my brain – or so the doctors led me to believe. Also, for me, it had no side effects that I was aware of, other than the soporific effects for two or three days in the fortnightly cycle. My uncle Michael, who had been on the same treatment until he passed away in 2013, joked that the drug had a reputation for being termed "dead-dicks-ol" – referring to the dip it caused in libido. (This never seemed to happen to me. Perhaps if I was not on the drug, then my sex drive would be off the scale, but who can tell if that would have been the reality, or if I was just trying to massage my own ego with this very palatable idea.)

***

It was on this Monday, when I made what seemed like a monumental effort to stir myself and rise from my warm and cosy double bed to get ready for work. I followed my usual ritual of breakfast and then ablutions. There was one addition to this routine, which would always enhance my day if I could fit it in. That was the joy of meditation. I knew that the power of the drug would not allow me to succeed in creating a daily morning meditation ritual. I really understood the benefits that it could bring me if it was kept at moderate levels – particularly for me. Above all else, I really enjoyed the quietude and spaciousness it afforded me.

As I drove to work along undulating country lanes slowly waking up to the bright morning sunlight, I skipped between Radio 2, a classical station, and a rock station. The rock station would quite often play some enjoyably, gritty and dark songs. Occasionally, I would listen to Radio 4 for more cerebral topics. Normally, it was all about the music, and what appealed to my emotions or general mood at the time. Generally, my grasshopper mind would have me hopping between stations to find the most appropriate tune or interview.

That morning I arrived at Knowle, where the Architects firm was based. I would always park a little outside of the village. I would then make a brisk walk to the offices at its heart. I was the second person to enter the firm that day. I was satisfied that, in my first two weeks, I was making a good impression with timeliness and with what I also felt was the volume of work that I was producing. This knowledge gave me a spring in my step. It made me feel happy and valued.

Unsurprisingly, Brian, the owner of the company, was the first person to have arrived that morning. He was concentrating hard on his screen when I entered the space that me, him and two others shared.

Brian's practice was the first company I had gone to for an interview, because my urge to leave Warwick had been stronger than the potential downsides that were intimated by his website and the projects they were working on. In Brian's office there was not much communication at the start of the day, other than saying "good morning" to each other. The previous Friday, Brian had set me an assignment with respect to a large factory complex in Brazil, which his company was in the process of undertaking. Unless there were any questions to be asked about it, we would both leave each other alone.

I had quite an interesting desk in the office, as it overlooked the main high street. This meant that, when people passed by, they would often look in inquisitively. Consequently, I could not resist the temptation to meet their gaze and have a direct visual encounter. At first, it was exciting to see if I got noticed, but then, slowly, over time, it became tedious. Above all, it was a distraction from work. I did have the ability, if I wanted, to zone out from the pedestrian footfall, but in my first couple of weeks, I often got carried away by the impulse to see if there was any attractive woman walking past – hopefully looking with interest in my direction. This would naturally be a way to bolster my ego.

Through my Buddhist practice I had begun to grow weary of searching for a partner or a soulmate. I had resigned myself to a life of quiet solitude and healthy friendships with people who shared my values and ideals. Good, wholesome friends, normally with members of the same sex, were what mattered to me. They were what gave me psychological and spiritual nourishment. I was also very much able to enjoy my own company. I would relish indulging in a good film at the weekend and reading the weekend papers or a good book.

The latest film with which I had been enamoured was of Italian origins and, at that time, had just come out in the cinemas. It was called *The Great Beauty* by the director Paolo Sorrentino. It was a sumptuous, dazzling film, which followed the creative life of a one-time successful writer. It was also a poignant tale of death and grief, as he had lost the woman he had had a romantic fling with in his youth. She still pulled his heart strings of connection and love. The film was, above all, a tale of the brevity of life, but also accepting the joy of simple pleasures.

Next to me in the office, I could perceive a high degree of architectural ability in Ben. He was always dressed in snappy elegance. Occasionally he would recount to me how, at the weekends, he would go to London to mix with celebrity types. Lots of women desired his cheeky sense of humour and powerful physique. He got lots of solicitations from keen female admirers. He did, however, have a steady girlfriend to whom he showed loyalty and devotion. He also had two daughters, whom he doted on, often finding it difficult not to spoil them with gifts. There were times when I looked carefully at his work and admired how he carefully suffused his drawings with detail and colour, giving them life and credibility. Often, he would gloat that a lot of people in the area came to him for the quality of his architectural submissions, which he produced for the planning stage. I could really believe the authenticity of his claim.

This morning he was quite subdued, as he had spent a lot of the previous evening burning the midnight oil on a particular commission. His computer was perpendicular to my desk. At times this could be a touch disconcerting, as I could not be sure if Ben was looking at me or at his monitor. In previous offices, this desk arrangement would have bothered me a whole lot more, but now it felt only like a minor inconvenience to which not much heed was paid.

I was particularly pleased about having experienced and come to terms with a large, open-plan office at the University of Warwick. Starting my time there, I felt very self-conscious while speaking on the phone, but gradually I had grown in confidence. In the last few years of my time at Warwick, I no longer had any qualms about speaking on the telephone to people. I had a particularly loud and commanding voice. Sometimes, I had no idea that I could be heard from the other end of the office. Even when my booming speech had been pointed out to me by a colleague who sat close by, it had not deterred me from still engaging warmly and confidently with anyone I spoke to on the phone.

I turned to Ben and asked,

"You look very tired. How late did you work 'til?"

"I think it was about 3 o'clock when I eventually headed to bed. It's interesting, but I've been working on a planning submission for a couple who are having a few issues with neighbours. You wouldn't believe it, but the neighbours had caught wind that this couple want to build an extension onto their house. They've been threatening them, saying that if they go ahead, they'll make their lives a misery," he said incredulously.

"That sounds positively wicked – in the pejorative sense, that is!"

"Another thing I couldn't quite believe is that the neighbours, who are making the threats, are not in their 30s or 40s, but they're retired pensioners, of all people!" he said, shaking his head.

"Just because they're pensioners, doesn't mean that they are going to act any more ethically than younger people. Wisdom doesn't necessarily come with age, I'm afraid."

"I guess I've always had it in my head that older people are harmless and wiser, and would never resort to violent means, due to their frailer years. How wrong I was."

"I think part of the problem with older people – not all, mind you – is that they very much get stuck in their habits and emotional tendencies, and find it much more difficult to break out of those constricting modes of behaviour. It's as though, through their lives, they've been forming deeper and deeper ruts or grooves of their habits. They become entrenched and find it very difficult to let go. When something comes up to throw off their equilibrium, they can become very reactive and aggressive because they are so trapped in their routines. Just thought I'd share that with you, as a snippet on the psychology of aging," I added, letting out an involuntary exhale.

It turned out that the environment at the Architects was a great deal more parochial than the one I had left at the university. This difference of size and diversity only seemed to confirm to me that my time at this office might be limited.

I was managing a few projects beyond the factory and offices in Brazil. I appreciated these smaller schemes as a complement to the larger, more unwieldy assignment, especially when the budget for the Brazil project was continuously being reduced due to the client's financial constraints. The client was a large, prestigious car manufacturer making inroads into the Brazilian market. It was becoming a bleaker prospect to produce the factory offices with any sort of architectural finesse, due to the continual tightening of purse strings.

While parked in front of my monitor at the office in Knowle, a slightly sinking feeling of not being happy and fulfilled in the world of architecture was looming. Over time, it had started to grate. I then thought about a speech I had given about a week previously to a fellow Buddhist friend who was embarking on a four-month-long ordination retreat in the Spanish mountains. A couple of senior order members had praised me afterwards on what I had read out to the assembled gathering, remarking on its content and the clarity of the prose. They asked if I wrote in my spare time, and had I ever thought about writing a book. I began to wonder if I could make a living out of writing. It was definitely food for thought, something I would seriously consider in the weeks and months ahead.

CHAPTER 3

WONDER WOMAN

It was a Saturday, over a week and a half later, when I noticed how my mind was slowly becoming more excitable. There had been a string of evenings where I did not get a good night's sleep. At the time I did not question my state of mind, as I had made a visit to the nurse at a doctor's surgery in Leamington, which I had recently registered with. I had placed complete trust in the nurse, as I had done with all the other nurses and doctors at previous surgeries.

I did something completely out of character compared to my normal weekend activities. After checking the inbox with my e-mails, I found a seductive thought rearing its head. It was tempting me to check my junk inbox, knowing full well that there would be messages from porn sites and links to them. Was this going to end up being a seedier evening than I had planned?

I found myself drawn into the world of pornographic webchats. I found an ostensibly reputable site where a constellation of prospective women flaunted their physical beauty. I had only one thing to go on and, of course, it was skin deep. I was particularly drawn to the Eastern European types, who had a slight air of mystery about them and penetrating, twinkling eyes.

On that Saturday evening, one woman stood out to me from the vast selection of women from all over the world. She was from Latvia. She had a fiery, sultry look and a tantalizing display of cleavage. Her eyes were bewitching. I thought, "*What have I got to lose?*" and decided to log on to her site. She was planted behind an angled computer with, again, a very flattering V-neck top. There was a colourful, contemporary painting hanging on the bold purple wall behind her. I was immediately hooked by her look and screen presence. I decided to communicate a very short message, with a degree of trepidation.

"Hello, you look good," I typed with not much hope that she would respond to me out of all the other men online who were messaging her, too.

I watched her type and then messages would appear on the screen. To begin with she was answering other men, and then after two or three, she answered me.

"Hello, Alastair! How are you on this fine Saturday evening?" which she sealed with a wink emoji. My first thought, after reading some responses to me and other men, was that she had a strong grasp of the English language. Her writing was indeed very skilled. There was a feeling of exhilaration in getting her attention. It seemed, by the fact that she was responding more quickly to my messages, that she was starting to show greater interest. It probably didn't hurt that I was extolling her patently desirable physical attributes.

I then noticed that, with the press of a red button, I could start a private web viewing. However, I let the conversation develop a little more before I decided to embark on a private, one-to-one exchange. It could potentially cost a lot of money. Slowly but surely, I was getting sucked into her fascinating world. I was thoroughly enjoying it. I had not felt this good in years. I took our conversation as flirting, as our texts were peppered with emojis and kisses, and we were both lavishing praise on each other. Although I was cognizant of the fact that she could not see me, I was nevertheless stimulated and intrigued by her compliments and our dialogue.

Beginning to feel reckless, I said to myself, *"Let's throw caution to the wind!"* I then pressed the red button for a private chat. Here it would just be me and her in a scintillating, gorgeous exchange. Normally in these private viewings, the woman would undress and bare all; however, she was determined to keep sitting behind her monitor and keep typing. I was also keen to do the same. What interested me most was to flirt with and flatter this beauty queen!

"Has anyone ever said that you look a lot like the original Wonder Woman from the 70s TV series? You could be a dead ringer for her." I messaged. I was speaking from the heart.

"I've never come across the word 'dead ringer' before. That's a new one to me. You do mean that I look identical with her. A few people have commented on my look being similar, but none have been as outright and gracious as you have been," she wrote, while smiling radiantly.

Finding no desire to halt this courtship, I gradually became more and more locked in. I proceeded to tell her about my grandfather, who I had a very close relationship with. I messaged,

"My grandfather was German and a very small part Swiss-Italian. He was a very successful doctor in the region, and he had a particularly gifted touch in healing people. This might have been partly due to the fact that his own father was an eminent GP in the area as well. My grandfather loved big German cars. In the 60s, he had a large black Mercedes, which was one of several very desirable cars in those days. He once showed me a photo of it. It looked identical to a car that a mafia boss would have driven. He was a man with fine tastes, and funnily enough he would still drive very fast on the German Autobahn, up until the last year of his life. Personally, I drive a small sporty car, and it suits my needs perfectly. Do you drive?" I was pleased that I had painted a rosy picture of my grandfather leading the high life. This would be one more story to reel in her heart.

"Yes, I do drive, but nothing fancy yet. I hope to also purchase a German-engineered car, as they're nearly always well-built and have a good and quick performance. Tell me more about your relationship with your grandfather. What was his name?"

I replied, *"His name was Theodor. He was a lovely man to get to know. He was confident but also sensitive to a wide range of people. When I used to walk with him in the streets, so many of the public knew him and acted in a friendly way towards him – normally by engaging in animated conversation. He would always stop for everyone, even if he was under pressure to get somewhere. He nearly always had time. He would exude empathy and compassion. The other two notable qualities that he possessed were a great sense of humour and a distinct charm that radiated from him."*

"He sounds amazing! What a lovely relationship you must have had. You must have a very positive view of your childhood and growing up."

"Yes, you're right there," I said, *"yet school was a little more difficult though, especially the boarding school that I was at. So, it was not all plain sailing, but is life ever like that anyway?"*

"You're right. Life is always bittersweet, but it would be nice if it always ran smoothly though," she replied wistfully.

The whole time she was live on the webcam, she played current songs. One of the songs that caught my attention had lyrics about shining bright like a diamond. It was by the artist Rihanna and was entitled "Diamonds". Mentioning that I particularly liked that song, I asked her to play a couple more times. Later that evening, I went so far as to say it was our song. Gauging her reaction to this remark – she remained expressionless – I sensed that it was more mine than hers. This did not prevent her from obediently playing my request; plus, I was paying for our conversation. I had heard the tune being played on other occasions before that evening and had been immediately captivated by its melody but listening to it with her gave it even more gravitas.

Quite often that night, I would write messages without letting any internal anxiety hinder the fluidity of my typing exchange. The rush of adrenaline in my system was contagious. As soon as I felt the message was complete, I would hit the "send" button with a flourish, exulting in the confidence I was exhibiting. I was glad that I had found someone on one of these sites who preferred a civilized yet scintillating conversation and was drop-dead gorgeous but was not willing to bare all.

What I was experiencing in myself was truly revelatory. I could not stop the conversation with the kick I was getting. Two and a half hours passed with little time for respite from tapping on the keyboard. It had reached 2am in England. On the other hand, she said she was starting to feel exhausted, as she had started her shift at 9pm Latvian time, and it was nearly over. I respected her wishes, but still felt a slight pull to just continue the conversation a little longer, eking out as much gratification from the evening as possible.

Eventually I knew I had pushed it as far as it could go but ended by suggesting she play our song to conclude the exchange. We just sat silently and motionlessly, except for the dramatic chords of the music playing. I was mesmerized by her beauty and charming personality. I wondered if, while she was reclining in her high-backed leather armchair, she was imagining what sort of man I might look like. I had tried to paint an honest, but ever-so-slightly exaggerated picture of myself, likening my jaw to that of Superman's, indicating that I was a perfect height, and that I had greyish-blue eyes. These were all appealing features, which would draw her in as much as I had been sucked into her world.

That night in bed, I found I could not sleep. I endlessly played the Rihanna song in my head with a mixture of joy, mild frustration and annoyance, the latter sentiments arising because I could not unwind properly. I felt the song was now indelibly linked to us. I skipped through the thoughts of what I had written, and the delight and thrill she and I had expressed. This feeling of euphoria was beautiful, as there was no nudity, just mutual appreciation and attraction – at least on my part. Anticipating a hefty credit card bill, I had no idea how much it would cost, but I would not normally let money get in the way of unadulterated pleasure and quality time. Being an architect, I was sure that, for one night, I could bear the cost.

The following Monday, after I had taken myself off to bed, I let temptation get the better of me. I decided to see whether the Latvian beauty was working that evening. Knowing I had to go to work the following day, I felt impelled to just communicate with her again. I thought it would just be for a short while, nothing more.

However, that night I got drawn into a two and a half-hour conversation with her. After I indulged in a slew of frivolous and jocular exchanges, I thought I would bite the bullet. I asked her, *"Would you like to come to London for the weekend. We could sample a few of the many delights the city has to offer?"*

She replied, *"That sounds like a great idea! I would be up for that. Do you have any ideas where you and I could stay?"*

"I have a few hotels in mind near the centre of London, in places like Soho and Mayfair. I would pay for your own room, and all the food and drinks. All you would need to do is pay for the flight to the Big Smoke." I was letting myself

be free and uninhibited in my gestures of generosity, even though nothing was set in stone. I felt that I wanted to pull out all the stops to make it a very memorable and romantic weekend for us both.

"Don't worry," she said, *"I would not expect you to pay for everything, but it is a very generous offer. You're a charmer you know!"*

"I try my best, and especially as I get a good vibe from you. What do you think you would wear out on your visit? Or more to the point, what sort of clothes do you like wearing?" I asked.

"It depends on where we go into town, but I would probably wear some tight-fitting jeans with a shirt that hugged my bosom, and just for you I would have quite a few of my shirt buttons undone, to get you wild with excitement. What would you wear?"

I responded, *"For the evening, I would wear some colourful trousers, a white shirt, a blue suede waistcoat, and then some appropriate shoes. Unlike you, of course, I would only undo the first couple of buttons to give a hint of my moderately hairy chest. In the daytime, I would probably wear some comfortable jeans with an understated T-shirt – no flashy logo emblazoned on it. I find that, in the clothing department, simplicity is normally my preferred option, but with a varying degree of colour, either bold, muted or a combination of both."*

To this, she replied, *"I'm also a fan of tracksuit bottoms and a jogging top, to be worn in the daytime for leisurely strolls in the city or park."* Once she had sent this message, I could feel my psyche reeling at the inappropriateness of the attire, especially on a romantic weekend in the city. I quickly changed it to the subject of hotels. I knew it was undoubtedly my class snobbery – stemming from my boarding school days – rearing its ugly, misshapen head again.

When I was speaking about my clothes, I was aware that I needed to keep the descriptions sparing, so I could keep a semblance of mystery intact. I believed, from what I had read in magazines, that a lot of women were drawn to the mysterious. Then again, I believed that this quality also appealed to men, but probably not quite as intensely as it did to women. It was probably because a lot of men smothered that faculty of wonder with more mundane interests, such as sport, cars and video games, to name a few. It was hardly surprising, given the sheer complexity that modern life had become for so many. Both men and women's minds were becoming more stressed out, sped up and compulsively active due to the bombardment of advertising, the effects of the continual presence of social media and other distractions. Most people were being brought to the surface of themselves and living lives of more and more superficiality. Most of my Buddhist friends shared an interest in the mystery, magic and wonder of people and the universe, but I believed none of them could surpass my passion in this domain.

CHAPTER 4

THE MONOLOGUE

About a week before I was to suddenly depart from the Architects
Office, I had been driving particularly fast, to the point of
displaying a high degree of recklessness. My dangerous yet skilled
driving, which I put down to quick reaction times, had been fuelled
by listening to rock music on the car radio. Some of the songs fired
my passions. I was still experiencing a degree of restlessness. On top
of all this, I was still getting very little sleep, which was affecting my
ability to concentrate at work. However, on this day I did not feel
the need to show off, or drive at an aggressive speed.

I was going to a meditation class that morning. Later, I would be
meeting a Buddhist friend, Daire, for lunch. He had been ordained
into the Triratna Buddhist Community, formerly the FWBO, with
which I was affiliated. Getting ordained was becoming a priority in
my life, as I had managed to build up a very steady spiritual practice.
About a year prior to this, I had asked my friend if he would like to
be my private preceptor, or spiritual mentor. There were hints that
he might formally accept my wish of becoming my private preceptor
very soon.

One of the thoughts bothering me while driving to Birmingham
was the belief that, after accessing the porn site, I was somehow
being watched, and my every movement was being scrutinized by
intelligence agencies. Seriously believing that this might have been
going on for a very long time, my mind started to develop wild
imaginings. One idea I came up with was that the Government

Communications Headquarters (GCHQ), which employed some of the smartest minds of our time, were trying to track down someone who they thought would be the devil on this earth by deciphering symbols and scrutinizing predictions. They had been doing this for years, even before I was born. The belief that consolidated in my mind was that the authorities were convinced that I embodied all the characteristics of what they presumed a devil would masquerade as: namely, an individual who could be charismatic and intelligent, and would feign kindness and humility. He would defiantly disbelieve in the existence of a creator God (a belief to which I, however, very much subscribed). At times, this devil could also be radical in his nature.

I thought my life might be in mortal danger, were it not for my strong faith in the gods from other world systems, who gave me special protection. This was because I was sincerely treading the path to enlightenment. These gods were just as near as they were far. Magic was their exalted form of power. They could perform miracles over distant galaxies, as some of the higher, more elevated gods had intimate, experiential access to each living being on this planet and innumerable others in different world systems. With time, I would grow to become more confident in exposed public areas because of the love and compassion of these numberless gods.

Over the previous two and a half years, I had been involved with the leading and supporting of meditation classes in Birmingham. Prior to this Saturday, I had asked Damien, one of my friends, if he could lead the meditation class that day. I did not feel emotionally stable. This was a wise move, as we were in a room called the Garden Shrine Room, which was a relatively tight space. The numbers had swelled that day to about 16. This would have been really unsettling for my state of mind if I had been leading the class. I could now sit back, relax and just listen.

Those of us on the team had a ritual we'd do an hour before the class started: We would chant refuges and precepts, and then share with the group any issues that we had.

When it came to my turn, I said tentatively, "I hate to say it, but I'm not feeling all that well today. I'm sure you can probably tell." I wavered slightly, feeling the enormity of what I was about to express to the group. I then decided to take the plunge. I began to articulate,

"I strongly believe that the British government and governments around the world want to eliminate me, due to their misguided belief that I am the devil or the anti-Christ. However hard they try, their attempts will always be thwarted by the intervention of the gods. I think that the truth is that I'm destined to become Maitreya, the future Buddha – not in this lifetime, but in hundreds of lifetimes to come."

Damien, who was leading the class, became seriously disturbed by my disclosure. He said very little in response to me. I noticed his visible agitation, while I was enunciating the words. A similar reaction from the others was not perceived by me. I pondered whether the other two were keeping their emotions in check to keep the mood as calm as possible, to hold a semblance of harmony.

Very few, if any, of my Buddhist friends – even those closest to me – shared these sentiments about the presence of gods in our human lives, I would come to realize.

I finished the class and was relieved that I did not have to teach that day. Daire was waiting in the Buddhist Centre's small but inviting reception area, as I came striding towards him from the back of the building. We warmly embraced. Without any extended delay, we left the building for a charming French restaurant in the centre of Moseley.

Daire had a slow, deliberate gait, whereas I preferred a brisker pace. I was happy to match his gentler speed. I always tried to work with people and not against them, endeavouring to meet them at their level. This allowed me to develop a degree of humility to those I met.

I had no desire to share the story of my little confession that morning in the restaurant. Instead, I suggested to him that we retreat to his residential community, and then I would spill the beans on my current views.

After polishing off lunch and then walking back to his abode, I got settled into a slightly tatty but comfortable armchair in the community's living room. I waited for my friend, who was making tea.

He entered the room and carefully placed one of the mugs on a silver coaster by my side, whilst grasping the other with his powerful right hand. He then parked himself in a seat opposite. Although I was tall, he was even taller, and he had a broad frame, which magnified his imposing stature. When he spoke, his words were thoughtfully chosen and enunciated deliberately, at a slow pace yet suffused with warmth.

"It's good that we're in a nice quiet space here, so we won't be overheard, as some of what I'm about to tell you is very personal," I opened (although at the back of my mind I had a niggling thought that I was being eavesdropped by GCHQ). I thought for the sake of this discussion, I would not qualify my opening gambit.

"Yeah, it's a nice, cosy space here. I agree with you, we were a little exposed in the restaurant, sitting behind that large party of slightly rowdy couples, who I could sense you were feeling uneasy about. So, tell me more... what's been troubling you? How are you feeling?"

Daire was a kind man who listened carefully and attentively. I was communicating some of my deeply held views, which, to lots of ears, would sound bizarre and strange due to their radical nature. These views consisted of the gods keeping me from harm, GCHQ, MI5 and the government, who were trying to employ covert ways of ending my life. After delivering a lengthy monologue and feeling that most of what was necessary had been said, I watched as he carefully deliberated. He then replied, "I can see why it was bothering you, and why you wanted to wait until we were in the privacy of our own space – here in the community." He took a short pause, collecting his thoughts, then continued, "Do you really think that the intelligence services would be interested in you? Don't you think that they'd be more concerned with catching terrorists and spying on them, than knowing what you're doing? You're not a terrorist or someone with grievances to bear, are you?"

"No, I'm definitely not!"

I had explained that the trigger had come about from my exchange with a gorgeous-looking Latvian woman. Gradually, I had pondered the significance of our communication, after which I thought that the intelligence services might be monitoring me for engaging in such a random and out-of-character act. Doing a lot of reflection in my life, I had thought for a long time that I was a particularly special individual. I had mentioned in my speech to him that the security services had a misguided belief that I was the devil or anti-Christ. Hairs on the back of my neck rose. I knew that divulging this thought was for the best – I wanted to try and deepen my friendship by being completely open and honest.

Once I had finished sharing with him some deep-seated views, I watched as he calmly took it all in. He paused before answering,

"I really don't think you need to worry yourself," he said with a soft, consoling tone. He continued, "Have you spoken to your doctor about your medication recently?"

"I really don't think I need to see my doctor about my medication," I said with a degree of restrained composure, yet feeling just the faintest hint of resentment at this suggestion. I carried on by saying, "Having said that, I do feel as if I've not been sleeping well in the last week or so. I can't explain it because the medication should've kicked in by now. It could be that having had the webcam exchange has excited my mind, yet I hadn't been sleeping well before that, either. However, it might be possible that the nurses at my new doctor's surgery might've administered the wrong drug, or instead deviously and knowingly didn't give me the correct medication."

Over the previous week, I had mulled over something I found a bit strange: When the nurse called me in to her treatment room, she already had the syringe loaded and ready to go. Why did she feel that I should not be present for the opening of the ampoule and loading up of the syringe? I could, after all, have had a friendly dialogue with her, and got to know her a little bit! The more I ruminated on that situation, the more uneasy I felt. I recalled how the nurse seemed rather distant and aloof, while also acting very seriously towards me. Later that day, when I had finished saying a warm goodbye to Daire, I thought to myself that I would still give the surgery the benefit of the doubt – for now, at least.

He ended our conversation by asking me about the webcam lady. "How much did you pay to speak to her? I'm sure you're aware that those webchats are expensive. I think you said that you'd been communicating with her for over two hours, on two separate occasions. Just be careful what you're getting yourself in to!"

I replied, "They are expensive, I know. I think I should probably refrain from continuing my exchange with her. Although, she is so gorgeous. I'm positive I've already run up a hefty bill. You're right! I should probably sever that link before it gets out of hand, but I do love our communication…"

"You don't even know if she really likes you. She's probably just seeing you as a way of making money. She can't even see what you look like!" he said with an increased volume.

I had decided earlier that week that I would spend the whole day in Birmingham both with Daire, and then with another order-member friend called Saraha. I had arranged to meet Saraha at about 4:30pm for a walk and an evening meal afterwards. So, after Daire and I said our goodbyes with a big, hearty embrace, I went off to meet Saraha.

Saraha was a particularly inspiring individual. Not only was he a very gifted teacher of Buddhism and meditation, but he was kind to others. He really worked hard on improving his mental and emotional states. Being a playful man, he liked to tease me in a loving and gentle way, which I appreciated and responded to with an equal lightness of touch. One physical characteristic of his was that he did not bother with a clean-cut look. His hair would normally be dishevelled, and he would sometimes be sporting a ragged-looking beard. When it came to dress sense, he always had an eye for colour and tones in an unfussy and uncomplicated way. I loved being in his company. One quality that united us both, which I had expressed to him on a few different occasions, was our mutual idealism and commitment to the goal of enlightenment.

I had gone for a short walk in Canon Hill Park to kill time between my two meetups. I was slowly sauntering back from the Midlands Arts Centre. I loved the beauty of the park and being around so many wise and ancient trees. Anyone with any sensitivity and empathy had to be amazed by such magnificent beings – so grounded, immovable and majestic. The sky was blue and free from clouds, except for some wispy stragglers skirting across it.

I exited the park. I was gradually approaching the zebra crossing on the way to his community, when I noticed a couple of large, expensive and angular-looking black cars with blacked-out windows, one behind the other, driving towards the crossing. I had no idea what make of car they were, even though I was quite familiar with different car types. In the past, I had tended to feel I had the right of way, so I would boldly enter the crossing. I would then raise a hand towards the driver as a mark of acknowledgement and gratitude. There was also a degree of presumption and foolhardiness involved.

However, today I felt there was something slightly sinister with these two cars. Something in me said, *"You need to wait and let them go."* Strangely enough, as I approached the crossing, I waited for a brief second and both the cars just shot straight over. The next car in line, a small and dainty vehicle, stopped to let me pass. I was particularly struck by the kind expression on the woman's face, as she smiled sweetly. Her warmth was further accentuated by the juxtaposition with the previous two shadowy vehicles. This sparked in my mind the lightly held thought that these faceless drivers had strategically planned this apparently random occurrence, seeing as I had my mobile phone on me, which had a signal that could be tracked. Of course, I could not be sure, but my inner voice was hinting that this idea might, in fact, be correct. I managed to shelve this view and calmly continued walking.

I pressed the buzzer on the door of the community, having arrived five minutes early. I wondered whether I would be greeted with Saraha's friendly face or someone else's.

There were, in total, six people who lived in this large early Victorian house, which was quite a common build-type in Moseley. They all lived in harmony, based around shared values and commitments to a relatively simple Buddhist lifestyle.

The door to the house opened very slowly. Saraha had one eyebrow raised in a mock-serious expression.

"Hello, can I help you?" he said in a very croaky voice, as if he was some wizened old man. His head was squeezed between the leaf and the jamb of the door.

"I have come to meet the legendary man called Saraha. Does he not reside here?" I responded in an equally affected accent, stifling a laugh.

"Yes, he does. That is I. I've arranged to meet a man called Alastair. Is that you, I wonder?"

It was then too much to keep up the pretence. We both dissolved into fits of giggles. After a moment inside, we went for a long walk together into Canon Hill Park and the adjoining Highbury Park.

Despite his sweet and gentle side, he was a courageous and very capable man. While we walked briskly, I felt a great sense of appreciation for his straightforwardness and bravery. I remembered on one occasion, in one of his classes, he shared a wise aphorism with the assembled group: "Bravery was feeling the fear and doing it anyway." Since I had come into Buddhism in my first year at university, I had experienced fearful situations, yet was always on the lookout for new scary challenges – predominantly in the realm of communication.

After our bracing and invigorating walk, we were walking around the centre of Moseley, trying to decide which restaurant we should go to. Before we chose where to eat, we stopped into Java Lounge, a local coffee shop.

There were few customers inside. After ordering our drinks, we sat down in the middle of the space. For some reason, I had not ventured to explain to him my alternative views during the walk, as I wanted a bit of time between my first meet-up and this one to process my thoughts. I had really appreciated being able to clear my head during our reflective movement through the two parks. Obviously, we did converse on our walk, but we stayed clear of weighty topics. Instead, we entertained ourselves with short bursts of comparative small talk.

Somehow, in the coffee shop that late afternoon, I possessed a great command of the English language. I felt a strong surge of confidence and strength. It rarely came my way, but that afternoon, it was as if

I was on fire with an eloquence and verbal dexterity. Reflecting later in the car back home, I thought that this might have resulted from my avid reading habits over the previous 24 years, and my regular teaching practice at the Buddhist Centre, which gradually helped me overcome some of my psychological demons.

While we were sipping our coffees, I began expressing my theories to him on gods, the devil and the situation for our current humanity, in more depth than I had previously articulated to anyone else. I watched how he was progressively taking in my thoughts, all very calmly and impassively.

"The first thing I want to mention to you is how the gods arise. These gods had, at one time, been humans living a very similar pattern of existence to us, with their world revolving around material wealth and consumption. However, they'd been part of the population that wanted to grow and develop spiritually by leading a more ethical life. They used meditation as a tool for transforming their minds to reach greater levels of awareness and consciousness, while also cultivating wisdom. There were also those humans who were just looking for something more meaningful in their lives than materialism and consumerism."

My emotions were completely galvanized. The gods in my story supported the ideas I was trying to define and bring clarity to. But sometimes I was unaware of how much my voice carried. As such, I was probably being overheard by most of the customers. I continued my explanation, with him murmuring from time to time to suggest that he had not stopped listening.

"Hate and negative energy had been gradually growing in their world, and there was a devil that was feeding off this gross negative and unhelpful energy. He was consequently becoming more and more powerful. He existed on an alternative plane of existence to the one humans or gods were on," I went on, not allowing him to interject.

"I want to explain to you how a devil arises in the cosmos. There've been innumerable devils in the past in numberless world systems. The story of the arising of a devil figure is not too dissimilar to the story in Milton's *Paradise Lost*. It started with a being, who had advanced himself in the spiritual world of the god realm to such a degree that he was almost on the brink of realizing supreme enlightenment. This is a truly mighty and awe-inspiring state of mind and heart. This path of continual spiritual progress and development lasted for an unfathomably long period of time, culminating in a final stage, which could only be described as a state of complete universal consciousness or, in other words, supreme enlightenment. Almost on the brink of enlightenment, he was suddenly thwarted by a huge upsurge in extreme pride that was none other than Mara – the Buddhist name for one's own spiritual devil – assailing and gripping him in feverish intensity. Everyone in the cosmos possesses a spiritual devil. He or she is always being tempted, seduced, belittled or whatever evil we could think say, or do. This Mara is always in opposition to our Buddha nature, a gentle and compassionate yet heroic and powerful force that is also a part of us. The side of us that succeeds is the one that we feed. To undertake goodness and purity takes effort and goes very much against the grain of Mara and his or her armies of psychological demons. They prefer the easy option or a lazy acceptance.

"The supremely developed being died instantly. He was then reborn in a hell realm, where he suffered great mental and physical pain. While a god, he'd developed all sorts of magical powers. One of those powers was the ability to see into his numberless previous lives. He was still in possession of these many magical abilities while he traversed through the depths of hell. Over time, he conquered his fears and physical pain. He could also see where he had originated from, and who he had been before in countless previous lives. Over time he amassed more and more hate and negative power, which, over a vast expanse of time in hell, became greater than the monumental love he had built up in the god realm.

"Once the hate became greater than the love, he transformed into a negative power and forcefield. He had the ability to extricate himself from hell, where he was residing. He then emerged on another completely unique transcendental plane. The devil then coursed through the cosmos, and finding the most suitable world system, latched onto it.

"Each of the innumerable world systems in the cosmos either have or will have their own distinct devil, and our own specific devil has been feeding off the negative energy of this world for thousands of years. In the process he has been getting ever stronger and more powerful." I was curious to see if he was registering all of this with an open mind, but I inwardly felt that it was a case of information falling on deaf ears. I nevertheless continued with expounding my deep-seated views.

"The devil is very close to descending onto this earth. This will be accompanied by a terrifying display of thunder and lightning bolts, in which he will present himself as an incandescent behemoth – a highly intelligent one at that with no regard for the sanctity of anyone's life.

"The people in this world who are in search of some higher, spiritual and more liberating goal, will be plucked from this earth by gods in their spaceships and transported to their heaven worlds. The gods will descend just before the devil strikes to whisk them away to earths like ours, but how ours was about a million or so years ago – that is beautiful, heavenly paradises.

"As you and I know, nothing is permanent in existence. Although these gods live in these heaven realms for an extremely long time, it is nonetheless limited. There are also multiple levels of bliss and happiness, corresponding to their different spiritual attainments. I think we can see distinct evidence of the gods' presence through the numerous reports of UFO sightings, where they are trying to make contact, either indirectly or directly, with humans whose minds are open to higher dimensions of consciousness. As I'm sure you're aware of, there's more and more hatred and fear manifesting on this globe. Change is now rife. I think, for some, life is too much of a struggle, and something must give.

"The beings who'll be left on this planet will be immersed in increasingly evil ways, becoming demonic in appearance, as well as strong and powerful by conquering their physical pain. Eventually, all in this hell will possess total disregard for life. They will pounce ferociously on the expression of any miniscule sign of weakness displayed by the weak. The world will escalate in temperature to unimaginable proportions, to which the demons would be impervious and concerned with just one thing – their own twisted souls.

"One quality that both the gods and the demons share is a sense of freedom. The god realm is considered a place where beings work together in harmony. They are always seeking the welfare of each other in a place of beauty, both outer and inner peace. I would term this a constructive or positive anarchy. In the realm of the demons, nothing is sacrosanct. Nothing is off-limits, with destruction being waged not only on life, but property and possessions as well. This I would term 'destructive' or 'negative anarchy'.

"There is a third category of being living in this present-day world that I need to explain to you. There are those in the world of finance, politics, business and the skilled professions, who are very intelligent and able individuals. They have surmounted variously sized obstacles throughout their careers. They are now extremely successful in their respective fields. They are all extremely competitive. They're all concerned with their own personal gain and quasi-enlightenment. The sexes polarize themselves, so the males are generally aggressive, butch men, but with a high degree of intelligence. The women have great intelligence, voluptuousness and charm that ensnares the men in their web of entrapment and control. This type or class of being will also be transported away from this earth just before the devil arrives, by what Buddhists call 'jealous gods' or 'titans'. Their environment is mostly stationed in their spaceships. They endlessly course through the depths of space, visiting and passing by all sorts of different worlds. They've always been in continual civil warfare with the heavenly gods, by forever attempting to capture the tree of abundance and magic – a wish-fulfilling tree that is only accessible to the heavenly gods.

"The jealous gods will never succeed in gaining access to this mythical tree. Their attempts will always be thwarted from time immemorial into the unceasing future.

"I thought I'd also tell you about the female counterpart to the devil. Before both of their descents from the pinnacle of spiritual evolution, they were soulmates to each other. They lived together in a blissful union. They were spiritually androgynous beings, which meant that they possessed male and female characteristics in equal measure. They were completely content and complete in themselves, without needing to be fulfilled by the other gender's distinct qualities. This goddess also lived for an eternity in utter bliss. Like the god, who would become the devil, she was seized by a substantial pride just before she was about to realize supreme enlightenment. However, the goddess lacked the substantial drive and energy that the male god possessed, and she formed into the planet Earth as we know it today. You always hear talk about Mother Earth bandied about in New Age circles. I believe that this concept is completely real and true. This planet is alive just like the trees, plants, animals and so-called inanimate objects that inhabit this globe."

I sought to round off the informal speech – and reassure him – by saying,

"We've all been so many people and types of being, right from the most powerful in conditioned existence to the most miniscule. This has always come into being due to an infinite network of conditions at play in the universe, both arising, playing itself out and ending. There was a revered Vietnamese monk, Thich Nhat Hanh, who, as I'm sure you know, had been friends with Martin Luther King Jr. He once stated that the effects of a few claps of one's hands, has an effect into faraway galaxies. A good friend also once told me that science posits the theory that each atom, with their corresponding electrons, is inextricably linked to all the other infinite number of atoms in the universe. If one atom is affected, either positively or negatively, then that'll have either a positive or negative effect on all others.

"It's so important now in the world we're living in, to try and perform as many acts as possible of kindness and love for each other and the environment, to counteract the negative energy that is steadily accumulating in this world. The essence of existence boils down to a cosmic battle between the forces of good and evil. However, goodness will ultimately always triumph over evil."

Finally, I thought I had explained enough about my views, in as much detail as I could muster. The coffee shop did not steadily increase in numbers during my monologue, so I felt comfortable with this limited audience. A few eyes had orientated themselves towards me. Although I had been aware of a few customers trickling in and out during my speech, I had been lost in a kind of heady vocal trance.

Later that year, Saraha confided in me his impressions of the afternoon and early evening. He said how I had left him very little room to speak. I had seemed totally self-absorbed to the point of there not being any dialogue. Instead, there was just a very lengthy monologue. It was not surprising after our meet-up that he appeared emotionally drained, extraordinarily withdrawn and taciturn. On the other hand, I had felt totally engaged and energized by what I thought was my eloquent discourse. There were some moments in my life when my powers of explanation and speech were inspired. On that afternoon, I loved the sound of my own voice. It was a thrill, but not one to be repeated for the sake of forming deeper connections with friends.

Before the monologue, I had mentioned the Latvian lady who I was besotted with. I explained to Saraha how I was entertaining the idea of meeting up with her in London. As we walked back to the community after our dinner, I raised the issue again, expressing my fondness for her, even though we had never met in the flesh.

"I really felt we had something special between us and that we were being drawn together," I said in an impassioned way.

"I can assure you that it won't lead to anything. You'll have spent a great deal of money communicating with her in vain. After all, she's making a business for herself and is probably preying on people like you who will fall for her," he said gently and kindly, being respectful of my infatuation.

"Okay, you know what – I'll now make a vow to you. I'll never communicate with her again. I'll also not go on that website or any like it again. I want you to be my witness." I said this with a deep and heartfelt conviction. I understood that a genuine vow in the Buddhist tradition was a serious undertaking. Once made, it should never be broken. It could potentially have grave repercussions if it were to be breached.

"I hear and witness your vow, brother. Do you think you'll be able to honour it?" he delicately enquired.

"I realize the importance and weight of a vow and I believe I have it in my power to accomplish it. I'll now rescind my involvement with her, and that you can be sure of." I had no doubt in my mind that it would be accomplished. I went home that evening, satisfied that something truly positive had come out of our meet-up – an exchange I could be quietly proud of.

CHAPTER 5

COFFEE AGENTS

One of my routines at the weekend would be to while away some of my leisure time in coffee shops in the centre of Leamington. It did not bother me that one of the coffee houses I frequented on a regular basis was Starbucks. I appreciated the friendliness of the staff that worked there. The décor was simple, uncluttered and unpretentious. It was also a light and airy space, which I liked.

It was a bright, cold Sunday morning, the day after my trip to Birmingham. Sauntering past boutique shops along Livery Street, with a somersaulting joy within my heart, I entered the relaxed setting of the coffee shop. I ordered my beloved coffee, a flat white, a choice I very rarely deviated from.

As I sat down on one of the timber chairs and planted my book, which was a meditation handbook, onto the veneered circular table in front of me, I became aware of the woman sitting opposite, neatly ensconced in a corner with a view out of the window. She was an attractive middle-aged woman with fine features and a good figure. I had seen her on quite a few occasions over the last couple of years, nearly always sitting in the same location. As she arrived often before me and others, she would quite regularly get her pick of the seats. No one would ever accompany her on her visits to the coffee house. She appeared to be a very self-contained woman, rarely expressing emotional colour – at least not to me.

She would always be reading one of the Sunday papers, which was a ritual that I began in my university days and still follow to this day.

On this day, she was wearing black jeans, a black fleece and a black beret. She would quite often wear black, a complement to her austere demeanour. She would very rarely meet my gaze. When she did, it would normally be with a stern look. I imagined that she could pass for an assassin – trained to kill – and be able to leave a scene of death and destruction without a shadow of remorse at the enormity of her crime.

I questioned why an attractive woman, with what seemed like a hearty dollop of class, would always be in this coffee house. Would she not be more suited to an independent coffee establishment? Or did she appreciate this shop for the same reasons that I did? She seemed intriguing, but someone who I was not willing to get to know.

My imaginings about this woman spiralled outwards. *"Could this woman, normally clad in black, be working for MI5? Was the only reason she came to this coffee house because of me?"* All it needed was to go off to the bathroom, and she would be able to slip some poison into my drink. She would then make her way back to her seat, calmly sit down and immerse herself in the Sunday papers again.

Licking my lips, with a satisfied look on my face, and believing that this woman posed little threat to my life, I tried to get the attention of the female staff to say my goodbyes. I always tried to be courteous and pleasant with those I met. I had developed a particular fondness for the staff. On this occasion, they were busily attending to a couple of different customers. I thought it was futile to interrupt their flow, so I left in silence. I had at times, a wonderful timbre to my voice. It would occasionally be a very harmonious pitch. But the degree to which this occurred would fluctuate greatly, depending on my moods. At my peak, it was unrivalled in quality and texture, lending itself to clear and articulate formal presentations and public speeches. In the past, my parents had mentioned the clarity and beauty of my voice. I was convinced that they were not lying, and it was indeed a genuine sentiment of theirs.

Ambling leisurely towards my next coffee shop – Caffè Nero, another well-known outlet – I started studying the architectural details of the buildings around me, something I loved to do whilst meandering through towns and cities. This included historic as well as modern architecture. Often, I would walk along the pavements, looking up to study some quirky detail in an architectural design and notice the interface of other disciplines. I had read once about how Antoni Gaudí, a famous Catalan architect, had met his demise by being run over by a tram in the centre of Barcelona. I could really empathize and understand how that would be possible, especially as an architect myself. I shuddered at the thought of living in a city with trams. On a couple of occasions, I had experienced close calls with them when visiting some German cities. Admittedly, the problem in those instances was that I did not look the right way, and I was just a little impulsive in crossing the street.

Entering Caffè Nero, I loved having the chance to interact with one member of staff, who was a bright, intelligent and good-looking blonde. She was very welcoming to me, as her eyes appeared subtly wider and more lustrous on seeing me. I wallowed in this frisson of pleasure and would normally delight in our short exchange.

"Hello, how are you?" I dutifully asked.

"Quite well, thank you. How are you?" She responded with a warm smile that I later savoured while drinking my coffee.

"Pretty good, thanks," I replied.

"What's the book you're reading?"

"Oh, it's a book on meditation," I said with cheeks reddening.

"I tried meditation recently, but I didn't think I had the patience for it, and I got very frustrated. I don't think I'm able to do it," she proffered.

"I believe everyone is able, if they put their minds to it, to be mindful, which is primarily the quality one is trying to cultivate. Even you can do it, I'm sure. Just persevere – if you wish, that is. There are no 'should' or musts in Buddhism, thankfully, only guidelines and advice to be accepted or rejected according to circumstance."

"So, now then, onto more important matters, what would you like to drink? Let me think… could it possibly be a regular latte?" she said narrowing her eyes.

"How did you guess? Can you read my mind, I wonder? I guess you'll be predicting where I'll sit as well," I ventured.

"Just there on that comfy armchair," as she extended her left arm and pointed towards the window at the front of the shop.

"In fact, yes, that's where I had in mind. You're a terrific mind reader." I thought of adding, *"Next you will be telling me what colour underwear I'm wearing,"* but I stopped short of expressing this, for fear of being too risqué, and because there were other customers waiting in the queue.

"Here we go – one perfectly formed latte." She placed the coffee on the ledge in front of me.

"You've even given it a heart shaped froth… how romantic," I enthused. Now experiencing a degree of sexual arousal, I reluctantly acknowledged the other customers who were waiting to be served and prised myself from the conversation.

As I sat down in the predicted seat, I opened my book. I began to read. I tended to sift through the text quite slowly, to try and absorb the concepts and ideas more readily, but also to experience joy on occasions when the author had beautifully phrased sentences or had used delightful metaphors and similes to explain ideas. I would also have moments where I would pause from my book, sit still, and try and reflect on the topics. At other times, I would just get distracted by the array of different personalities that entered the coffee house. As T.S. Eliot once stated, "We are distracted from distraction by distraction."

On this Sunday morning, I noticed something slightly odd about a couple who had entered the coffee shop just after me, while I was comfortably positioned in the leather armchair. Both had severe problems with their legs. They were using crutches to get around. The woman, who was elegantly attired, almost as if she had just been to church, looked over to me. She gave me a warm, deep smile. The man, who I presumed to be her partner, had a very serious look on him. He was wearing black tinted glasses. The quality that struck me most was their stoical and uncomplaining nature. They both had severe physical disabilities, but they were resilient in the face of them.

I started thinking how they might have got their serious injuries yet remaining so impassive. I had just watched a series, called *Homeland*, about CIA spies, and the thought of agents being in the field came to me. An initially tenuous view emerged that they had once been acting as special agents, located in a volatile region of the world. They had both got injured in the line of duty. They were now working for GCHQ, which seemed to me to be entirely plausible. It started gathering momentum. Had they come to spy on me, or even check me out at close quarters, to assess how much of a genuine threat I posed to the authorities?

The more I churned this circular story over in my mind, the more I realized that I would only go to that coffee store for one reason only: to talk and flirt with that blonde member of staff. Otherwise, there would be no pull or draw to enter its premises. I came to suspect that there was something up in my world. It seemed I was only starting to scratch the surface of this web of entanglement and intrigue that, up until recently, I had been blind to. I experienced a momentary dread engulfing me, but just as quickly as it had materialized did it then dissipate. I thought whether I could be a number-one target for all governments around the world. Could this be true, or was this just a symptom of my schizophrenia, and my consequently creative, yet at times, fanciful imagination.

Out of the two of them, the woman was more overt in her interest towards me. On several occasions, she continued to give me heart-warming smiles that I willingly reciprocated. What I also observed was their serenity – they did not seem to feel the pressure to indulge in idle chit-chat. Instead, they just savoured their coffees and their environment, with a few exchanges of necessary but hushed words.

I was also conscious of the book I happened to be reading, which was called *The Heart*, written by a person called Vessantara from my Buddhist movement. The book explained a universal loving-kindness meditation with a wonderful depth and clarity. It was in a resplendent red colour, which was emblazoned all over. I noticed myself thinking about whether they thought this was a book I was particularly drawn to because this colour symbolized devilish passions. This is not how I saw it at all. Instead, it was a colour that embodied love and compassion; predominantly in the Buddha Amitabha, a deep, red, ruby, and archetypal Buddha figure that existed in Buddhist teachings.

More than anyone else I knew, I responded very favourably to this loving-kindness meditation practice. I profoundly resonated with the idea of Metta or universal loving friendliness that the Buddha had encouraged in all his followers, all those years ago. A lot of people who had grown to know me picked up on this quality of friendliness and kindness, which normally manifested as warm, connecting smiles, and helpfulness to nearly all I encountered.

Once I had left Caffè Nero, with the peculiar occurrences still playing on my mind, I ventured back to my spacious flat. I was starting to feel a little emotionally unsteady with these two coffee shop incidents. I walked tentatively but deliberately through Jephson Park, the local park near the centre of town. I loved the variety of trees that were assembled in its park. I would commonly stop and sit on one of the many benches that were available. On this Sunday, there were quite a lot of people making their way very leisurely through the picturesque grounds. Quite a few of the benches had been snapped up, but I managed to spot one bench, which seemed to be basking in the sun's rays. I parked myself on it. I just quietly and mindfully absorbed the sounds, aromas and visual delights of that wonderful resource for a brief 15-minute spell.

I sometimes thought that these grounds acted like my own substitute garden. Although I had a garden at the back of my flat, I spent very little time using it, partly due to its small but elegant parameters, partly since it was directly overlooked by both neighbours' kitchen and bedrooms, and partly due to me possessing a tired, old timber table and chairs, which I had inherited from the previous owners. They were gradually falling apart. I felt all three of these conditions lent themselves to a sense of claustrophobia in my back garden. I basically preferred the resource of the wonderful open space of the park instead.

CHAPTER 6

THE ATTACHÉ CASE

The following day back at work, I started to act differently. Being aware that I was probably on show at least to the intelligence agencies, I made a point of dressing more flamboyantly. My mood was becoming more hyper and manic, with the by-product being an increased heart rate. My mind was beginning to buzz with more and more discursive discourse.

I wore a white cufflink shirt with a single-breasted navy-blue blazer that had gold buttons, and stylish, smart grey trousers from Zara. To complete the look, I had my newly purchased polished black shoes. These would make a strong click on the ground because of a metal cap on the undersole, and also due to my tendency to drop my feet first on my heels, and then the rest of the foot.

I would always park at the edge of Knowle village by a small, wooded patch. This backdrop gave me a little cause for concern because someone could lurk in there and ambush me while getting into or out of my car. I knew I just had to trust that I was being completely protected by unseen forces at play in the universe.

It was a sunny day. There was a completely clear blue sky that morning. Both the weather and my attire gave me a spring in my step. However, it was partially tainted by my restlessness and anxiety. Although it was quite a cold day, my blazer, which had a figure-hugging tight fit, kept me sufficiently warm so that I did not need an overcoat. The desired look would have been spoiled if I had to don a thick overcoat on top of what I was already wearing.

As I entered the office, Elaine, Brian's personal assistant, had already arrived. She had an ordered pile of papers in front of her that she was carefully and meticulously sifting through.

"Morning, Elaine," I uttered in a very strident, military tone that was very reminiscent of my boarding school days.

"Morning, Alastair." She was quite a pretty girl but not very self-assured. She had told me on a couple of occasions that she did not really enjoy her job. I pondered whether this was the cause of her low self-esteem. At times she could be quite nervous around me. This was nowhere more evident than when I was making coffee or tea for myself. I would be standing silently in the kitchenette, waiting for the kettle to boil in a moment of mindful contemplation, when she would appear at the entrance door. She would get a short, sharp jolt of fear – triggered by my quiet presence.

"You're in early today? What possessed you to come into the office at this hour?" I said cheerily.

"The admin was getting on top of me, so I felt I needed to grab the bull by the horns and do something about it. I wouldn't normally come in so early though. It's a little unusual for me." She replied with the side of her mouth curling upwards.

"I think that's commendable of you. It's healthy to have some dedication to your work, at least at times!" I said emphatically, with a partial grin also emerging.

Sitting at my computer, after about an hour and a half of half-hearted work, many thoughts, ideas and images scurried around in my consciousness. This time, more than usual, I observed the various passers-by filing past my window. Sporadically, I would start to smile to myself as the thought crossed my mind that I would not be beaten by the authorities. To me, it was a like a game of giant unwieldy cat and nimble mouse. At other times, I would try my best to muffle outbursts of laughter. I would then instinctively look over to my right to see if Ben was clocking my peculiar uncontrolled behaviour. He appeared not to be taking any notice, yet I was unconvinced.

One woman who walked by the office stood out for me. She was a distinguished-looking older lady wearing a cream-coloured mackintosh, all buttoned up. She carried a long, thin, black umbrella in one hand, and in the other hand, what looked to me like an attaché case. She just did not seem to fit the mould of the country folk in this large village. She appeared as if she was someone who could easily be working for Scotland Yard or MI5 because of her dress sense and purposeful physical movements. What also struck me as different was that she looked directly at me. Then as I clocked her, she hesitated – gazed in the direction she had come from, and then focussed her head on the original direction of travel. She then walked briskly on, as if to suggest she was unfamiliar with the town. This felt like a warning shot being fired across the bows.

From this brief instance, I thought that the jaws of the undercover world were slowly starting to lock onto this shadowy figure named Alastair. They would slowly try to grind me down until I was gasping my last remaining breath.

There was a back exit from the office through the car park. It was the shortest route to a local supermarket that I would sometimes use to buy my lunch. There were places for people to hide behind pillars and cars, but I seized the opportunity to face my demons. At lunchtime, I went through this back alleyway, pushing through the internal obstacles I was facing. I went to purchase flavoured rice, a packet of crisps and a chocolate bar at the supermarket. A suspicious idea popped up out of the blue, while standing before the aisle where the rice packets were located. The scurrilous thought hinted that the first packet of rice on display might have been tampered with by the intelligence services. I believed that they knew which rice I preferred, since while I had been at the office, I had always picked the vegetarian option of that particular brand. I then reached right to the back of the selection of packets. I felt emboldened in the belief that I was now managing to outsmart them.

After eating my lunch in a small, relaxed seating area in the office, I had the intention of continuing my regular routine of a briskly paced walk around the village. On this Monday, the bright and clear morning had started to cloud over; now, it looked like it would rain. I decided I would still give it a go. I started to make my clockwise route around the village, which would normally last about 20 minutes.

As I approached the end of the first leg of my customary lunchtime route, just on the edge of the high street, it started spitting light drops of rain. I took this as a sign not to continue my walk and did an immediate about-turn. I then proceeded to head straight back to the office.

As soon as I had done this sudden change of direction, I saw two quite muscular men look at me very intently while passing me on the high street. They could only have been about five meters behind me before I made this abrupt change of course. During the brief walk back to the office, a thought surfaced: These two men might have been seriously intent on doing me extreme bodily harm, but the weather had shifted at just the right time to protect me.

Having about 20 minutes to spare before my lunch break was over, I decided to access my e-mail account. Very assuredly, I sat back down at my desk, typed in my password and pressed enter.

"*Incorrect password – please try again,*" came the response back on the screen in red. I was sure I had typed the correct password. I thought I must have been mistaken. I promptly went through the same procedure again. Like before, the same response flashed up on my screen. Instantly, a surge of panic gripped my body tightly. The intelligence agencies were now playing a game with me. They were enjoying themselves. I could feel myself blushing, thinking they were all having a good, old laugh at my expense. I believed that they were now flexing their mighty muscles at this lone, vulnerable man. At other times, before this event, I thought I had control over my life. Now I pondered how I could ever be any match for such an enormous machine as the government.

Ultimately, I did not want to harm anyone, but I did deeply feel that the authorities were intent on terminating my life because they saw me as an insidious threat to their hallowed view of democracy, which I saw as being built around selfish interests and motivations.

The following day the weather was overcast. I was not put off by the seemingly stealth actions against my life and took a walk on my lunch break around town again. This time, however, I avoided my normal route through town, opting instead for a route through the park. I was wearing my duffel coat and I had the hood up. At one point, near where I started my amble through the park, I slightly hesitated, thinking I should go back the way I came and continue the remaining stretch on more secure territory. Deciding against this, I strode through the park. I defiantly said to myself that they were not going to get the better of me.

The part of the park I was walking through was a fairly open area with a few spindly immature trees, evenly spaced to define the tarmacked pedestrian route. Approaching the last stretch of park, where I had to go through a small car park, I saw two refuse collectors from the council. They were busily emptying the contents of one of the bins into a big green polythene sack. I was no stranger to the antics of MI5, feigning to be workers to make a raid or hit. I had watched the spy programmes on television, after all. Although they were not all factually correct, quite a lot were probably based on reality.

One of the operatives shifted his head from his task to meet my gaze. He wore an expression of curious bafflement. The other operative was focussed on the bin and was also carrying out more of the strenuous lifting, so was not paying me any attention. My heartbeat started to quicken to a rapid-fire procession as I got closer to them. As I passed close by, I maintained a fixed focus on the way ahead. After about four or five meters past them, I could hear them whispering to themselves. They then both laughed heartily. This prompted me to relax a little, thinking they were probably genuine workers from the council and not MI5 agents in disguise. They were probably finding hilarity in the sheer peculiarity of what had just transpired.

That week on the Thursday evening, I had gone to bed early with the intention to get up in the middle of the night and do various things, like wash the dishes, meditate and read a book. I had grown accustomed to this singular habit over the last couple of years. It seemed to work well for me. It was not a habit I indulged in regularly, but every now and then, when I felt tired, early in the evening, I would take myself off to bed. I would then sleep for about two to three hours, rise from my slumber, and then busy myself with activity for about two to three hours before going back to sleep again.

I rose from my early evening sleep, glugged down some tap water and then proceeded to brush my teeth. I set myself up for meditation in front of my shrine, which featured a beautifully detailed copper statue of the Buddha as the centrepiece and a few postcards embellished with a few different Buddhas, both archetypal and historical. I saluted the shrine with a verse common in the Buddhist tradition. I then knelt on my yoga mat, whilst kneeling with the aid of my meditation stool. I found that regular meditation just seemed to calm me down, help give perspective over my life and lessen my feelings of restlessness and agitation. If anything, it evened the pace of my heartbeat to a faint but nevertheless punching rhythm.

About halfway through the 50-minute sit that I had scheduled, I felt, what I thought, was a moment of clarity and insight. What if the intelligence services were not the only people viewing my life? Could it not be beyond the realm of possibility that governments had opened a channel on digital devices and an app for smartphones, devoted to this peculiar and curious individual? Was my every movement being filmed, whether outdoors or inside buildings? They would have the most cutting-edge and sophisticated technology at their disposal. Through very advanced thermodynamic and satellite systems, they could effectively spy on any individual in the world, showing a complete clarity of picture resolution to a wider global audience. Could this be why a girl at last New Year's celebrations on a Buddhist retreat displayed such a hostile reaction towards me? Could it also be why members of the public displayed a deep curiosity about me when I passed them on the streets? I harked back to their sense of fascination, that at the time I had not been aware of – I thought that was how they looked at everyone. I wondered how long I had been like a *Truman Show* protagonist.

After my 50-minute meditation, I was nervous and overwhelmed by the prospect of being on show to perhaps millions, if not billions of people around the world – all judging me in their own way, and thereby being either praised or criticized in equal measure. The world would scrutinize every area of my life – seeing me with all my foibles and idiosyncrasies, as well as my more flattering attributes, which in my mind would pale against the murkier aspects of my character and habitual tendencies.

I remembered my father – whose name is Kevin – relating to me what the registrar of the University of Warwick had said to him on one occasion. My father was a tall, handsome man doing part-time work in a senior role at the university. He said that the registrar had commented on me, describing me as an onion, in that whenever you thought you knew my character or habits, another layer would peel away to show a deeper and more complex side. The registrar had said to my dad that he found me to be a very complex and interesting individual. He was therefore unable to predict my behaviour. Where did this view come from? It was almost as if the registrar had first-hand experience from making this assessment. I had only spoken to the registrar on one occasion, and although it was friendly, it was nevertheless short. It could be that he had been fed information and anecdotes about me from other senior people in the university hierarchy. But I was sure that the registrar and others were viewing my life like a Big Brother-type spectacle.

I walked into my kitchen after meditating and saw the stack of dishes piled high. Immediately, I had a strong aversion to clean them all. I had left it a few days but realized if I did not wash them clean tonight, then I would have to resort to takeout. Fortunately, I very rarely let it get that bad. Whenever I left them to the breaking point, I would nearly always step up to the mark and do the necessary household duty.

But before I tackled the dishes, I was drawn to the idea of playing some music to accompany my domestic activity. Standing in front of my relatively large collection of CDs, I opted for the album *Music* by Madonna. I loved her music. She would always reinvent herself with new musical styles, like a chameleon.

While I was engaged in the washing-up, I felt a lot of energy welling up, so I let it go in a free dance expression to the sound of her voice. I paid particular attention to one of the songs, called

"Impressive Instant", with its psychedelic melody and its lyrics about the universe spinning out of control and being in a trance. This song just ignited in me an unadulterated joy. I expressed this with an exuberant display of wild and free dancing. This was enhanced by the strong belief that I was a televisual spectacle in the ongoing drama that was my life.

After the dishes were done, I went to bed. Sitting up half under the sheets, I spoke to a perceived global audience.

"Hello," I opened in a kind, jovial tone.

"I know you're all watching my every move. I guess you thought from my usual serious expression that I was a man with evil or malicious intentions. This could not be further from the truth. I've always loved humanity. I believe very much in helping those who are in need. I believe in kindness and honesty especially." I paused for a moment of deliberation, feeling a weight of emotional pressure and nerves bearing down. I then continued, "I must make a point of talking to you more often, rather than keeping my thoughts to myself and secret! I'll have to make myself more transparent in future. It's time for me to go to sleep, so goodnight to you all." I ended there. I then tried to get some shut eye.

The following day, Friday, 14 March, I left the offices in Knowle because of the perceived risk to my existence by Ben, my then-new work colleague who did martial arts and seemed to start working at the office as a direct threat to me. I then made my excursion to London to challenge my shadow side.

CHAPTER 7

THE SPY?

I held the landline phone in my hand, poised. I felt very worried about what I was about to do. Over the course of last Friday, when I had left my job to travel to the centre of London, through to the Sunday, my thoughts proliferated around the subject of spies. The idea that my every action might well be televised to many people around the world was fast becoming a larger and more powerful mental whirlwind. I had now started to believe that even my father was in on the act of deceit, as he had worked for the Ministry of Defence a few years back. He had, on one occasion, told the family that he had interviewed special agents and the Chief of Military Intelligence. I imagined it would not be too far beyond the realm of possibility to think that my father had been briefed about me. They would then have enlisted his cooperation.

I was sitting on my sofa with the landline resting in the palm of my hand, for what seemed like an age. Beads of sweat were slowly building on my brow and palms before I managed to build up the nerve to ring my parents and speak to my father. He was the first to come on the phone. Immediately, he answered in a very positive and upbeat tone, which he was prone to do.

"Hi Alastair. How are things going?"

"I want to ask you something, Dad. I want you to tell me the truth!" I uttered solemnly. Immediately, my father switched to being very concerned. The agitation in his voice was palpable. This made me feel physically uncomfortable, and not to mention a little queasy.

"Oh no! What's wrong?!? What's happened?!?"

"Are you a spy, Dad?" I came straight out with the question that was on my mind, without mincing my weighted words.

"What do you mean, a *spy*? I worked for the Ministry of Defence but…" I felt he was evading the question. I was very suspect with his answer, so I very forcefully interrupted him, by repeating the question. I then followed it up by saying, "Just answer yes or no dad!"

Again, my father tried to avoid replying categorically yes or no, which increased the worry in both of us. Finally, after I had pursued this quite rigid line of approach in a confrontational manner, my father suggested, "Alastair, I think you should come over to ours straight away and speak to us face to face about all the concerns and issues you might be having."

I sensed that he was deeply affected by this accusation. So, I agreed that speaking in person would be a good idea. As soon as I had put the phone down and had collected my thoughts, I left my flat for Crick, the village that my parents lived in. It was a medium-sized village, boasting a small supermarket, two pubs, a gastropub and a restaurant on the outskirts.

I drove carefully and considerately to my parent's home. It was a very smooth and easy ride that was made stiller by not playing the radio. However, the closer I got to my parent's residence, the more the anxiety and expectations of what would await me swelled. Might mum be in floods of tears? How would my father be towards me, after what could be conceived as a thinly veiled recrimination?

I parked the car on the gravel driveway and, out of the corner of my eye, saw my father making his way from the side of the house to the entrance gates to close them.

Dad had been a very successful person in business. He had climbed the ranks from the bottom, to become managing director and later chairman of a few companies. In terms of worldly life, he was very accomplished. This had given him an assurance that occasionally teetered on the edge of smugness. I was indeed very impressed with his achievements, especially the ability to overcome himself and his foibles with grit and determination. He was someone who was not worried about what other people thought of him. He was his own man. This heroic streak ran through me as well, which I had particularly nurtured once I had left school.

He opened with a trivial but relatively comforting question, but which ominously masked the more serious and weighty conversation to come.

"How was your journey over here?"

"Good, thanks," I replied with a bitter and nauseous feeling squirming in my gut.

"Let's go in and speak to Mum as well and raise your concerns. By the way, Alastair, I've been shaking quite violently with what you've said. It has moved me to the core. You must realize that both me and Mum love you very dearly. We only have your best interests at heart. We only want you to succeed in life."

I hugged and kissed my mother, who was sitting in the study area where they habitually watched television. I sat down at one end of the room, in a low-lying tanned leather armchair, while my mother was seated on the opposite side of the room. My father, who had been trailing behind me, now nestled into his favourite high-backed upholstered armchair, in which he would often park himself in to watch television and read the papers.

Before anything was uttered, I had a profound sense that we had a much larger audience than ourselves to this ensuing conversation and discussion.

"How are you, Alastair? We were really concerned about you when you called, but we're glad that you decided to come and see us, and not wilfully and dogmatically stay in Leamington." My mother, Marie-Louise, eased in the question and statement tactfully, and with a maternal sensitivity.

"I really haven't been sleeping well for the past two to three weeks. I suspect that the nurse at my new surgery in Leamington has either willingly or, out of sheer incompetence, not given me the correct medication," I proffered.

"I knew it was a bad idea for you to change surgeries, especially as you were changing jobs. There was a lot of upheaval in your life," she said with muted anguish.

"What's done is done, and we can't change the past, but perhaps you might be right, as it seems so out of character for you not to be well. Hasn't it been almost two months that you've been with this new surgery?" Dad enquired.

"I think it's been about six weeks. If I'm getting my medication, I should be healthy and sleeping well, but it hasn't been happening."

I felt a deep reassurance from and safety with my parents. This feeling of comfort and ease was amplified by the warm ambient lighting in the room, and the temperature being at an optimum. It made me feel very much loved and supported by my parents in their homely environment. I had always appreciated what a loving and stable family I had grown up in. I really did feel that, at least, my mother had always had my best interests at heart, by steadfastly trying to encourage and nurture my talents, but not in a pushy, overly domineering way.

"One of the things the nurse at the new surgery did strangely was having the syringe fully loaded and prepared before I entered her treatment room. There wasn't much in the way of dialogue. She didn't seem to be particularly interested in me as a person."

"Kevin, what do you think? That doesn't sound genuine. It does appear to be a little suspect with the practice's procedures. Have you seen the doctor who is meant to be referred to you yet?"

My mother was a beautiful woman. She had had exquisite eyes in her heyday, but they had slightly lost their lustre with the inevitable ageing and passing of years. I noticed this particularly when, a few years back, I saw a photo of her that was taken after she had got married to dad. I was particularly drawn to the utter beauty of her eyes. Her skin also had a very healthy glow to it. She was an extremely strong-willed woman, who ruled the Gamble household with an iron fist, but she had a soft, gooey core inside the shell of her defiant exterior. This was probably down to her Germanic origins. She was a considerate woman to her family and friends, and I was aware of her compassionate side when I would watch her respond to people's suffering on the TV. Quite often she would be moved to tears.

"No, I haven't, and that is also something very odd about the practice's state of affairs," I replied.

"And also irresponsible for that surgery not to demand it, considering they were bound to have realized that you've been on medication for a long period of time, and considering you'd filled out a registration form when you joined," my mum noted.

"Alastair, on the phone you were suggesting, from the sounds of it, as if you thought I was a spy, working for the government to keep tabs on you. What makes you think that I would ever do that to my own son?" He tried to say it calmly, but his voice belied the undercurrent of anguish that came with this question.

"Well Dad, you did work for the MoD. You did say you'd interviewed the Chief of Military Intelligence in an underground bunker at Whitehall. You then mentioned how you had spies in the secure room who you were interrogating or asking questions to, obviously related to your area of national security. It didn't seem to me like too much of a stretch of the imagination to think that they had roped you into their world of subterfuge and espionage. I really don't think that mum in any way has a clue about your involvement. She is completely innocent."

"You're right, Alastair, I did interview those people as you mentioned, but I was never interested in what went on in the world of MI5 or MI6. I was obviously aware of their departments. I sometimes worked in the space next to them. Quite frankly, I was just intent on doing a good job for the MoD, and nothing else," he said with what seemed to me like genuine wholeheartedness.

I paused. I suddenly felt convinced that what dad had just said was true and accurate. If he had been recruited by MI5 to spy on his own dear son, he would be inwardly torn and frustrated at his despicable deception. He had always been such a loving and dear father to me that I believed he would never be able to undertake such a massive betrayal of trust. I also reckoned, in that instant, that the secret services knew about this real tenderness that overflowed from my father towards me. They would, therefore, never ask him to carry out such a reprehensible act, which the authorities would assume he could not properly execute.

"Dad, it has just come to me that I now truly believe you're innocent. I really believe that you and Mum are genuine in this overall game of subterfuge. I do think that I'm like the character out of *The Truman Show*, with my every action being televised around the country and possibly the world. Isn't it too much of a coincidence that I've a passing resemblance to the main protagonist of that film?!?"

With strained control, my father replied, "I'm glad you now believe your parents would never do something as awful as spy on their own first-born son. We've only wanted to see you succeed in your life and be the best you can be. Anyway, what makes you so special that MI5 should want to know your whereabouts, and that you should be a continuous television spectacle to the world?"

"I believe that governments around the world have a real concern about the threat from a possible radical lone individual who could rise and dismantle this present world order. They mistakenly think that this individual is me. Having said that, I think I'll become a Buddha in future lives. I also believe I am destined for spiritual greatness in this life to come. It was prophesized by the Buddha that someone would emerge in this world. He'll be called Maitreya, and I believe that someone is me!"

"You're not going to be a Buddha. You're so unlike what a Buddha would manifest as!" Dad replied indignantly and mockingly.

"How do you know, Dad?" I collected myself before I continued. "You really do not know the qualities I've developed over my life that resemble that of the Buddha's. Before he became the Buddha, it's stated in the scriptures and biographies that he had an almost super-abundance of talents at his command. As you know, I've got many aptitudes and talents. When I read the accounts of his early life, he also had an abundance of material wealth. He was handsome, not too dissimilar to me. He was part of the warrior caste in Indian society. I too am an inheritor of a lot of material wealth in this family. It is interesting to note that our family stems from the landed gentry with our motto being *'Moriens sed invictus'* – *'Dying but unconquered'*. This implies bravery, courage and valour, like that of the warrior caste of the Buddha's time. The other name that Maitreya goes under is Ajita, which literally means 'Unconquered'. I think this synonym of Maitreya's, and its link to our family motto is more than a coincidence, don't you think?"

"Still, Alastair, you're not going to be a Buddha. There are many more people in this world who would be a candidate for that title before you!" My father said with a disparaging tone.

"I'm not going to be able to convince you both, but I believe it to be true,". I wearily stated.

My mum then suggested to me, "I really think you must change surgeries to be back here in Crick. The surgery here has always been so good to you, and you really liked the staff there."

"I agree. I'll ring the surgeries up tomorrow or sometime this coming week."

The realization sprung on me with a short, sharp kick to my innards that they did not know that I had left my job last Friday. I was adamant about not going back. I did not want to divulge this crucial piece of information for fear of the presumed backlash that would ensue, and the possible vitriol that this would engender towards me. I was, of course, dwelling in a tender and fragile state. In my mind, I was thinking that I would give it a few more days until I told them. I would then feel more comfortable to withstand their anger and anxiety, which I perceived would be the natural corollary of the bold decision I had made.

After a little more bandying about ideas and discussing the way forwards, I said to my parents that I would retire to their small sitting room. I then read one of the latest issues of *House & Garden*, an interior design magazine that my mother religiously bought every month. I loved looking at other people's homes, not because I desired to possess one or do up my own place, but just for the sheer pleasure of savouring the designs and elegance of the interiors. I really valued seeing the grandeur of some of the many homes or flats that people lived in. I also appreciated the articles that were written. I would occasionally read some of the issues from cover to cover, intensely wallowing in the overall delight of the publication. In some ways, I preferred this magazine to the multifarious architectural publications that largely focused on the architectural shell. I pondered on this for a moment. I thought that I might have been a more accomplished interior designer than architect, as I had a genuine aptitude for colours and textures. I also possessed a gift in draughtsmanship. The overall form and spaces that could be achieved seemed less interesting to me now than the quality of their interiors, and what could be achieved within a defined building shell.

CHAPTER 8

THE GIANT

The following week I arranged an appointment with my doctor
at the Leamington surgery so that I could explain matters and my
concerns. Rather than going back to the surgery at my parent's
home, I wanted to wait until I had this scheduled meeting. I was
still not getting any proper, decent sleep. My meditation was the
only way to salvage some glimmer of peace and cope with a slowly
mounting restlessness, which, at that point, was still partially
contained.

On the Wednesday morning in Leamington, I had a very strong
idea pop into my head. It emotionally hijacked me and began to
snowball with momentum. I started to consider the possibility of
going to London early that afternoon with my meditation stool, some
warm clothing and some food provisions. I would venture off into
London's Hyde Park. I would then find a majestic tree to sit under
and meditate well into the night, just as the Buddha had done before
his enlightenment all those years ago. I felt on this occasion that I was
very much following in the noble footsteps of a great spiritual warrior.
I was trying to overcome some fears in a very exposed location.
Also, it would be the middle of the night, which would add to my
intimidation.

That morning I rose from my warm, sumptuous bed. Before I had
breakfast, I did my morning ritual of meditation. In a surprise turn, I
decided to indulge myself, to give me as much strength for the ordeal
I would be facing that evening. Normally, I would have a shower

in my roll-top bath, but this time, I felt the strong desire to use the bath as it had been originally intended. I allowed hot water to pour from its thin stainless-steel spout. I then found some bath liquid to create a luxuriant foam, which magnified the level of pampering and indulgence. This felt good. I was relishing this intense satisfaction. My physical movements took on a slower and more deliberate nature.

I filled the bath as much as I could before my conscience hinted that I might now be starting to waste water. I had a strong ethical sense that had been developed over 21 years of Buddhist practice. I delighted in the warm embrace of this early morning bath. All I needed in this instance would be to have a few scented candles to light the bathroom, rather than the comparatively harsh light to which I was more accustomed.

In the afternoon I was about to set off on my momentous trip to London. I was sitting in my comfortable wickerwork armchair when my landline started ringing. Rather than thinking it might be a cold caller and not answering, something impelled me to reach for the phone to find out who was on the other end of the line.

"Hi, Ali," my sister Christina said.

"What are you doing?" she enquired with a soft and low sternness. I immediately wondered how she could possibly have known to ring me just before I was about to embark on a serious adventure – unless she was also party to the televisual display of my life. If she was not involved in this big conspiracy against me, then why did she ring when she must have known that I would probably be at the office?

"Hi Chriz, I'm okay, thanks."

"Why aren't you at work?" she asked in a tone that suggested she was trying desperately to keep herself a measured, calm and responsible presence on the other end of the line.

"Well, I've decided to give up work for a while, as I felt I wasn't safe in that office environment. I really feared for my life. I felt the only sensible thing to do was to completely remove myself from it. I would then live off my savings and the inheritance that we will be getting."

"Don't you think that it's a little foolish giving up your work like that? I also think that it's very unlikely that you were in danger of losing your life in the office. It just seems to me to be unbelievable and completely far-fetched and fanciful!" she said, bristling with worry.

While she was speaking, I hoped that she would not ask what I would be doing that evening. I could only be truthful. The disclosure would be reported straight back to my parents, which would cause loud alarm bells to go off in all their minds.

"I just think I need a break from working for the time being. My leaving the office has been the trigger for that."

"Have you taken your medication recently?"

"It's interesting you should mention that, as I was with Mum and Dad last Sunday and I told them there was something fishy about the surgery in Leamington. Mum, Dad and I think it would be better to go back to the surgery in Crick because they've always been good to me. As Dad said, 'They cared for patients rather than processed them,' which is a quality that's becoming more unusual today." I said this with hope that this would go some way to relaxing her concerns.

"Oh well. That's a good step at any rate. Would you like to come and see me today?" Inwardly, I felt the panic assault me, thinking my cover would be blown. She would then discover what could only be called my mission for the unfolding afternoon and night ahead.

"I can't come to see you today, as I'm doing other things, but some other time might be better," I replied, trying desperately to suppress the tension in my mind.

"It'd be really good to see you, though."

"Really not today, but definitely some other time, Chriz." I was now just willing the conversation to end due to my extreme awkwardness. I had a train to catch, which would be leaving in about ten minutes.

"Okay, whatever, Ali. It's your life. I can't tell you what to do or what not to do. Just take it easy, and hopefully I'll speak to you soon."

"Will do, Sis. Thanks for your concern. Speak to you soon then. Bye." And with that I hung up the phone.

I quickly grabbed the rucksack that I had earlier filled with the necessary provisions, put on my warm duffel coat, locked the flat and lightly jogged towards the train station. Nothing would prevent me from changing my course of action now. I deliberately did not take my mobile. There were two reasons for this decision. Firstly, I did not want my parents or sister to have the possibility of contacting me during a momentous night, and thereby spoiling my heroic undertaking in the blackness of Hyde Park. The other reason was that I did not want my movements to be so explicitly tracked by the intelligence services. I wanted their potential efforts in locating my whereabouts to be made that little bit harder, rather than having my coordinates given to them on a plate.

I was walking into the deep unknown: the mysterious, exhilarating yet frightening void. Nonetheless, I felt surprisingly calm about what might await me.

On the train journey there, I found myself mulling over why I had picked Hyde Park as a destination. I had been there before quite recently. I appreciated the proximity to Oxford Street, Soho, Mayfair and the Marylebone Rail station. I was convinced that I would find the ideal tree to sit under for my late-night meditation after a wander around the lush open space.

The journey to London was uneventful. Everything ran efficiently and smoothly. The carriage I was sitting in was quiet and empty. This helped in giving me space to think clearly about how to structure my evening, with a vaguely coherent plan of attack. I had decided to wear warm, practical items of clothing – nothing flashy, like my previous visit to the capital.

On this day near the end of March, it was particularly sunny and warm, which was a relief, considering I was going to be out in the open air for most of the night. After having walked very briskly from Marylebone station to Oxford Street, I continued to head straight for the interior of the park and have a good look for that elusive timber giant that was to become a haven of tranquillity.

I came across quite a few people in various locations, groups huddled together, or couples stretched out on the ground, catching some much-needed rays. I sauntered past them. I was keen to find somewhere more secluded and in a slightly denser, woodier part of the grounds.

Then, as I was walking into a more tree-covered and partially overgrown area, at least on one side of the path, I spied a tree that a young couple were under. Very little could be heard from them. They were talking quietly. They were about a good 25 meters away from where I had stopped in my tracks. Behind them was another row of trees. I noticed a very majestic oak tree, which had no one under it. It felt suddenly like a strong force was impelling me to choose this being out of all others. It was its proximity to the path that I was standing on and its grandeur and energy, which seemed to be completely in accordance with my sensibilities and intuition.

I pulled the fold-away meditation stool out of my rucksack. Laying out a warm blanket on the ground in front of me, I planted the meditation stool on top. I began to sit in a meditation posture for all who passed by to see. The tree was a good 20 meters away from the path that snaked alongside the undergrowth. As a relaxing and comforting thought, I mused that there must be many eccentric people who passed through this park all year round. I was just upholding a long-standing tradition. *"Anyway, what was such big a deal about meditating in public, in a quiet setting like this?"* I pondered. At the beginning of my meditation, I was overwhelmed with jangling nerves. My closed eyelids fluttered vigorously – albeit to my awareness. Their quivering nature did slowly subside, but an echo still lingered for the duration of my time on the stool.

I knew that I was nowhere near the development of that of Siddhartha Gautama before he became the Buddha. About 20 minutes into my sit, I could feel myself getting restless. I felt a desire to explore the city. The realization slowly crept up on me like a shadow as the sun moves: I needed to do what my heart desired, which was to venture into the thriving metropolis. I knew I had found the most appropriate tree. I could now go wandering as if I was a lone predator and find somewhere to have a meal to keep me sustained for the evening's surprise instalment. As I was aware that the nocturnal drama was fast approaching; this made me slightly less calm than I was earlier on in the train. The stark reality was steadily dawning.

Carefully re-packing all the contents of my rucksack, I made my way along the path back to Marble Arch, where a great multitude of nationalities were speaking in unarranged groups, taking in the warmth and beauty of the weather, and the city's hustle and bustle.

I spied Pret A Manger, which I knew sold vegetarian meals with ingredients that had always enlivened my taste buds. While I lingered inside the store just in front of the sandwich selection, I felt the glowing warmth of the sun beating on my back through the plate-glass window. Inwardly, I delighted in the simple pleasure of the heat and golden mellowness that had spread over me with a bear-like embrace. I appreciated the simplicity of it all, and the fact that this was amongst the turbulence and complexity of what modern life had become for many people.

As I made my way out of the store, I thought that I would eat my sandwiches just at the front of the building, among the snaking throng of shoppers, workers and holidaymakers. There were no seats. I felt emboldened just to stand to the side of the pavement and eat my meal in full view of all who walked past. I had planted myself firmly at the edge, among a constant moving stream of bodies in muted colours, interrupted by splashes of bold, vibrant colour. Only a handful were taking time out to pause near me. I set about wolfing down my supper. I thoroughly relished the exhibition I was making.

I wallowed in the gorgeous nature of this spot, not only because I had a view of the beautiful park, but also because the sun was enlivening my face and body. However, the contrast could not be starker between me, feeling still and composed, and those around, who appeared to have varying shades of anxiety and stress inscribed on their faces. I felt so happy to have ditched my last job, and to have taken the leap into the unknown. I did hope that my previous employer would not be picking up too many loose ends that I might have left. I hoped his architectural business would continue to flourish.

After polishing off my meal, I washed it down with some water. I dutifully waited for the traffic lights to change to allow the crossflow of pedestrians over the busy street. Quite often as a teenager, I would try and dodge traffic when it was the vehicles' right of way. I very rarely attempted such foolhardy behaviour while in the heart of London. I remembered back to one occasion when I was at the Oxford Circus junction heading southwards along Regent Street in my late 20s. I had walked out into the road to suddenly see a double-decker bus come to a screeching halt – within a few inches of my life. After that incident, I became much more aware that I needed to abide by the green man signals at pedestrian crossings and not take the law into my own hands.

After having parked myself on a stone slab that ran in segments by Marble Arch, I suddenly became aware of my own inner landscape. I felt very alive and present in my experience. My heart was charged with a fire and heat. This was not a confused or erratic heat, but one with a genuine, sustained force behind it. Still, I could not help but think about what was in store that night. I felt my pulse quicken fractionally more than before.

Over the last two to three weeks, the fire in me had been getting progressively stronger and more powerful in expression. I still wondered whether I was getting more muddled in my thinking. Was I breaking through to new levels of insight and awareness of the world around me? Not entirely sure, I thought that the primary symptoms of my illness were manifesting themselves, which I had never experienced in the 17 or so years that I had been on medication.

I turned my mind away from what I would say to the Leamington surgery, gradually weaning myself off a negative train of thought that could cause me to spiral. Instead, I let go of any need to be anywhere other than the present moment. I appreciated the warm, penetrating sun and the paradoxically peaceful yet frenzied melee occurring around me. My worry for now was plateauing.

CHAPTER 9

THE MEDITATION

After I had been sitting on a deck chair, freely available for anyone to use in the park, dusk was starting to set in. The tendrils of remaining light around me were steadily fading. I had decided to sit back in my original position below that magnificent oak tree, grabbing something sweet to eat that I had brought with my provisions for the evening. I stood attentive to the sights and sounds playing around me.

After a while the sky had completely turned black. It was a clear night. The moon and stars were visible from where I stood in the park. I laid out my warm blanket before me. I then donned a very thick jumper, as well as my trusted duffel coat that had remained on me most of the afternoon and early evening. Unfolding my meditation stool, I quickly established a comfortable and relaxed, yet upright and dignified posture on the knobbly ground.

Closing my eyes, I could hear sounds of boisterous laughter at the end of the path, where it split off in my direction. No sooner than I had become aware of it did it start to diminish in volume. It was then that I acknowledged that, in this part of the park, at least, I was now on my own. I was now experiencing a mixture of emotions. On the one hand, I was tense about the possible threat from a group of rowdy delinquents. On the other hand, I was delighting in a joy that would come to me in waves. After 30-or-so minutes sitting quietly and firmly on the stool, I began to grow agitated again. I said to myself kindly that I was nowhere near the development of Siddhartha

Gautama. I could excuse myself for feeling unnerved and wanting to move from my spot.

I thought I would change tack. I made a firm resolve to sit on for another ten minutes, doing the practice of mindful breathing in which I had been engaged. This practice improved the integration of one's many different selves or sub-personalities into a harmonious unified self. It also cultivated concentration.

The idea that surfaced was to venture into Mayfair and sample the atmosphere in a couple of the pubs in that quarter. I thought that it was not too late. By experiencing city life a little that evening, I would be nearer the stealthily and possibly deadly action that might confront me.

After having ordered my second soft drink at O'Neill's, I occupied myself by making overt glances in the direction of a few pretty women, not being particularly discreet. When I was distracted like this, most women I encountered would not meet my forceful gaze. It was sometimes close to being an outright stare. My sister had confided in me on a few occasions that this bold eye contact could be viewed, by a lot of women, as intimidating. I had always maintained that I was only being true to myself. I would only act out how I was naturally. In recent years, I did temper my focus by looking away every now and then. I somehow sensed that people probably saw me as different, eccentric and odd.

I left the pub. I then let myself be spontaneously guided in my choice of the next venue. I did not have any plan, but chose dark, quiet roads to test my nerve as I walked towards unknown drinking establishments. There were moments on this stroll when I started to sense what it might be like to be a fearless warrior. I felt exhilarated in the courage I was displaying. I slowed down my walk towards a bar, prosaically called Bond Street. I fancied the idea of having a swift alcoholic drink amongst those who I thought would predominantly be city highfliers. Glancing at my watch, it was coming up to 10:30pm. I was glad that it was becoming sufficiently late. After one more drink, I could head back to the park, and then resume my late-night meditation. All this evening's entertainment was a prelude to the real reason I came to London that day, but still all vital. I crossed the threshold into the invitingly lit bar and saw nearly all the seats around me taken. I did not feel intimidated by the quantity of handsome and possibly materially successful young people. As I entered the space, I paused for a few moments. I surveyed all around me, in a cursory way, the whole lively spectacle. I then proceeded to head straight for the bar, where I patiently waited my turn to be served. I ordered myself a bottle of beer. It was going to be my one and only drink that night. I would slowly savour it and allow the alcohol to relax my nerves a little.

I found a two-person table with wooden seating, located by the entrance to the bar. Casually ensconced in one of the chairs, I leant part of my back against an ornate free-standing timber partition. I felt self-assured and confident in this setting, even though I was sitting all on my own. My body language displayed this quality: partially splayed legs, open shoulders and one arm languidly hanging behind the back of the chair. I faced my body towards some of the other customers in the bar and the entrance doorway.

A good ten years ago, I would not have even contemplated going to a bar or pub on my own, let alone a smart, well-to-do bar like this one. But the last two to three years that I had been teaching at the Buddhist centre had given me a much greater measure of inner robustness. My work at the University of Warwick was also invaluable in building my confidence, as I quite frequently had to chair meetings.

I sat in my seat, feeling very integrated. I spotted a small group of 30-to-40-year-old women, engrossed in what seemed like a meaningful discussion. I wondered what they were talking about. Instead of them conversing about current affairs, or something of a more serious nature, I imagined they were probably dissecting and sharing tales of their partners' peculiar but annoying habits. They looked the types to have other halves, as they were not distracted by other men around them. They were content to be absorbed in each other's company. They seemed mature and sophisticated, a well-heeled bunch of women.

One of the blonde women did steal a look in my direction, but quickly averted her gaze when I turned my head towards her.

Registering her barely noticeable interest, I tried to pursue a subtle, visual flirtation further. She did not reciprocate with playful, wandering eyes, although, as I was getting close to sipping the last remnants of my bottle, she got up and walked past, flashing me a warm smile. I relished this moment on my journey back to the giant in the park.

Looking at my watch, I was just about ready to get into my meditation posture underneath the dark, black, impassive colossus. I observed it was now just after midnight. I had leisurely made my way back from the bar. On a few instances, I took the opportunity to gaze upwards at the wondrous cosmic display. It was not the brightest glimpse I had ever had, but it was enough to inspire my imagination and child-like wonder.

Settling down on my meditation stool and getting comfortable, I made a resolution to sit for at least 50 minutes without shifting. I thought that if I gave myself a realistic target, I would then be more likely to achieve that aim, than to proceed with the wishful and vain hope to meditate indefinitely into the night. The total reality was now thrust upon me. Nearly always in times of existential crisis, I would rise to the challenge with a grit and determination. Although there was a hint of worry, the major emotion was feeling emboldened. The open-air scenario lent this emotional strength to my situation. As I sat there with the very faint thrum of vehicles diminishing in intensity, a profound silence slowly began to descend.

There was a Zen story about an abbot who had been told that newly accomplished Samurai warriors would often test the swords they were given on homeless vagrants in certain parts of Japan. Their way of testing the swords would be to sever the vagabonds' heads. The abbot spent some time with the homeless people. He decided one night that they should make themselves scarce, while he would sit in the location where the Samurai warriors usually appeared. He was not deterred by this threat to his life. Instead, the abbot calmly sat in a meditation posture in that place. While he was positioned in that spot, a Samurai warrior nimbly and quietly came towards him. He unsheathed his sword, and then exclaimed in a loud voice, "Prepare to die!" The abbot did not flinch at all – he continued sitting like an immovable rock. The Samurai warrior was so shocked at the strength and courage of this individual that he panicked and then fled from the scene, not having the courage to carry out his threat.

Zen Buddhism was often about sharing these stories, and paradoxes, with people and monks. This specific story had lodged itself firmly in my psyche. I too felt that I could be as strong-willed as the abbot in the face of impending danger.

I wondered whether there were agents with guns, staring at me through the crosshairs from the protection of the adjacent bushes. They would be patiently waiting for their orders to fire their weapons. These mercenaries would be as silent as was necessary for me not to hear their furtive movements. I could not be sure, but with the past week's events, I would not put it past the secret service to be involved in such a malicious strategy. I still believed that they considered me to be a threat to the whole of civilization.

About 10 minutes before the end of my 50-minute sit, there was a deep stillness that had descended everywhere. I heard behind me a branch snapping as if someone had accidentally trod on it. Suddenly, a fear gripped me tightly. I now knew this was the moment of truth. I would just act like the abbot had done all those hundreds of years ago. Although, I felt fear, I continued to remain rock solid. There was no exclamation or spoken word uttered, just a resounding tranquillity in the depths of the park, and yet what I imagined was a looming menace in proximity. I was open to the possibility that it could have been a fox. Somehow, I thought that the sound of the branch snapping was more akin to a heavier weight being loaded onto the wood. It sounded like the timber breaking had a deeper resonance than if a fox had landed on it. Although I could not be sure. I waited with bated breath - still sitting like a staunchly defiant yet motionless king. The terror gradually dispelling into a refined calmness.

Looking at my watch with the help of a light, I observed that I had been sitting very still and poised for almost an hour. I could not, however, sustain a longer sit. My body was feeling the discomfort with the knobbly surface beneath.

Lifting myself slowly and gradually from my stool, I delicately unfurled my legs from my meditation posture, being careful to allow my ankles to adjust to a normal standing position. I needed to be kind to my body.

From where the sound came, I could only see complete darkness. I presumed that whoever had made the noise had secretly retreated to a more secure vantage point in a well-trained and managed operation.

Finding the path with relative ease, I followed it to where it split off, where a pool of luminosity covered my frame in a ghostly wash. I paused briefly. I deliberated on which path to take. Was I going to follow the tried-and-tested route or else go towards the more unfamiliar and somewhat alien territory in what was total blackness? I chose the former, but as I came nearer to the Marble Arch entrance, I veered off towards the other end of the park, still maintaining my alignment with the established pathway.

After walking for what seemed like a couple hundred meters, a lone, slim, dark figure shot across the path about a hundred meters in front of me. It disappeared, without there being a single iota of sound. It was almost dreamlike in its apparition. This ghostly appearance rattled me, because up until then, I had not actually seen anyone. I suspected that this singular person was one of many lurking because of my presence that night. How many more were there watching my movements?

This specific observance prompted me to flee from the confines of the grounds immediately. My breath had now become more audible and shallower, as again, the harsh light of reality was announcing itself. Changing my orientation, I headed straight for the nearest park fence. It was very ornate and refined in appearance. They were particularly high but fortunately, there was a low-standing wall below the wrought-iron posts, which I used as a ledge to give me a prop up. Being quite a tall man, and having sufficient muscle power in my arms, I managed to lift myself up to its highest level. I slotted my trainers between the arrow heads on a flat piece of wrought iron. I was positioned at the corner of the railings. I was balancing precariously at a great height.

Thinking that the best approach would be to now jump off onto the dimly lit flagstone floor below, I wavered for about a minute before taking the plunge. Just as my body lurched forwards, my right trainer got momentarily stuck between the arrow heads. This caused me to land almost squarely on my right knee, while the left foot landed directly onto the ground. A sharp and searing pain shot through my right knee and leg. I instantaneously worried if I had broken it, due to the impact. I rolled up my jeans to where the blow had occurred. I saw that blood had started oozing out of my knee. I then began to unroll my jeans. I hoped that, over a short period of time, the jeans would absorb and stem the flow of blood. Although I felt decidedly tense and worried at this juncture, a kind voice whispered that my wound would heal with time. I did not need to fuss over it. Another voice suggested I could liken myself to the mythic spy, James Bond. This was all part of the trials of my night-time adventure. It was as if I was the shadowy spy fighting a lone struggle against the system that had created me. I then had conceited notions that I really was that mythical superhero spy. I felt convinced that the agents would have attempted to have a pop at me. The streets were now deserted. I imagined the scene to be like something out of an end-of-the-world apocalypse.

While I hobbled with no destination in mind, but keeping a steady momentum going, my thoughts would intermittently gravitate towards my injury: *Would it heal?* For all the bravado of me thinking I was like the archetypal secret agent, I still felt vulnerable and slightly stupid at my fanciful imagination.

After spending about a good hour and a half – or what seemed like that length of time – aimlessly ambulating through the streets of London, I stumbled across a small park area, demarcated by some high hedgerows. I made my way to a bench within the public garden plot. Reclining on the bench, I wondered whether I could catch a few winks before resuming my meandering path through the heart of the city. I felt empathy and compassion for all the homeless people who struggled to find decent places to sleep in built-up areas. I thought how lucky I was to be able to go back to a warm flat at the end of this ordeal.

About five minutes into my rest on the bench, in an uncomfortable and awkward position, I intuitively believed that I really needed to push on. It was necessary now not to delay in finding my way back to Marylebone station. I felt very confused as to my orientation. I was not at all sure that I would be able to successfully navigate my way back. Suddenly, after having resumed my path on the streets again, with a huge stroke of luck, a taxi drove by with its light on. It came to a halt at the red traffic lights about 50m (around 150ft) ahead. Immediately, I sensed that this was my moment to flag it down. With all my reserves of energy and with a hobbling momentum, I moved as quickly as I could towards the taxi, shouting for him to stop and give me a lift.

"Hello there! Thank you so much for stopping. I'm after a lift to Marylebone station please."

"Sure! You're very lucky, as I was just about to finish my shift and head home. You're out late tonight. Been anywhere nice?" he asked.

"I've been in Hyde Park. I then decided to wander the streets." I thought that there was no point in lying to him, but I was nevertheless being a little cautious about sharing the whole truth.

As he continued to speak, I felt he was a friendly man, so I felt very safe. He was quite talkative without being excessively so. He was quite happy to keep the conversation light-hearted, without delving into the reasons for my midnight excursion. The conversation just seemed to glide by effortlessly. There was no suspicion on my part that he might be taking a circuitous route to build up a greater charge. He just seemed very honest and decent. I expressed this, just before alighting at my destination, with a generous tip.

Once I had raised my hand in gratitude, the taxi disappeared into the distance. I was then left at the entrance to the station with an eerie, otherworldly silence, yet with a profound peace in my heart. I would now bide my time by loitering in the vicinity before catching the first train back. I assumed the train journey back would be a very quiet and subdued affair.

The pain in my knee still throbbed. I felt the main part of my adventure was now over. The rest would now be comparatively plain sailing. I could now remain mindful and vigilant during the ensuing hours, feeling very awake and alert to my environment without needing to be particularly worried or fearful.

I rested my body against a metal electrical box and folded my arms. I just observed the surrounding architecture, imagining the problems and issues that the construction teams would have had to overcome to achieve the architect's vision. I admired the black wrought-iron filigree pattern of the large entrance canopy. I thought of how many hours of craftsmanship had gone into achieving these swirling, refined designs. I contemplated how many more hours of investment from all parties would have gone into these spectacular edifices compared to the time and cost parameters enforced today. In those earlier times, quality of product was the overriding concern.

After lingering against the electrical box for a good half-hour, I felt impelled to take a little walk around my immediate environment. Walking at a slow and deliberate pace, I came to the corner of the Marylebone Rail Station building. I turned into one of the side streets. I was suddenly aware of someone walking close behind me. I had not spotted him before. It did feel like an encroachment into my personal bubble. As I had done in the recent past, I fixed my attention on what was ahead of me to convey a degree of naturalness. It was as if it was a training that had been imparted to me in a school of espionage.

I had been shocked by this personal intrusion. My heart felt like it was trying to pummel its way out of my chest. My palms and brow became decidedly moist. I looked at the posters lit up in the windows to the side of me. I decided to adopt the ploy of moving in an exaggeratedly slow way to suggest to the other lone individual, "Give it your best shot, mate!" The man, who was dimly lit by the artificial light and thus unrecognizable to me, walked past just a little faster than a snail's pace. I spotted in the corner of my eye that he held what seemed like a can of some description. I presumed this was a powerful alcoholic mix. However, I could not detect any alcohol wafting in my direction, so I was open to other possibilities. I put aside the thought that he was a drunkard or homeless person, which was my initial impression on observing his can of fluid.

Still feeling a little shaken by this closeness to a stranger at that hour, I felt no real desire to then continue down the side street. It was not because I feared for my life, but just because I felt I did not have anything to prove to this unkempt individual, who languidly walked away from me and the station. I gracefully did an about-turn and headed back to the entrance.

There were streetlights lighting the entrance area. A solitary *Metro* paper was gently rustling on the ground in front of me. Bending over to pick it up, I started reading some of the columns. Although I was generally a serious-minded individual and concerned with the world's situation, I could be, at times, a sucker for the trivial – specifically, what was going on in various stars' lives. A column captivated me right away. It was about George Clooney, a suave and sophisticated actor getting married after all these years of living a bachelor's lifestyle and being adored by a massive female fan base. There was a flattering photo of him. I thought he appeared devilishly handsome in the photos, although I felt there was a certain vulnerability to him that he was keen to conceal from the public's watchful eyes. I felt he had a charm that was not altogether sincere, but I sympathized with him, thinking that that was the *modus operandi* of so many famous people around the globe. The moods and attitudes they displayed in public never quite matched their character in their private moments. To get a truly all-round authentic person in the public arena was a rarity.

Checking my watch, it was coming up to 4:30am. There were lights on in the station concourse, and a staff attendant filed through the large metal gates that were slightly ajar. I felt very appreciative of all the many people making my life easier in every respect. This was fundamentally the law of conditionality taught by the Buddha, commonly spoken of as dependent origination, or even as the Tibetan Buddhists sometimes termed it, interdependent origination. It determined the reality of every being's existence. This law manifested as a vast infinite network of causes and conditions that contributed to each moment-to-moment experience of every living thing in the cosmos. These conditions would arise, play themselves out and then cease, in a state of continual flux. Each living thing was in some way connected to and not isolated from everything else in the universe. One of the Buddha's first disciples, called Aśvajit, had enunciated this in a very pithy phrase. He was asked by Sāriputra, a man who was a truth seeker, what the nature of reality was. Aśvajit responded with these succinct words:

"The Buddha has explained the origin of those things, which proceed from a cause or a condition. Their cessation too he has explained. This is the doctrine of the great shramana (a wandering monk, who labours, toils, and exerts himself)."

Another way this truth has been enunciated is: *"This being, that becomes; from the arising of this, that arises. This not being, that does not become; from the ceasing of this, that ceases."*

Sāriputra, who was a very evolved man, had an instant spiritual awakening on hearing this truth. It could be seen by most to be a very elementary concept, but to directly see, experience and realize its implications was to see it as unfathomably deep and complex. This concept, which allies itself with the concept of impermanence, goes to the very core of Buddhist teaching.

So, seeing that the large entrance door was left open, I thought this might be an invitation, allowing me to enter. Feeling a little calmer after my earlier encounter with the stranger, I tentatively entered the station. Finding a metal circular bench, I slumped into its unforgiving steel support. I continued to wait patiently. My mouth was starting to dry from lack of fluids. I then remembered the bottle of water that I had brought with me from home. I had completely forgotten about it because the night's events had swallowed me up in an encircling flurry of muted activity and drama.

I waited for a good hour and a quarter on the bench, shutting my eyes from time to time for what I hoped would be a short nap. Unfortunately, no such luck was in store. Admittedly, I still felt alert and present at this hour. I then saw a couple of separate men making their way onto the station concourse. They immediately darted for available seats nearer to the digital screen display than I was, all while appearing to be in states of half-slumber.

The coffee stall attendants had arrived. They were slowly setting up shop. I was now desperate for a cup of coffee. I got up, made my way closer to their stall and sat on another steel bench. Almost a few seconds after I had sat down, quite a large and tall guy decided to sit directly next to me. Immediately, I was seized by dread – I saw this as a very odd move. Without a moment's hesitation, I lurched forwards out of the seat and found a spot among the coffee stall's tables and chairs. It would be highly unusual for someone else to sit with me there, as it was a compact arrangement.

Earlier, I had stuffed the copy of the *Metro* inside my rucksack. I decided now was a good time to retrieve and sift through the paper again, to keep my mind active and my emotions engaged. During my reading, I looked up. I noticed a bleary-eyed office worker had parked himself a couple of tables opposite. He was flicking through the contents of his own *Metro*. I could not help but think that both the man who had decided to sit right next to me, and now this supposed office worker, might not be genuine. After all, they were at the station at such an early hour. *Might they be undercover agents monitoring my movements at very close quarters?* Although the suspicion was rife, I inwardly said to myself that I needed to try and let go of these unhelpful thoughts that were crowding my consciousness. Even if these two men were spies, they were just trying to do their job. They believed that what they were doing was the right course of action. All they wanted, or anyone else for that matter, was to be happy. Ultimately, their happiness was misguided, but the same could be said for so many other people on this planet. Happiness was not dependent on external circumstances, but on an inner contentment and peace that comes about through a transformation and development of self. This view was so self-evident to me. It was also unsurprising, due to my 21 years of on-and-off Buddhist practice, which had finally stabilized into a path of consistent, regular steps and a well-established spiritual routine.

After delicately sipping the very hot coffee I had bought, I looked at the digital display for the next train to leave for Leamington Spa. I observed that one was already waiting to depart from platform four.

With a huge relief, I left the *Metro* by the coffee stall, took my coffee, slung my rucksack over my shoulder and went to board the train. I now felt my mission had been accomplished. I could sit back restfully and feel contented for the journey back. However hard the intelligence services had tried to kill me off in a stealth operation, the more I would be protected by the benevolent gods.

CHAPTER 10

THE MESSAGES

The morning after returning from my intrepid trip to the heart of London, I started turning my thoughts towards the Buddhist movement that I was affiliated to. *Could the ordained members of the Buddhist community really be who they say they were?* I believed wholeheartedly that the founder of the movement, Sangharakshita, was of pure and noble intent, but as for some of his followers and disciples, I could not be so sure. Although they taught a principle called "Metta – universal loving kindness – I felt that certain order members did not display this principle in the slightest way, even though they claimed to practise it in meditation. A friend of mine, who had gone on one of the Buddhist courses, remarked that she found one of the order members to be close-minded. She alleged that he dismissed the claims she put forward to him in a slightly condescending manner. She had espoused those ideas to me. I had been a lot more receptive and open to her views, even agreeing with a lot of them.

As I continually mulled over the various members I had come to know, I became more and more certain that there was something untoward with certain people and their activities. *Had they been set up with their sole aim to find a convenient way to eradicate this elusive figure?* I still believed that the teachings of the founder were exemplary and perfectly suited to the Western mindset, but I felt that a few of them were only paying lip service to the teachings. They were half-heartedly living them out in their own lives. My associative train of thought began imagining the group I had joined as a sort of covert religious cult. I had been completely taken in by their web of deceit. They were probably part of the spy world's conspiracy, to do away with a genuine, warm-hearted individual – one who possessed real potential for enlightenment and Buddhahood.

When I pondered their characteristics, even ones belonging to those I had come to know and respect, I became aware of attributes that could make for very effective and lethal secret agents. Most of them were well educated. Quite a few had been to boarding schools, while some had gone on to study at leading universities. They were mostly slim and wiry individuals. Some of them could be very assertive and bold. They were mostly very competent and capable people.

I considered that the further up the ostensible spiritual hierarchy it went, the more deadly their attributes became. The most senior order member in the movement, just below the founder, was an extremely charismatic and gifted speaker. He had an astonishing command of the English language. He was above all erudite and eloquent in equal measure. He had attended a prestigious boarding school. He also had an uncle who had been an admiral in the navy.

I remembered how I had been on retreat over half a year ago with this order member leading it. He had, for the whole ten days, worn the same smart, grey waistcoat. I convinced myself that this article of clothing was what a secret agent would wear. He also liked to don a black fedora, which made him look even more suspect.

I wondered whether some of the order members were secretly trying to plot my end with the most seemingly accidental of causes. On the same retreat with the man in the grey waistcoat, another leading order member had suggested that I could go and talk to him. As I remembered this incident, I shuddered at the idea that, if I had done so, my life might have been in peril. I surmised that this man would have had no qualms in inflicting a killer blow, either with a sharp blade or a gun with a silencer.

Over the next few hours, I allowed these anxious thoughts to proliferate and cement themselves into what I saw as a vicious reality. On that Thursday afternoon, it dawned on me that I now needed to extricate myself from this Machiavellian Buddhist group. I would write an e-mail setting out my views. I would send it to those I knew in the movement without hesitation or deliberation. I was becoming more assured that I had seen into the truth of the matter. Getting out my laptop, I waited for what seemed like an age as my computer started up. After logging on to my Hotmail account, I proceeded to write vigorously.

Dear All,

I have had an epiphany moment, and certain things have become clearer to me. This comes after 21 years of reflection on the nature of existence and the law of conditionality, as it applies to all beings. This includes trees, plants, animals and what you would normally see as inanimate objects. I see all life imbued with energy and consciousness.

I truly believe not all of you, but quite a lot of you in the movement, are not genuine, and your motivations are not pure. I believe you have been recruited by government bodies to dismantle the very structure of what Sangharakshita has espoused. This has been done very subtly, adeptly and, dare I say, skilfully and intelligently. Any person who can take this teaching further and lead us into a new society is, in your eyes, truly a threat to the established order. Although you preach a new order, you do not want it transpiring. You have been recruited to eliminate any real and genuine hopeful to the emergence of a new order. I believe you are all aware that this person is me!

One of the things that has given your game away, is that you are all too bloody confident! In my years of reflection, this has always stumped me, but now I can truly say it is clear to me. Most of you are just FRAUDS!

I am aspiring to be a true Bodhisattva on the path, and I truly believe that the Buddhas and the gods are protecting me on my continual journey through the realms of the cosmos, with their great compassion for the sufferings of all beings.

With compassion to you all – may you one day realize the unadulterated bliss of release and liberation.

Alastair Gamble

I realized that Metta – and its development in meditation – was one of the movement's defining standpoints. I believed this principle was just a front for the more wicked aspects of the organization.

I was sad to have to write this e-mail. Over the years I had developed a real fondness for the people I had met. I knew now that I was formally severing links. There was no way I was going to reengage with them. I was now fully aware that I was on my own. I would perhaps have to explore other traditions or movements to try and continue some semblance of Buddhist practice.

I also wrote a letter to my sister, as I believed she was also duplicitous in my drama. I was extremely reluctant to write it, as she was family, but I could not ignore what I saw as her grand deception the day before on the phone.

Dear Christina,

I really did not want to speak to you on the phone until I had formulated my thoughts in an e-mail to you, thereby setting them out coherently.

We have all heard of the prophecies, namely that there will be a second coming, a Jesus-like figure that Christians believe would come to save humanity or the future Buddha that Buddhists trust will appear one day. There is the Devil, who is often portrayed as waiting for the right moment to come to Earth, once evil has increased sufficiently.

GCHQ, MI5 and MI6, some of the most brilliant minds in this country, were trying to locate where this possible Devil character might be. I am sure the minds of GCHQ would have assumed that this figure would be deceptive and charming, and that they would not stand out too much, but still possess a lot of wonderful qualities – not only in terms of abilities, but also in terms of looks. For the record, I do believe in the Devil, but not as some charming man who is pretending to be humble, but instead as someone who is intent on world domination and has a gigantic ego. By the way, as a Buddhist, I am trying to diminish the pull the ego has on me. I am seriously trying to pursue the important idea of humility, which is essential in the spiritual life. The actual Devil will be a raging inferno of a being, able to overcome any extreme pain whatsoever. He will look like a true monster. He will be immense in stature, towering over all beings. I truly believe he will arrive with lightning bolts and thunder. It will be the start of hell on this planet, where he will rule supreme for many, many millions of years, with the planet getting progressively hotter and hotter and eviler.

I, on the other hand, would want to be part of a new world order, amongst the realm of the gods, basing my life on the three qualities of love, contentment and wisdom, and fundamentally aiming to lead a truly ethical life.

Returning to the point of GCHQ, I imagine that when they find or found this potential Devil figure, they would tune into every part of his life, from the moment he was born. They would use the government's sophisticated satellite technology to watch him, and then take the footage and create a new reality TV show of this character that could be displayed all around the world. I hasten to add that this would not have been shared with everyone. There are people on Earth who are longing to lead spiritual lives. These particular people – there are many of them – would not all have access to this reality TV show. I believe one of the key messages from this show, which would have been displayed whilst it played, is: "If you meet this person, then terminate his life!"

(As an aside, is it not interesting to note that when The Truman Show came out, the main character had a passing resemblance to me? A couple of people have commented that I look a little like him! I do not think this is just a coincidence!)

Back to the reality show I mentioned before, those watching would have to sign official secrets act to state that they would never divulge this piece of information to the person being watched – namely, myself. They would not be able to discuss it with anyone who was not in the know.

On Wednesday afternoon, I received a call from you, which was very odd for you to do. How would you know that I was in my flat? Would you not realistically have assumed that I would be at work at that time, and there would be no point in ringing me? You then opened the dialogue with, "What are you doing?" and not, "Hi, Alastair, I was not expecting you to be at home at this hour," in a friendly, congenial manner. In my opinion, this slip-up on your part gave the game away. It proved to me that you are in

*on the conspiracy to terminate my life!! I am convinced, though, that Mum
and Dad do not know what is going on. I can fully believe in their care and
concern for me.*

*With this knowledge that I have gained, I can truly say – hand on heart –
I do not want anything to do with you, David or Theo ever again. I will
not be making any visits to your lovely home in Oxfordshire. It is not your
fault. You are just a pawn who has been sucked into this world of duplicity
and deception. I am sure you feel you are doing the right and noble thing for
your country. Ultimately, there is no one to blame. It is just the way things
are and always have been. We are all on this wheel of life together, making
our journeys through the cosmos, constantly being reborn until, one day, we
reach the end of our immensely long journey and find inner contentment and
supreme peace.*

*I hope that you fare well in the endless rounds of existence, and some day
you will find your complete liberation and bliss. This also goes for the whole
of humanity in this world, and the innumerable beings in other worlds. My
notion of space and time is vast and epic. We are all guided by two desires –
namely, to be happy and to be free from suffering.*

With compassion to you all,

Alastair

After this explosive letter to my sister, I managed to salvage our
relationship in the months to follow. I was told that she had been
called by my previous employer just before my Hyde Park outing, as
I had put her down as my next of kin. My employer had said to her
that I had not appeared in the office since that last Friday. He was
very concerned about my welfare. On discovering this important
fact about my sister and after giving her a few soothing words of
reassurance, I was able to resume a very friendly relationship with
her and her whole family again.

CHAPTER 11

BELBROUGHTON

The following day after sending my two explosive e-mails, I desperately needed to turn to a genuine companion and friend in this time of need. I racked my brains. There was a particular woman, who I had got to know from first meeting her at a meditation class. She was open to alternative points of view. She seemed genuinely spiritually inclined. Her name was Susan, and she worked as an independent filmmaker.

After looking up her contact details on my mobile, I decided to call her. I would see if she was free that evening, as I could really do with someone lending me a sympathetic ear.

"Hi Susan! How are you?"

"I'm doing well, thanks. It's nice to hear from you. Is everything okay?" She could tell from my trembling voice that all was not well.

"I'm in a little bit of a pickle. I have left the Buddhist movement I was with, as I suspect they aren't genuine, and they aren't who they claim to be. I think that they probably have some ulterior agenda that is of a sinister nature." I confided.

"I'm really sorry to hear that," she said with authenticity.

"I'm also in need of some friendship. You're the first person I thought I could genuinely turn to, as a trusted friend. Would it be possible to come and visit you this evening, I wonder, if it isn't too much of an imposition?"

"Yeah, sure! I haven't got anything on tonight. You'd be more than welcome to come over. If you want, we could go out for a meal?"

"Thanks, Susan, that would be lovely! I'll tell you more when I arrive at yours. Can I come over about five-ish?"

"No problem! I'm working from home today, so come over whenever."

"Thanks, you're a lifesaver!"

I was truly grateful for her willingness to meet me at her place. From what I knew of her, she was a loving and caring woman who would lend a very sympathetic ear to my plight. Although I was sleeping a little better with the help of my meditation practice, I still had a heat inside. It was as if I was a human pressure cooker simmering at a low temperature. I was still convinced my life was being played out on satellite TV in most people's homes around the world, and that my life was still in mortal danger.

Susan lived in Belbroughton. My journey there was very mixed. To begin with, along the stretch of the motorway, I drove considerately and responsibly. But once I got off the motorway, I drove as if someone had given me a shot of pure adrenaline. It was as if I was the protagonist in an action film having a car chase. My driving was very skilled, but on the dangerous side in these closing miles towards her house.

Finally arriving at her place, after some wrong turns, I got out of my car. I ventured over to her front door and rang the bell. A few seconds later, the oak door opened. I was greeted by a gentle smile, with the slightest amount of worry detectable in her eyes.

"Hi Susan! I'm not too early, am I?"

"No not at all. As I said you were welcome to come over at any time, but now is perfect, as I'm just wrapping up my editing for the day."

"Great! Thanks for being able to see me. I see you as a friend and someone who I can truly turn to, and someone who would probably be supportive of my problematic situation."

I started to relax a little in her homely and comfortable abode. Before I proceeded to tell her about the recent unfolding of events, I started to become a little more agitated, thinking that what I was going to say would be viewed and judged by millions of people. This thought remained during the early part of our chat.

"I really believe that my life, and what goes on, is being shown to millions, if not billions of people around the world, as if I'm some *Big Brother* spectacle. Already by saying this to you, I feel uncomfortable with the knowledge that I'm being judged harshly by so many. I know there will be some members of the public who will really get me, but so many will not. My view is also that some members of society won't be party to this secretive world – like you, for instance."

"I really have no knowledge of what you're saying, but that doesn't mean it isn't true," she said tactfully.

I found it suddenly very difficult to go on. I took a deep inhalation of breath as a strong tension manifested around my heart.

"I don't expect you to believe what I'm saying. All I would encourage you to be is open-minded."

"Don't worry. I'm listening to you with an open mind. Do you want to tell me about your thoughts on your Buddhist friends?" Susan enquired in a maternal way.

"I'd placed so much trust in my Buddhist friends. I'd also become so fond of them that to find out they have hoodwinked me into thinking they were *bona fide* Buddhists – it really hurts. They claimed to preach Metta, or universal loving kindness, as being as elevated as mindfulness, but most didn't seem to embody that quality much, if at all."

"I agree with you. The order members I met didn't seem to be as kind as I was expecting them to be. In some ways they seemed to be a little on the gruff and serious side, not really showing much love or open heartedness."

"I also believe that some of the order members have sided or are working with the government to help eliminate me. I believe they agree with the authorities that I'm a genuine threat to the established world order," I added with anguish on my face.

"I'm sure the order members aren't in collaboration with the government to terminate your life. Do you really think that you pose such a threat to the established world order?" She asked sensitively.

"I just think they've been monitoring me for a very long time. They see a lot of idealism in my nature. I am sure they spotted and took notice of my YouTube video, which I aired last year," I said, as my internal tightness started to mellow a little. I assumed that, to her, it all appeared a little far-fetched, to say the least, but I imagined she was still listening attentively to my theories and responding sympathetically where appropriate.

We both went to her office on the first floor. I talked to her in sporadic bursts, while she busied herself with completing the remaining tasks on her computer. She partly concentrated on her work, whilst lending a slightly distracted ear to my more mundane concerns. The day was ending on a particularly warm note. I was enjoying the stillness of her home. The low setting sun's inviting rays reached out over the green pastures, while we conversed.

She suggested we eat out. I jumped at the chance. She gave me a couple of options. A restaurant with a regal name sounded, by far, the most appealing of the selection in Belbroughton.

After about 20 minutes of wrapping up her editing, we both agreed that we would go for a drink at one of the pubs in the village before having a meal at the royally labelled restaurant.

We walked a short distance into the heart of the village and called in at the local pub. As we entered the invitingly lit old pub, which had been given a contemporary makeover, a woman was sitting in one of the leather armchairs. She was in her 50s. She greeted Susan amiably and asked her who the young man was she had in tow.

"What's your name?" the woman asked me.

"Alastair. What's yours?"

"Joan. I bet you're an architect. Something tells me that you are," she enquired in a direct and forward manner.

I was starting to think, *Here is my first example of a woman, who knows the intricacies of my life, but has few qualms about revealing in small part her knowledge of me.* I went along with the charade. She did not divulge any more ostensible guesses about my history but kept remarkably restrained towards me for the rest of my time there.

As Susan chatted with Joan, a man with short, brown hair and a kind and inquisitive face looked at me and smiled affably. I suddenly felt that this is what the upside of being famous would be. I responded with an equally endearing smile. I got into a short conversation with him. I thought to myself, *This man is finding me equally as fascinating and alive, as I am finding him. Can these two short exchanges be further evidence to me that my life is being streamed to millions or billions around the world?* The counter thought still did emerge from time to time that I might be seriously deluding myself with this seemingly outlandish idea. *Can such a claim really be genuine?!?*

After one drink, Susan and I headed for the restaurant, which was delightfully situated by a gently flowing stream and against a dark wooded backdrop. She and I both agreed how comforting the sound and sight of a meandering stream was to us.

"So, this is the restaurant – The Queens. A very regal name it is, too." I felt kingly in stature by exclaiming this fact.

"Do you know that I have only been here once before for a drink, so I'm not sure what to expect from the food here?" she stated anxiously, as if she was going to be judged harshly by me for her choice of restaurant.

"I'm sure whatever we have will be excellent and very tasty, what with a name like this. I'm sure we can't go wrong – don't you think?"

"I'm sure you're right. Let's go in and hopefully enjoy its culinary delights." She and I motioned towards the large oak entrance door.

Once we went in, we were invited to sit at a two-person table, against a floral wallpapered wall. I sat with my back to it. I had a good view of the other guests seated among us.

We looked through the menu and decided we would each have a starter, as well as a main course. Interestingly, we both opted for the same fish dish for our mains. We both chose a glass of red to accompany our meal, with an accompanying bottle of sparkling water.

A thought of an objectionable nature arose. *What if the chefs now had the perfect opportunity to poison me with either my starter or my main?* I did not confide in Susan this idea of poison, but instead chose to try and dispel the low-level worry that was lightly bubbling beneath my composed exterior. If I mentioned this to her, it would only mar the beauty of our evening together. I was sure it would cause her to feel utterly disturbed. I just hoped that if the chefs were going to sprinkle some cyanide or other deadly concoction, then the gods would exercise their magical powers in turning it into something neutral and harmless. I started to feel a little more at ease with this new reassuring thought.

As we ate our mains, I noticed a couple beside us not talking much. When they did speak, they were being discreet in what they did say. It was as if they were trying not to be overheard by the other guests and me. I think they were slightly embarrassed about sitting in such proximity to me. They very rarely glanced in my direction, but I felt they had a strong awareness of my indomitable presence.

Susan then said to me,

"How would you like to meet my spiritualist friend, who also lives in this village? Perhaps you can explain your ideas to her. She's a wonderfully warm and compassionate woman. She has a definite positive and radiant energy. One of the things she likes to do when you greet her is to give a big hug. She will undoubtedly give you a very warm embrace if you do meet."

"That sounds lovely. I need to meet more open-minded individuals, and those with depth and more rounded spiritual interests."

"I could take you there tomorrow if you like. I've spoken to her to see if it's okay. She's told me it would be fine for you to go over tomorrow morning."

I had earlier asked Susan if I could stay the night at hers because I did not feel up for driving back that evening. She was perfectly happy for me to bunk in the office, which doubled as a second bedroom. She said that anyone staying there normally had a very good night's sleep, as the room had a particularly good energy and orientation to it. I was still suffering from a considerable lack of sleep. I hoped that this night would prove to be different.

After I settled the bill, we both walked out into the clear night sky, with stars sprinkled all over the jet-black cosmic backdrop. Once we arrived back at her house, she offered me a tea. I opted for a camomile to help me try and sleep better. After a brief wind-down,

I polished off the tea, said goodnight and headed off to bed. She followed soon after.

Although I could feel a distinct calming and positive energy with the bed and its arrangement, I could not manage to quell my anxious mind sufficiently to get a good night's rest. The room's powerful and restful energy did however give me some broken sleep, which I was grateful for.

The following morning, we both went to see Susan's spiritualist friend, Linda, near the heart of the village. She lived in a relatively new estate, which had a front lawn beautified by a plethora of bushes, trees and flowers.

The meeting with Linda was everything I imagined it to be. She seemed to me to be larger than life. With a distinct, positive aura, she explained to me that she was in touch with heavenly spirits. She could communicate with them through messages sent via instruments she had in her possession. I was open-minded to these abilities, but I did not accept everything she suggested was in her power. Her claim to be living within higher states of consciousness and having to try to come down from these exalted states of mind, I saw as dubious. Internally, I remained a tad dismissive.

Susan had left early. She was only there to introduce Linda to me. After I had spent a while in the company of such a loving presence as Linda, I parted with a strong bear-hug embrace. This refreshing physical contact lingered for quite a few seconds. I confirmed that I would like to visit again soon.

Walking back to Susan's place, I was suffused with a warm glow. Thanking Susan for the stay, I got into my car, and drove back to my flat.

CHAPTER 12

THE CONFRONTATION

The following Wednesday, I was due to see my doctor and nurse to confront them about what I saw as scurrilous activity. In one way, I was sympathetic to their plight. I believed they were just following orders from the secret service and the government. In turn, the government were only conditioned by their misguided ideologies. I could really see how everyone was enmeshed in an unfathomably deep and complex web of conditioning. I should only be compassionate towards them all.

On the day of my appointment, I went about my newfound daily morning ritual, drinking coffee and reading a book in one of the coffee shops. As I turned the corner where the Town Hall proudly stood, I entered Livery Street. I spotted in the corner of my eye a man who was very smartly dressed and leaning expectantly against the wall of the hotel. My first impression was that he was some sort of diplomat. He had that air of calm assurance and carried himself in a dignified manner. On seeing me, he came away from the wall and hovered by the entrance to Livery Street. As I proceeded to walk at a less brisk and more measured pace than my walk leading up to the Town Hall, I saw that this distinguished-looking gentleman was now starting to follow me. So, I decided against entering Starbucks. I carried on to the next coffee shop, Bar Angeli in Regent's Court. The interior felt like a time warp, rustic yet sophisticated. It had a lot of dark timber panelling and pictures of screen idols dotted on the walls. Only two or three of the staff would communicate with me on a friendly yet disconnected basis. I was never quite sure if the staff regarded me with caution.

As I comfortably planted myself in a two-person table by the entrance door, the elegantly dressed man entered the coffee shop. He purposefully headed straight for the staff in the kitchen. He whispered some words into their ears, and then left the premises. At no time did he make eye contact with me. I noticed how he tried pushing the door away from him to leave the coffee shop – floundered – before pulling the door inwards to exit. Immediately, a powerful vice-like grip of terror seized me. I thought that this brief event could only mean one thing: The government wanted to try and poison me again. I thought it could be so easy for the staff to slip some of the toxic plant belladonna, also known as nightshade, into my coffee. It would take a few hours to kick in. Then, back at home, I would quietly pass away. The emergency services would then be told to put my death down to unexplained causes. They might even claim I had a heart malfunction that can strike people in their 30s and 40s to try and assuage the grief my devastated parents would feel. I had completely forgotten the comparative reassurance I felt with my meal at the restaurant in Belbroughton. This time, I believed that the possibility of success for the authorities seemed greater.

At once I decided I would take pre-emptive action. I politely said to the waitress, "I would like to change my mind about ordering the latte. Could you cancel my order?" The obtrusiveness of the man had been overwhelming. His little slip-ups, like not being aware of which way the door opened, helped obviate the possibility of my death in this instance. I was a little shaken up by the incident and was struck by the reality bearing down on me.

Later that afternoon, I walked to the surgery from my flat. Over the last two weeks, I had been experiencing an expanding heat and fire inside. I felt in control, yet a little out of control at the same time – a dichotomy of moods. It was not that I felt terribly anxious, just an experience of undeniable heat.

The receptionist at the surgery had reddened cheeks, which I put down to the stress of the job. Ultimately, she looked frazzled. She wore a stern expression.

The nurse called me into a different treatment room from her usual one. She sat down behind the desk, while I sat adjacent to her. She then enquired in a mock serious way – at least, that's how it appeared to me (I couldn't be sure if it was my bias towards her that was clouding my judgement).

"What can I help you with, Alastair?"

"I need to say something frank to you. It relates of course to my medication." I paused to muster my inner resolve, before launching into my accusation.

"I believe you haven't been giving me the correct medication at all. For the last three to four weeks, I've been experiencing sleep-deprived nights, which has caused my performance at work to deteriorate, and for me to subsequently give up my job. I've been on the same medication for about 17 years. Nothing like this has ever happened to me before. I can only put it down to one thing: You've been negligent in your duties." Before the nurse could retort, I continued in a demonstrable fashion with my line of reasoning.

"Ultimately, I don't think you're at fault because you're only following orders from the authorities," I expressed vehemently.

"I can assure you that I've in no way given you the wrong medication. I'm sure you are just imagining it," she retorted. I was convinced that she was lying, yet found this conversation futile, as she would just stand her ground, and so would I.

"The proof of the pudding is in the eating. The symptoms of my condition have been manifesting themselves over the last four weeks. How do you explain this?" My voice was becoming amplified.

"I really don't know. All I can say is – hand on heart – I didn't tamper with your medication," she responded in a deadpan way.

"There's never been a time when you've let me come into the treatment room and then shown me the ampoule you were extracting the medication from, before subsequently injecting me," I said with an escalating confidence.

"This is the procedure I follow with all the patients I see."

"Well, that procedure is ultimately flawed!" I retorted, finding my riposte very satisfying.

I thought if that was the case, then I had no other option but to withdraw myself from that surgery and return to the one at my parent's home. I did not divulge this to the nurse. I said that, in the future, and especially tomorrow when my injection was due, I would want to witness the nurse drawing out the Depixol drug from its ampoule, as a definite priority. She confirmed that she could oblige with this request.

After talking to the nurse, I went to sit in the upstairs waiting area until it was time to meet with my doctor, who I had not ever met. Once I was ushered in, I started to spill my thoughts about the spies that were out to get me. I maintained that I still felt at ease with myself, due to my steady Buddhist practice.

I highlighted that I was an intelligent man. I saw the world with sense and reason, even though my views might sound extreme. I got the impression from the doctor's body language that she thought I might be seriously loopy, but I also wondered whether she couldn't reveal the truth to me because she had been instructed by the government to keep silent. These conflicting ideas seemed to ricochet in my head. I was a little unsure, as to what the actual reality was. Was I a crackpot or was there truth in what I was confiding to the doctor? Ultimately, I felt a little unsteady in my opinion while talking to her so intimately. I was speaking to her for the first time. I barely knew her.

The following day, I had my injection with a different nurse. This time a petite, anxious-looking woman showed me the ampoule before administering it. With her hands trembling and her demeanour jittery, I wondered whether my seemingly outlandish views had been bandied about by the staff and caused this nurse to be intimidated by my presence.

After a couple of days of receiving the medication, I started to sleep better. This was long overdue, considering it had been a good four to five weeks of sleepless nights. My worried parents called to see how I was. There was overwhelming relief that my sleep patterns were slowly returning to normal. I told them that the nurse showed me the ampoule on this occasion. Both my parents and I were convinced more than ever that the surgery had either been negligent, or else they had been underhand in their dealings with me. But we both thought it would be futile to press charges. *What evidence would we have against them?* All I knew was that I would immediately stop being a patient there. I would return to the Crick surgery, where they were much more understanding and sympathetic. After all, I had, over the years, developed a friendly relationship with the nurses and doctor at my former surgery.

CHAPTER 13

THE SPIRITUALIST

I went to see Linda again, the spiritualist woman, without meeting up with Susan this time. I wanted to discuss my views and beliefs of a supra-mundane nature. The last time we had met, I was reluctant to mention my intrepid trip to Hyde Park, either to her or Susan. It was then so fresh in my mind that I needed time to process the experience. This time, I had managed to absorb it into my life. The pain in my knee would still throb sporadically. It looked as if the knee plate was set slightly different to how it was before, due to the impact from the fall. Intermittent feelings of worry enveloped me about the healing process. *Would I be able to run as before and play tennis easily? Had I disfigured it to the extent that practical concerns might even become an issue?* A more positive but quieter thought countered the negative train and soothed my anxiety. For now, I would live with this constant ebb and flow of painful sensations, which I had begun to get used to.

When I had last visited Linda, I felt the house possessed a strong, even powerful positive force, which was her energy leeching into its fabric. I thought I might make quite a habit of this, dropping in to see her for a chat. I could then explore ideas about us, life and the universe. I knew she was just as fascinated by these things as I was.

Once I had pressed the doorbell, the door opened evenly. There was Linda with a big, beaming smile. She appeared otherworldly, with what seemed like the faintest impression of a halo around her head.

"Hello, Alastair. Lovely to see you again!"

"Hi, Linda! It's lovely to be here again," I said as I entered the living room. I gave her a very warm hug. Linda offered me biscuits and tea, and then we engaged in small talk for a few minutes. She then asked in a curious and interested way, "Alastair, what would you like to talk about this time?"

"I thought I would tell you about my excursion to Hyde Park. I went there two weeks ago, just before I first met up with you, to test my nerves and try to overcome some of my fears. I sat in the middle of the park in the middle of the night and meditated, while also making a point of sampling some of London's nightlife. I really believe that I wasn't alone when I was sitting in the park. There were probably secret agents trying to shoot me dead, although I can't be sure. I did, however, see a lone silhouetted figure race across my path about 100 meters in front of me, just as I was making my way out of the park. In the ensuing drama, I damaged my knee quite badly from climbing over the park's railings and jumping down from them." I began to roll up my jeans to show her the darkened reddish-mauve scab encrusted on my knee.

Linda replied matter-of-factly, "I know what the knee injury signifies. It means you were being too wilful, and not listening to your kind inner voice. Sustaining an injury like that, with the brief story you've just described, usually implies stubbornness and being too headstrong."

I nodded and murmured in agreement, realizing that she could well be correct in her assumption. I knew no better.

"What mental condition did you say you have?"

"I'm diagnosed with schizophrenia, but I'd been well and functioning in a healthy manner for about 17 years, until a psychological upheaval happened in the last few weeks. All I can put it down to is that the nurse at the surgery where I live did not administer the correct treatment, for one reason or another."

"I will fetch a little device, which divines your actual symptoms. You could, of course, suffer from a bipolar condition and not schizophrenia." On our last meeting together, Linda had shared with me that she had been a nurse before turning her attention to spiritualism later in life. She came back from her bedroom with a pretty and bejewelled object.

"This object needs to be balanced. First, you determine which rotation stands for yes, and which rotation stands for no – either clockwise or anti-clockwise. You then pose it a yes-or-no question. If it rotates clockwise, with the question being asked, then that implies a 'yes', and if it revolves in an anti-clockwise direction – then that means 'no'. Obviously, I'm posing the question to the angels, or as you had termed them, 'the gods'." I had always been extremely open-minded in areas of the unexplained and mysterious. I felt that I could only go along with her mysterious diagnosis, thinking that, with this divining, there would be a definite and irrefutable truth presenting itself.

"As I thought," she murmured. "The pendulum rotates clockwise when asking it if you have schizophrenia, and anti-clockwise when asking it if you have a bipolar disorder. This means that you have schizophrenia and not bipolar." To me, this was disconcerting to hear. I would have far rather been termed a bipolar sufferer than a schizophrenic, with all the latter's accompanying negative and unhelpful associations. I talked more with Linda, but I was feeling a little deflated by the outcome. Now I would feel forever wary of mentioning my condition, unless it was to those friends of mine that I deeply trusted. I realized that the stigma attached to mental conditions was becoming ever more eroded, but the mention of schizophrenia still seemed to play on a lot of people's doubts and fears. There was still a lot of uncertainty surrounding this condition.

I shared with her my belief that I was being filmed 24/7 like a *Big Brother* contestant, and the idea that the authorities saw me as the devil incarnate, masquerading as a spiritually minded figure. I tried to explain my theory that reality embraced both dark and light aspects of life, albeit rejecting evil acts of body, speech and mind. I explained how I believed that wrathful energy was within us all, and that this energy should ultimately be harnessed for the goodness and purity that was essential to leading a spiritual life. This energy had the force to drive us forwards with immense power and momentum. I then told her how I listened to dark, gritty songs on the radio or in my CD collection as a way of evoking the passionate and wild flavour of that energy. Also, its energy could be expressed in eccentric, flowing and staccato dance movements, while at home or in clubs. It could also manifest in the honesty of my personal exchanges with friends. My teacher Sangharakshita had once stated in a pithy maxim, "Rather honest collision, than dishonest collusion."

Linda replied calmly and unruffled, "I'm happy to meet with whoever comes through my door, whatever their beliefs or underlying motivations are. I feel very safe and protected. I've no cause to worry that any harm will come to me."

I took this to mean that she was a little disturbed with my open, provocative and revealing dialogue. Also, she had now established that I had schizophrenia. I sensed that she was indirectly admitting that she found me a mild threat. Her tone of voice remained constant, and it did not suggest any underlying concerns she might be having. I tried to dispel any fear she might be labouring under, confirming that I only had honest and honourable intentions with her – and anyone else, for that matter.

She suggested I pay some money for her time, which she had not asked for at the start of our encounter, but it was implicit that this was the form these meetings would take. I realized that it would forever be a spiritual consultancy service and not a friendly meet-up. I parted from her with a little feeling of resentment simmering away below the surface, as I could not now meet up with her as a potential friend. A financial transaction would always come between us. I felt that this was probably the last time I would come to visit this remarkable woman; however, I had thoroughly appreciated the wise counsel she had imparted to me in the small time I had got to know her.

CHAPTER 14

THE PSYCHIATRIST

After knowing that I had been given the correct medication this
time at the Leamington surgery, I had made swift and pressing
moves to change back to my old surgery in Crick. I knew I could
rely on the Crick surgery to do the right thing, as I had witnessed
in the past. They were truly responsible and caring in their actions.
The main female doctor at the Crick surgery suggested that I look
up a psychiatrist by the name of Doctor Goodyear, who worked at
Northampton Hospital. He had come highly recommended. She felt
this would be the best doctor from whom to seek good psychiatric
advice.

I had polished off an Americano, which was now my preferred
coffee of choice. I had grown used to a stronger, sharper and more
bitter taste, compared with the flat whites, which were slightly too
sweet for my maturing taste buds. I left the coffee shop and hung
around nearby to make a discreet but much needed call to the
hospital.

Once I got through, I asked the secretary to book me an
appointment to see Doctor Goodyear for a consultation. Even though
I was ringing on Tuesday, 8 April, a space in the doctor's diary had
presented itself on that Wednesday. I jumped at the chance to have
myself booked in on that close and convenient date. An evening slot
was arranged at 7pm.

I got back to my flat and then contacted my father to tell him of
the appointment, as my father had requested.

"Hi, Dad. Just to let you know, I've booked an appointment with the psychiatrist, who'd been recommended to me. I managed to get an appointment for this Wednesday at 7pm. Would that time and day suit you?" I said with a hint of resentment that my father had to tag along.

"I can definitely make that date and time," he said, audibly relieved.

"You know, Dad, it isn't necessary for you to come with me. I can go on my own," I said, feeling as though my independence was being usurped.

"I think I really need to be there, at least for the first part of the meeting, so I can set the scene. I need to explain things about you and your potted mental history. I don't intend to be there for the duration of the meeting, but I will allow you, once I've finished, to tell your side of the story to the psychiatrist."

As I ended the call to my father, I contemplated how I was sleeping so much better, and how my thought patterns were becoming more cogent. I was not seeing the sinister nature of my predicament as much. I was becoming more and more positive to the people around me and my surroundings. Not everyone now seemed like a threat to my life.

Once my father and I had parked in the empty car park at Northampton Hospital, we wandered up a flight of stairs to the first floor in a modern brick building. The reception counter was diagonally opposite the top of the stairs. A friendly secretary asked me if I could fill out my name and the details of my car registration. Although I found her pretty, I noticed how uncomfortable I felt because of my mental condition. *Might I be perceived by her as fragile and of a nervous disposition?* I knew this could not be further from the truth, but I laboured under this perceived interpretation, with all its prejudices and judgements.

As we waited at the top of the stairs in a small waiting area, I noticed that one of the walls had been painted a purple colour. I wondered to myself whether this colour was deliberate for putting the minds of the patients at ease. Or was it that the staff chose it for its more upbeat qualities. I appreciated the colour. It was one of my favourites.

After about five minutes of waiting, the door to the corridor leading to the consultancy rooms opened, and a young boyish man greeted us.

"Hello! You must be Alastair Gamble," he said, looking at me in a gentle but direct way.

"Yes, I am. My father wanted to come along as well –"

"Hello Doctor Goodyear," my dad interjected before I could continue. "I would like to tell you my side of the story about my son and his mental history. I would like to also explain my brother's condition, which was very similar to my son's. Then, I thought I would leave you two together, while I work on some papers I've brought with me."

"That's quite alright with me. Are you okay with that, Alastair?" Doctor Goodyear asked me in a professionally considerate manner.

"That's perfectly fine with me, thanks," I said reassuringly.

My father and I were positioned in the chairs provided, opposite Doctor Goodyear's, which stood behind an oak veneered table. The psychiatrist offered us both water. I accepted the offer willingly. I saw it as an opportunity to stop my mouth from becoming parched while speaking about my past mental history.

My dad took the lead and talked to the doctor about his brother and his history. Dad explained to him how his brother had suffered from bipolar and not schizophrenia. He had taken the same medication as I was taking. My father said he was convinced that my medication did the trick in keeping me consistently healthy, both cognitively and emotionally. He mentioned the concern both he and my mum had about the surgery in Leamington. Things for me were getting markedly better, now that I knew I had been given the correct medication in the last instalment. Dad also explained how we all felt more comfortable with me going to the surgery, by my parent's home. They were very supportive.

The doctor listened and transcribed feverishly as my dad was speaking. After my father felt he had explained enough about what was pertinent, with regards to mine and his brother's mental health, he suggested he would leave us to talk to each other, while he retreated to the waiting area.

Once my dad left the room, Doctor Goodyear said, "It would now be good to hear your side of the story. Firstly, what did you make of what your father said to us just now?"

"I would say most of what he said is spot-on. I would like to think that I'm like my uncle with a bipolar condition, but I had a spiritualist woman tell me, with the help of a divining instrument, that I have schizophrenia and I don't suffer from bipolar."

"I will endeavour to investigate that. As I said to your father, these conditions can overlap with one another. It does sound, however, that you experience manic as well as psychotic episodes, but as your father stated, you do not seem to experience the lows or depressions that often come with bipolar and schizophrenia. However, it is possible to be bipolar and only experience manic phases without the low points. It does also seem that the manic episodes are not without a degree of psychosis attached to them. This would effectively be termed bipolar affective disorder. This is one of the overlaps between schizophrenia and bipolar," the doctor reliably informed me.

"I thought I would also add that I'm never violent, hostile or aggressive to people when I'm having an episode. In the distant past, I would feel a strong wave of self-loathing. However, with this last episode, it was different. I felt more empowered, even though I believed I was locked in a struggle with the secret service. I found myself spiralling over what I thought were the government's secretive and malicious endeavours against me."

The doctor started to ask me to give him a brief mental health history from my upbringing through to the present day, highlighting the key episodes in my life. The doctor was quick at writing down the salient points.

After quite a long while of opening myself up to the doctor, I was relieved to have the glass of water by my side to give my drying mouth some much-needed lubrication. I wondered if the doctor was analysing my little mannerisms as well as taking notes, or was this my own misguided interpretation of the consultation process? I very much warmed to the doctor, who was a young man in his 30s. He was of a similar background and age, albeit a few years younger. The doctor mentioned how he had been to a concert with the band James that was big in the 90s. I responded enthusiastically to the mention of them and asked if they had played the song "Sit Down". The doctor, who loved the band, said he was a little disappointed with the concert, as they had not sung any of their hit melodies, especially that song.

The doctor enquired if I had anything further to add. I believed I had said everything that was noteworthy. We both stood up and shook hands. The doctor decided he would come to the waiting area and say his goodbyes to my father. "Mr Gamble, I'll be seeing your son in a few months' time, when I should have a better assessment of his condition. I suggested he go back into architectural employment to keep his mind busy and occupied. Hopefully, by the time I see him again, he will be gainfully employed."

My father replied with relief, "I'm in total agreement. There's nothing like work to give a boost to one's cognitive faculties and stop the brain from slowly wasting away."

"I'll see what I can do," I pitched in with a sense of resignation. I had come to appreciate the time and space I had to myself. I was reluctant to return to work so soon, although I knew it was probably a necessary activity.

CHAPTER 15

THE GANGSTERS

That Saturday I made another trip to London. The weather was glorious. It was surprisingly warm for that time of year. I decided to dress in a more visceral and rawer ensemble. I chose a black long-sleeved T-shirt; some dark blue jeans; a plain but stylish brown leather jacket; some comfortable but trendy-looking dark brown leather shoes; and an ochre beanie that fit snugly on my head to complete the look. Compared to my previous attire, it seemed more brooding and hinted at a dash of menace.

After arriving at Marylebone station, I decided to walk from there to the Tate Modern, rather than taking the tube to either Oxford Circus or even Charing Cross and then walking the remainder of the way to the museum. I felt impelled to see as much of London – and as many of the people who would pass me on my way – as possible. I still experienced a residual heat inside. This time, compared to a little over a week ago, it was a much more contained and subtle force.

While walking along the Southbank past the National Theatre, I was aware of how quiet it was at this relatively early hour. I had arrived at the Southbank before it had become busy with hordes of people, who would undoubtedly sample its varied food delights and its culture. I remembered that I had read an article about how the actor Bill Nighy thoroughly relished lying down on park benches or on the grass in parks. He would look up through the spindly branches and leaves of the trees to the sky above. He did this totally unselfconsciously. He had no concern for what other people thought about his antics. I very much admired the actor's self-assurance.

Seeing as it was not busy with the hustle and bustle of people, I chose a suitably clean park bench that overlooked the Thames. Lying down in a supine position, I gazed mindfully through the branches and blossoms of the tree canopies above me. I would then gaze at hints of the cloudless blue sky, just as the actor would do and had done. After indulging in this calm yet alert posture for about five minutes, a helicopter in the distance began to get ever closer and louder until it was hovering directly overhead. As far as I could make out, it seemed like a police surveillance helicopter or even that belonging to a special unit. This rather put me off the tranquillity I was previously basking in. I reluctantly moved from this spot. I wondered whether MI5 were continuing with their many attempts to erase me, through a sniper discreetly located inside the helicopter. I was not paying much attention to the details of the hovering machine and the occupants inside. Instead, I calmly rose from my seat. I walked nonchalantly from the bench and headed in the direction of the Tate Modern. Their weapons could not hurt me, as they would be continually disabled by the magical power of the gods.

Now, in this instance, I felt utterly safe and secure with this heartfelt belief. After a couple of minutes with the helicopter lingering in that aerial location, it then banked back towards the heart of the city.

While inside the Tate Modern, I arbitrarily ventured into one of the free exhibition spaces. Not being very focused on the artwork, I was instead a little distracted by the motley arrangement of people passing me by or going languidly in my direction. After about an hour of scanning the exhibits, it seemed to me that I was becoming emotionally saturated with the art on display. I also felt a little overwhelmed by the many individuals coalescing in small groups or meandering through the spaces on their own unique paths, like trackless birds in flight.

I went out of the exhibition area and found a comfortable leather armchair to relax on. It was situated on the middle level, with a large bank of windows opposite, from which to survey the large turbine hall.

Ensconcing myself in a rather indulgent pose, with my legs dangling over the side of the armchair, I directed my gaze – with a keen level of interest – towards all those who would wander by. It was slightly quieter on this level. The quantity of people walking past was inwardly more manageable for my softer temperament. I loved being inquisitive about people. I thoroughly appreciated trying to delve into the psychology of strangers and those friends and acquaintances I knew. It was as if I was drinking in their faces and physiognomy and gleaning some partially hidden truths about their histories, their hopes, fears, struggles and joys – the bittersweet symphonies that were their lives. My attention was not restricted to those who were attractive, popular or successful. I surveyed the whole gamut of people that fell under my radar with a feeling of Metta.

After enjoying the relative quietude, interspersed with sporadic bursts of couples or small groups passing me by, I left the building. I noticed from my watch that it was time for an early lunch. I crossed the Millennium Bridge. This was humorously termed the "Wobbly Bridge" after its opening because, when it first opened, it would sway precariously while people walked over it. The ensuing battle between the architect, Lord Foster; the engineer and the client was ironed out after considerable time and expense in lengthy court battles. The resultant action taken was to fit dampers to the underside of the structure. As I reached the other side, I ambled in the direction of St. Paul's cathedral.

Near St. Paul's Tube station, I spied Café Rouge, a French restaurant chain. I thought that would be the most appropriate place to get some sustenance. I walked in, and I was greeted by a very polite and friendly-looking woman. The restaurant was practically empty, seeing as I had arrived just after midday. She enquired where I might like to sit for my meal. I very much favoured the corner seat by the plate-glass window, so I could then have my back to it and face towards the interior of the space.

Almost about a minute after I had sat down and started perusing the menu in front of me, two very muscular and dominant males entered the restaurant. They looked towards where I was situated. They then chose to sit directly adjacent to me.

Immediately, a wave of fear seized me, as I tried to come to terms with what I perceived as two menacing presences. The person who was sitting with his back to the window seemed like the more dominant of the two. He was also the taller one. The other individual had blond spiky hair and a very smooth, translucent face. Although he was looking in the direction of my table, he could not seem to meet my concerned look.

I wondered about this. I thought that the blond brute probably had a guilty secret, of which he could not bring himself to acknowledge the reality. I also noticed that they both were speaking in what sounded like Russian. This fact heightened the drama in my mind, as I connoted their language with potential physical violence and maliciousness, due to the stereotypes I had seen in so many films. From their overall physique, they looked as if they worked out regularly in the gym, pumping iron and probably engaging in cardiovascular workouts to keep their bodies as fit as fiddles. The overall impression I got was they could do someone real damage, and the person on the receiving end was unmistakably me.

Once I had ordered one of the vegetarian dishes – namely, a croque monsieur filled with mushrooms instead of ham and a side order of chips – I did not need to wait long before the order arrived. I then proceeded to battle with my fears and demons by feeling very threatened and intimidated by these two perceived gangsters. I did not let the fear consume me, but rather chose, in my own inimitable way, to surmount the mental obstacles in my path. As I was eating, I did just that. Though I felt nerves and my pulse racing, I just mindfully pursued the task at hand. I did not need to engage in any mantra to give me solace. Just the act of eating with awareness was enough to keep my focus pin-sharp. I knew this moment would pass. There would be no violent repercussions from this close shave to my life.

After finishing my lunch, and having just paid, I got up from my seat and headed for the toilets. As I entered them, I did not let panic overtake me – I just went about my business. I was half-expecting the door to open, and one or both of the men to confront me. They would then clobber and maim me, possibly to my death. They would then run away from the scene of the event, and the authorities would have no desire to pursue these nameless thugs.

I exited the toilet to see no one coming my way. While I was ascending the second flight of stairs, the larger of the two Russians emerged at the top of the staircase. I chose not to engage in eye contact with him. I kept myself strictly to the left-hand side of the stairs, maintaining a tall and erect posture. We passed each other with no event to speak of.

I acknowledged the waitress and said goodbye to her courteously. She appeared to be reduced to a sweet, giggling, yet slightly embarrassed girl of her youth.

As I exited the restaurant, I took a moment to pause – take a deep inhalation of air and collect myself. I then advanced westwards between the large, opulent historic buildings. I decided not to look over my shoulder to see if the two men were following me. For a brief time, I heard no sound of footsteps behind me.

Suddenly, after about five minutes of leaving the restaurant, I could feel someone was directly on my tail. I smoothly turned my head round. I observed a man in his early 30s and of stocky build, looking sheepishly at his mobile phone, as well as making shifty glances at me. At this moment, I approached a juncture where there was a turning into a very quiet side street. I could choose to continue along the busier road with more pedestrian footfall, or else opt for the still side street with no discernible movement of human life. With a sense of courage, I chose the side street. Internally, I said to myself about the rogue individual, *"Let's see what you are made of. If you think you're so tough, let's see how willing you are to embrace the unknown."*

I purposefully strode down the quiet side street, deliberately not shifting my head to look round. I waited with bated breath to see if the man would follow. I just continued with my regular pace. I let go of my fears and worries within a matter of minutes. The man who had been by my side at the earlier specific junction had gone the other way. I walked past a site with building work happening. A large group of operatives from a firm of contractors were huddled together. They were discussing their build strategies. As I approached and sauntered by, their voices lowered. They all wore expressions with furrowed brows and looked straight at me.

Reaching the embankment, I decided to stroll along the Thames. I had no destination in mind. I was content to just absorb and appreciate the atmosphere, while maintaining a steady momentum forwards. It was as if I was some sort of lion on a quest to search for a pride of lionesses, which I would then become head of. There was even a leonine step to my gait, and what felt to me like an indomitable spirit.

After having passed lots of people, mostly sitting on the benches situated along the bank of the Thames and basking in the glorious weather, I reached the Houses of Parliament. There was a visceral response of awe and respect for the grandeur of its gothic architecture. The mass of people in this specific area was a little overwhelming. I managed to find a spot that was not so busy at the edge of the grassy square overlooking the side of the vast historic edifice.

Feeling a desire to lie down on the low stone plinth surround, I calmly and deliberately took off my shoes and made them as a rest for my head. I planted my tall frame on the very low wall. I then proceeded to close my eyes. I started letting the sounds of bodies walking by and the cacophony of the vehicles wash over me. I imagined what the public would be making of this comparatively strange occurrence.

The sun's warmth and light were a blessing. An overwhelming stillness seemed to descend into my heart. I was totally at peace with myself, yet all around there was the sound of the chaos of traffic and people frantically living out their lives.

After lying there in a supine position for about half an hour – and feeling utterly rested – I mindfully put my shoes back on. I favoured walking in a different direction. After skilfully negotiating my way across the wide, traffic-congested road, I headed towards Buckingham Palace along Pall Mall.

Arriving at St. James Park, I found a quieter spot in the open area of park. I lay down and closed my eyes again. This time I drifted into a short doze. I woke up with a startle. I lurched forwards onto my feet again, thinking I was in a very exposed situation. This would be a perfect opportunity for a satellite laser gun to pinpoint its terminal aim at me. It would kill me cleanly. I was now becoming a little weary of my endeavours that day. I plumped for making my way back home. I walked back along Pall Mall and into the centre. Once I spotted the first Underground station available, I found my way back to Marylebone station.

While sitting on the tube back, I observed a clean-cut, slim, handsome individual with an earpiece in one ear, sitting directly opposite me. He was not making any eye contact with me or anyone else for that matter. He had turned his focus inwards. He looked decidedly tense and nervous. I surmised that he might be a novice spy. He was probably given orders by central intelligence to get rid of me with a clean shot from a silencer gun to my heart. By his facial expressions, it was as if he was having a serious internal tussle, and therefore unable to act out the direct orders from central command. All I could feel was compassion for his plight. I wondered if, from the back of this crucial event, the individual's job would become more precarious, due to his slip-up in espionage.

A thought then crossed my mind. As much as my life was in danger, not one person could bring themselves to end it. It was not that I was invulnerable, just that my life was too precious in the grand scheme of the cosmos. Even if spies did have the gumption to try and end my life by whatever means available to them, then the gods would always miraculously intervene and prevent me from coming to any physical harm.

CHAPTER 16

THE SERPENT KING

I often went with my mood when it came to my choice of coffee shops. The Starbucks in the Royal Priors Shopping Centre in Leamington became my haunt in the mornings. The manager always engaged me in polite and interesting conversation, normally sparked off by my choice of reading material. There was also a very friendly Welsh woman, who was particularly keen on discussing my books and the ones she had been reading herself. They both lifted my spirits with their interest in me and enlivening communication. Somehow these were the only two members of staff I warmly connected to, while most of the others were frostier.

I had begun to go wandering a bit after my coffee. There was a nature reserve on the east side of Leamington called Welches Meadow. I had been to the grounds on a couple of occasions before, but on this day, something felt a little different.

It was a sunny day with no clouds present. I had with me a copy of the *Dhammapada*, which was a translation of the words of the Buddha. It was a profound discourse expressed in beautifully poetic form. As I approached the entrance to the open parkland, I heard loud calls and noises from youngsters in canoes on the river. They were shouting and yelping with delight.

As I walked near the edge of the river Leam, the path then took me to the middle section of a large expanse of grassland. After a pleasant five-minute stroll through the open parkland, I thought I would sit down on this gorgeous day and soak up the atmosphere.

There was a lovely view of the mature and majestic trees that marked the boundary of the open field. Within a couple of minutes of settling down into a comfortable posture, in which I crossed my legs and felt firmly supported, I heard a whistle go off. I could have sworn that it came from someone in the trees near where I was sitting and not the river further upstream. It went off again on a couple of subsequent occasions, each time within half a minute of the last. I could still hear the party of children in canoes. Their voices were faint, so I jettisoned the notion that the whistle came from their instructor. I heard behind me the sound of a few clicks. I was sure I also heard the subtle noise of rustling in the long grass, as if someone was trying to make their way very stealthily towards me.

I did not at any time turn my head around to see who was making the noise. Taking my book, I started reading the translation of the ancient and pure text. Hearing the clicking behind me again, I thought it might be coming from a weapon. Again, there was the repeated rustling of the long grass.

While I was reading, I noticed quite a strange feeling envelop me. I imagined it to be like an invisible serpent was climbing up my spine and offering complete protection to ward off attacks from outside. In Buddhism, there are such things as Nagas, which are mythical serpents that reside in the depths of the ocean of one's unconscious mind. They are thought to possess spiritual qualities. They are not of Christian mythology, as embodiments of evil. It was as if the king serpent Mucalinda was affording me complete insulation from harm.

After about 15 minutes of remaining extremely peaceful, I decided to make my slow but measured way out of the park. I was not perturbed by what I had just experienced. On one of my previous visits to the park, I had been sitting down in a similar spot. A bespectacled late-middle-aged woman had come by with her Yorkshire terrier. They both walked very near to me, and the woman carried on past me. Her dog, meanwhile, had frozen about a few meters away from where I was sitting.

Somehow, there was a force in me that the dog was sensing. The woman turned round to see why her pet had stopped walking and shook her head in bafflement. She went to grab his collar, confused and frustrated. She then dragged the pup past me while it strained at the lead. I wondered if all this was being picked up on satellite TV and transmitted to a billion homes around the planet. *What would everyone make of this event?* I thought it would stir up debate as to what my true intentions were. Personally, I would put it down to overcoming recent fears through a multiplicity of scenarios and events that made me much more in touch with my body and mind – it gave me a subtle but deep internal fire. I was sure that some would probably misread this event as a sign of something much more sinister.

On the day of the whistle noise, once I had left the park, it would be the last time that I would venture into the grassy field that year. The idea of strolling through the park and sitting in the middle of the expanse of land just did not continue to appeal. My activities on subsequent mornings became more orientated around the centre of town and its coffee shops.

I still wondered whether I was just deluding myself with all these theories about spies in the Buddhist movement. Over the course of the next month, I would slowly start to dismiss these views completely. My sleep patterns had pretty much returned to normal. The residual heat in me, over the weeks, would gradually ebb to a much cooler and more stable temperature. However, I still felt isolated by separating myself from my former Buddhist friends. I decided near the end of April to look up a different tradition that allegedly practised a modern Buddhism. Perhaps I needed to join another tradition, as I had followed the teachings of Sangharakshita for over 21 years, which was a good measure of time with one teacher.

After looking up the New Kadampa Tradition in Birmingham, I made plans to go and attend a short urban retreat, located in a large Victorian house on the outskirts of the city.

CHAPTER 17

NEW KADAMPA TRADITION

On arriving at the well-maintained Victorian house, I rang the bell and was duly greeted by an affable man.

"Hello! Have you come for the three-day urban retreat?" he enquired with a warm complexion and kindly eyes.

"Yes, I have. I hope I'm not too early arriving?" I said, being about 45 minutes early. I had deliberately planned this, so I could potentially speak to the senior monk or nun of this tradition. I hoped to quiz the individual about their practice and doctrinal viewpoint. I got into conversation with the man who had greeted me at the door. His name was Jay. After some much-needed pleasantries, I started asking him about pertinent aspects of his tradition. I interweaved the more serious discussion with dollops of light-heartedness, which seemed in line with the one-to-one and unfamiliar context.

I discovered that the monks and nuns wore robes. They had all made vows to observe the established code from the Buddha's time – a total of more than 200 rules. Already I pondered this fact. I thought that although they described themselves as modern Buddhists, they were quite heavily steeped in history and tradition. Their tradition placed high demands on monks and nuns compared to the laity. In our times of distractions here, there and everywhere, I felt it would be almost impossible to uphold all these rules, especially the vow about maintaining celibacy throughout one's life without subsequently denying one's fundamental life force.

Above all, I considered that we had to acknowledge where we were. We needed to try and walk the fine line between hedonism and an ascetic path. We had to think about the darker *and* the lighter sides of our lives. I understood these darker aspects to be primarily fear, hatred and desire. These shadow sides should not be suppressed; instead, one should try and turn towards, acknowledge, observe and experience them, with the aim of eventually letting go and transforming these strong forces. It is important, though, as much as is feasibly possible, to try not to mindlessly indulge in them. With gentle but steady effort, one should try to overcome these darker aspects of our psyche.

There were, however, dark elements in life, such as anger, which could have drive and power behind them. These could express themselves as uncomfortable truths in some music, films and sections of the arts. I also recognized these dark forces in understanding where we were in regard to sex. I thought very few could deny sex from their lives. Ultimately, this denial could lead to repression of one's baser forces. I was not in favour of a completely free sexual expression, though. Instead, I saw that it should be practised in healthy moderation to be set within an overall context of invaluable friendship with people who shared one's spiritual values of growth and development in consciousness.

I did believe that the more one was able to access and maintain higher states of consciousness through meditation – and therefore experience more and more profound contentment – then one could let go to a greater degree the attachments of the cruder and baser sexual urges.

In the movement I had left behind, I believed they had a much healthier understanding of the idea of the monks and the laity. They did not have a definite distinction between them. The people who were ordained into the order observed ten fundamental and overriding precepts, both negatively and positively formulated. These were considered training principles and moral guidelines. They were not generally taken as vows, but instead were areas of oneself, in body, speech and mind, which were there to be worked on and improved.

They were ultimately guidelines and not rules. The positive formulations were what the Buddhist practitioner could aspire to and forever better in themselves, until they became perfected when enlightenment was reached.

After about half an hour of conversation with Jay, the senior nun of the tradition came through the small but cosy seating area where we were sitting. She turned her head towards him and said that they would begin the retreat in a quarter of an hour. He said to her, "We've got one person here for the retreat. His name's Alastair. I'm correct, aren't I?" Jay said.

"Yes, you're right."

"Hello, Alastair," the nun replied. "Welcome to our place. Is this your first time here?"

"Yes, it is, but I've been with another movement before this. It was called Triratna. I've fallen out with them, as I believe that some of them might not be who they say they are, and I'm quite keen to now try your tradition and see what it's like."

"Sorry to hear that. Perhaps we might well be able to entice you into our collective throng?" she said with a half-wince and half-smile. It did not dawn on me that morning, but the more I reflected on this senior nun and others in their tradition, the more I felt that they were repressing a very strong life principle through the many monastic rules they had vowed to observe and uphold.

Another nun and a woman in her 30s named Leanne had joined the group. Jay made it clear to me that both Leanne and I would venture up to the large hut at the back of the garden, where the retreat would be held. We would then get situated in our respective spots, either on cushions or chairs. We would wait for the two senior nuns to arrive before taking up our sitting positions. The senior nun would then begin the retreat.

Inside the shrine room, Jay got the sound system ready, and cued up the specific music track he wanted to play. Once Jay, Leanne and I had got ready and waited silently for the two nuns to enter, I spotted an array of different unopened biscuits and sweets. They filled the shelving on the wall at the front, behind the raised platform where the retreat leader would sit. Among the biscuits were framed pictures of the movement's teacher. There were also lights that I later found out were permanently left on as a continual offering to their main living teacher and ancient Buddhist Je Tsongkhapa, whose teachings their tradition stemmed from.

I thought the assemblage of sugary foods and the constantly glowing lights were two odd practices in comparison to my more refined sensibilities. I understood the sentiment of using objects to show reverence for esteemed teachers, but not with biscuits and the other sweet foods that were on display. Also, they did not seem to respect the environment with their use of a continually powered electrical light source. I much preferred Triratna's simple gestures. There they would offer candles, symbolizing the enlightenment of the Buddha Shakyamuni, as well as our own Buddha potential; flowers to represent impermanence, as they are beautiful and scented one moment, but become faded and fallen in the next; and incense to symbolize the perfect community pervading in all directions. These I believed were more appropriate forms of offering, especially as the candles were always extinguished once the celebrations had been made.

To me, the sweets seemed to highlight the fact that the denial of sensory pleasures in so many other areas was in some way compensated by indulging in these sugary foods. I felt that, for Buddhists, there needed to be more a healthy balance with all forms of desire; not trying to stamp out some unwholesome desires while letting others run rampant as a way of keeping internal harmony. That was a path that Triratna followed, steering us towards refined and wholesome sensory pleasures, but without denying our strong base urges. I wondered if nuns or monks found tasty, sweet foods to be a source of solace, due to their many vows. In other words, I wondered if indulging in sweets would precariously keep them from breaching those many vows, passed down from ancient Buddhist tradition.

I believed that these historical principles and rules did not work well in our current age of mass information, communication and consumption. Other modes of operating, such as Triratna's approaches, were necessary as a Buddhist to meet with the modern Western mindset.

The two nuns entered the shrine room. Leanne and Jay clasped their hands and bowed their heads. I obediently followed suit. The senior nun assumed the position on an elevated platform, while the other nun sat in the audience. Jay fumbled with the electronic music device and experienced a little complication before succeeding in playing the right track. A few moments after the music started playing, all four of them broke out in song to a tuneful yet slightly syrupy melody. I wondered whether it was my past experiences that had me baulking at the sound of the tune, or just that the general atmosphere did not sit comfortably with me and never would do.

I thought it would help my slightly begrudging mood if I joined in. I used the book that had been given to me earlier so I would know what the words to the songs were. I tentatively joined in with the unified vocal expression. It helped me to get a vague understanding of their interpretation of the Buddhist teaching. This combined rendition of tuneful verses lasted what seemed like a good hour. Once the music ended, I waited with bated breath for the senior nun's first utterance.

I believed that this elevation of teacher over disciples that had been handed down from Tibetan teachers was something else that did not fit in with the spirit of exploration and openness here in the West. This act of formal separation between the laity and monks or nuns was, I thought, more a guard against their fragile egos – and not what was conducive to a healthy human exchange. I believed this was one more thing that was incongruous with our modern times.

The head nun spoke quite convincingly about karma, rebirth and the idea that all actions have consequences, interweaving stories from her own life to substantiate her valid points. I had no reason to call into question any of her views. In some ways, I responded favourably to all of them. I was encouraged by this exposition. I believed that there might be some merit in pursuing this tradition further.

After ending the talk, some more music played, and we collectively sang the verses. Then, once the music had stopped, the two nuns left the building. Jay, Leanne and I put away the cushions and mats while conducting a general clear-up. While we were tidying the room, Jay said to me,

"Did you feel the strength of the energy with the Vajrayana ritual we undertook? I noticed it. It felt quite strong."

"I perhaps found a little of the energy you are talking about, but I can't say it was anyway near discernible," I replied in a conciliatory tone, as I had in fact not felt even a glimmer of raw energy. "Vajrayana" literally means "the way of the thunderbolt" and was meant to be the third and last way to gain enlightenment. It was meant to be the speedy path to awakening but depended heavily on the guru-disciple relationship. If the guru was very skilled, and the disciple was willing and able, great progress could be made by the disciple through the guru's initiation and instruction. Great forces and energies could be invoked from the subconscious, yet if the disciple was not calm, tranquil and together in mind and heart, it could result in a mental collapse of the individual. The Vajrayana was not a path I was willing to explore in any depth. I preferred to stick to the Mahayana, with its emphasis on generosity, altruism and the will to enlightenment for the sake of all other sentient beings. The Mahayana adopted a steady but consistent development in all aspects of one's life, in one broad sweep.

I therefore preferred to adhere to meditation techniques that would cultivate concentration, integration and positive emotion, in the form of mindful breathing and universal loving kindness or friendliness, respectively. These were the basis of *samatha*, the Pali word for calm and tranquillity, from which *vipassana*, the Pali word for insight, could be established.

I stayed for lunch with all of them still present, but before the meal, I engaged in conversation with the head nun in the well-maintained garden. The weather was, yet again, bright – blue skies and wonderful sunshine.

"I would love to become a monk, but I feel the demands placed on all of you are extreme, with the many strict vows you have to abide by."

"If you find the vows too difficult, there'd always be a possibility to become part of the laity. They've a more restricted set of precepts that they follow and try and adhere to," she said, trying to appease me.

"The only downside for me would be that, as a layperson, I wouldn't have the opportunity to teach Buddhism or meditation, unlike the monks or nuns who are able to do so."

"That's not strictly true. We've several laypersons who teach just like the monks or nuns do. You'd have to go on a three-year course, though, and you'd have to teach in the style of our tradition, but if you felt we suited your understanding of Buddhism, and you were prepared to undertake the three-year-long course, which would involve some teacher training, then this tradition might well suit you."

"When you mention that laypeople do have the opportunity to teach, that fact really interests me. I had been teaching meditation myself at my former Buddhist place. I truly believe that, in my situation, teaching is so fundamental to my spiritual growth," I said passionately.

"If you wanted to know a bit more of our tradition, I could point you in the direction of some good books by our highly esteemed teacher. Or else, there is a spring festival and retreat near the Lake District at the end of May in three- or four-weeks' time. You could go to find out more about us."

"I think a retreat near the Lake District sounds very appealing. I'm pretty sure I don't have anything pressing around that time. How many people normally go?"

"You probably would find that it's attended by thousands of people. Most pitch tents, all dotted around the grounds. It's all very well managed. The retreat talks and meditations take place in quite a newly designed, decorative and harmoniously arranged large building, whilst other activities are centred in the old Priory, which is a vast historic edifice," she replied.

"The more you mention it, the more I think it would be ideal for me in my current situation. I also miss not being on retreat or at Buddhist festivals, so it would come in quite handy in my present circumstances," I said.

After more discussion about my situation with my previous Buddhist movement, we both went inside and joined the rest of them. They were beginning to tuck into a light vegetarian meal. I was encouraged by their vegetarian habits, which was not so prevalent in the more historic Buddhist traditions in Southeast Asia and the Far East. As I sat down among them and helped myself to the food on offer, I listened attentively to the ensuing discussion.

The subject was skirting around the issue of the mind and ethics. I felt suddenly impelled to mention the first verses of the *Dhammapada* that I had memorized on a previous occasion.

So, I said, "In my previous Buddhist group, we quite often stressed the first couple of verses of the *Dhammapada*, which was a sutra meant to be one of the most poetic and timeless words that the Buddha had ever uttered. It goes like this:

Experiences are preceded by mind, led by mind and produced by mind. He who speaks or acts with an impure mind – suffering follows, as the cartwheel follows the hoof of the ox drawing the cart.

Experiences are preceded by mind, led by mind and produced by mind. He who speaks or acts with a pure mind – happiness follows, like a shadow that never departs."

The other nun remarked to me, "That's a very beautiful quote."

"Thank you." I was happy that I had imparted this nugget of wisdom, although I wondered if the ramifications of what I had just said might percolate through their minds and not necessarily plant themselves and take root. The overriding view I had, though, was that their tradition spoke a similar language to my previous movement, but with different emphases, especially around the area of karma, rebirth and emptiness.

After lunch, I decided to leave, as I felt I had sampled enough of their approach to Buddhist practice, one with which I was not so familiar. That evening, back in my flat, I went online to book myself on their spring festival. I thought to myself, *Why not try them out?* I was now no longer affiliated to Triratna. I needed to get a sense of their festival format. If all else failed, I could see it as a holiday in lovely countryside.

CHAPTER 18

THE FORGIVENESS

Over subsequent days I spent quite a lot of time on my own reflecting, in a somewhat restless and isolated situation in my flat. *Were the people in Triratna frauds? Had my earlier unstable mind been subtly distorting reality?* The more I contemplated the facts, the greater became the realization that I had made a serious mistake with my interpretation of past events. From my experience of the Kadampa tradition, I strongly believed that the way Triratna explicated the Buddha's teaching was more in line with what my heart and reason were telling me. Triratna's approach was more progressive and modern than the Kadampa tradition or any other alternative, for that matter.

After days of deliberation, I took the bold step to write a very conciliatory e-mail to all those to whom I had sent the previous vicious e-mail. I had to, in some ways, try and heal the rift I had caused between me and Triratna. I proceeded to write:

Dear All,

Around the start of this New Year, I changed medical surgeries, as I receive a fortnightly dose of medication that is administered to me by a nurse. I used to attend a surgery close to my parent's home, but I then registered with a medical practice local to where I live in Leamington Spa, thus trying to further erode the ties that bound me to my parents. But a distinction could be made between the two surgeries: My previous place cared for patients, while the Leamington surgery processed patients.

By about the middle of March, I was starting to sleep less and develop ideas of being closely monitored by spies from intelligence services. I was starting to become paranoid and delusional. One of the main ideas I developed was the notion that I was a Truman Show-style figure being watched by millions, if not billions of people around the world. However, no one could reveal anything to me for fear of being prosecuted by the authorities. I was convincing myself that all the signs in my life pointed to this assertion.

It is interesting to note that the nurse at my new medical practice did not open the medication in front of me, as had been done in previous places. However, as soon as I walked into her treatment room, she had the syringe fully loaded with no ampoule in sight. I can only conclude from this that, probably on more than one occasion, she either diluted the medication, or else she gave me a different drug or even just water. What the underlying reason and motive was, I will never know. As the saying goes, "The proof of the pudding is in the eating," and this recent episode I experienced serves to substantiate the fact that I was not being given the correct treatment. I had been on the drug for more than 17 years, and up until this time, I had been well and healthy.

This brings me round to apologizing profusely for the last e-mail I sent all of you, and the worry and concern it must have caused. I also truly and deeply regret sending it. When I read it back to myself, my message sounds hostile and venomous in its content and delivery. This is the antithesis of my loving nature. In my defence, I was still in the throes of my episode with a confused head. I can assure you all that I am now 100 per cent recovered. I do not intend to ever go through that experience again. This time, I will have checks in place, i.e., making sure I witness the nurse opening the ampoule in front of me before administering it.

I lost my job through this turbulent period, but a few good things have come from this ordeal. I have upped my game with meditation, and now meditate 2 to 3 times a day, with each session lasting for 40 to 50 minutes. Now I am out of work, I can devote more time to the study and practice of Buddhism. I very recently inherited money from my uncle passing away last year, which could keep me comfortably going for the next couple of years while I look for the most appropriate architectural practice to work in.

I have left the surgery in Leamington and, for the time being, I have gone back to the one local to my parents' place, which I know well and trust. With my involvement at the Birmingham centre, I will start to attend events and courses very soon. All this re-engagement will be taken steadily and tentatively at first, but I want to fully immerse myself again with Triratna, and almost start where I left off – which seemed to be on a very firm footing.

With much Metta,
Alastair

Over the coming days I received several well-wishes from a few of those to whom I had written. They commented on how brave I had been in this last e-mail, and how the writings in my first e-mail did not reflect the person they knew. They only knew someone who was a warm, friendly and engaging individual, who had a lot of empathy for those he met. I was touched by the overwhelming support from a lot of my former Buddhist friends. This seemed to confirm to me their authenticity. I knew Buddha Day was going to be held on Sunday, 11 May. I decided that that day would be my first chance to meet and explain myself to some of my fellow companions on the Buddhist path.

A few days after I sent my e-mail, the ordination team in Norfolk sent me a message, stating that I would not be welcome on the Triratna retreat that I had signed up for that year. They had to seriously consider the well-being of the other retreatants. They needed to be thoroughly convinced that I had fully recovered, which they still were not. They suggested to me that I re-establish contact with members of the Birmingham Buddhist community. Only when the community felt comfortable that my health was fully restored would the ordination team feel reassured of my return.

I had asked for ordination into the Triratna order about five and a half years back. I felt that this dramatic episode was another setback to my ordination into the movement. Some of the order members highlighted to me and others on the path that we needed to view it as a process. We should try and enjoy the journey, rather than grasping after the goal of becoming ordained. They also shared that we did not have to be an order member to make spiritual progress. I was especially appreciative of my opportunity, over those two and a half years, to teach meditation to beginners at the Buddhist centre. It established a strong sense of purpose and confidence.

On Buddha day, I arrived about five minutes before the meditation in the morning with a mild degree of trepidation, but also an accompanying mild exhilaration. Here was a chance to re-engage my practice with a movement I wholly endorsed. Not only did they look far and wide, exercising critical evaluation of most Buddhist traditions and schools, but they also directed their gaze and focus on pertinent aspects of Western civilization, appreciating a lot of Western literature, philosophy and the arts. The movement cast their eyes on whatever artistic works surrendered their egos to higher, more visionary forces – works that were the realm of an illumined imagination, and not the product of a selfish or fanciful imagination. They also strove to become more socially engaged.

As I entered the café area, a bright sunlight streamed through the long skylight overhead and washed over the congregating group. I was greeted by Mahina, a female order member of a very pleasant and robust nature.

"Hello, Alastair. Welcome back," she said with a wonderfully warm and inviting timbre to her voice.

"Hello Mahina. It's good to be back. Sorry about what you had to be party to. I hope to never have to go through that again," I said, trying to raise her spirits with my newfound mental health, while wearing a smile that reached from ear to ear.

"We were all really concerned for you. There has been a lot of Metta towards you and your situation from all sorts of people who know you. It was lovely to witness their concern," she said, noticeably lifting me.

The day at the centre ended with a *puja*, the ancient Indian Pali word for a devotional worship. This consisted of reciting beautifully poetic verses and chanting mantras, which reflected the attributes of certain archetypal Buddhas and the historical Buddha. The verses that are recited are there to invoke seven different spiritual moods and emotions in the participant, ranging from worship to rejoicing in merits, and culminating in a verse to do with the transference of merit and self-surrender. This is enhanced by an exquisitely decorated shrine, as well as offerings of lighted tealights during the chanting of a particular mantra near the beginning of the ceremony.

Once we finished and completed the clear-up, I drove home. I pondered that although it was a very positive initial meeting with some of my Buddhist friends, it would take quite a long time for their wounds to properly heal. The trust I had earlier forged had been severely weakened, but thankfully not irreparably so.

CHAPTER 19

THE BUDDHIST FESTIVAL

The Kadampa festival and retreat was fast approaching. I decided that I needed to purchase a decent tent and some waterproof outdoor clothing. After buying a suitably robust tent that would not cave in or disintegrate with bad weather, I set about the night before my departure to pack a large travelling bag with all the necessary items. I planned for there being either hot or wet weather, so I stuffed as many different items of clothing as the large bag could handle. *Better to take precautions than be caught short of essentials*, I mused.

I never paid much attention to weather forecasts, but I was made aware by one of the members of Starbucks in Leamington that it was predicted to be a wet weekend for much of the country. My positive mental attitude kept me from feeling despondent about this weather report. It was the company of people that made a festival and retreat – or for that matter, a holiday – pleasurable.

It was the Thursday on the bank holiday weekend at the end of May. I had now let go of the view that I was a *Big Brother* spectacle for all to tune into. It was a relatively long journey on the motorway, and I made a few wrong turns near the destination. I spotted, as I slowly drove down the tarmacked drive, a large, highly ornate building. I knew from having flicked through their retreat brochure that this was their crowning architectural achievement. It was partially hidden behind a large, reclaimed brick wall, and set amongst some beautiful oak trees. The visitors' cars were parked in open fields outside the grounds. Two individuals, one young Scottish man and an elderly woman, greeted me at the entrance to the verdant makeshift car park.

"Have you come for the festival and retreat here?" the handsome Scottish guy dutifully asked.

"Yes, I have. You'd like to see my pass number that I got from the internet," I said, pre-empting what the Scottish guy was going to ask next and offering a warm smile in return.

"Thanks. That'd be great." I showed him my printed slip with the details. He then courteously waved me through.

The Priory was a gigantic and historic edifice. I was asked by assembled staff, dotted at various points along the route, to make my way to the reception area to register. A very tall spire in the middle of the complex hinted at the majestic nature of the building. I could only imagine what the rest of it looked like, as my initial view had been blocked by some two-storey dwellings that sat alongside the impressive hub.

As I was sitting obediently in the waiting area of reception, along with quite a few other festivalgoers, I observed how most of the staff, who were registering the procession of people, were wearing matte red robes, either as monks or nuns. I also became aware, over the course of my stay, how the nuns outnumbered the monks in this tradition by a considerable margin.

I had slight difficulty pitching my tent, although I had the instructions laid out before me. It had been many years previously, whilst in my teens, when I had last pitched a tent. A young South African man was also starting to pitch his tent nearby. He could see that I was struggling. He asked me, "Do you need a hand with that?"

"That would be brilliant if you could help. I haven't put these up in a very long time."

"I do a lot of camping, so I'm very familiar with how to put them up. Back in South Africa, there've been many opportunities to go camping,"

"Whereabouts in South Africa do you live?"

"Johannesburg. Where do you live?

"Leamington Spa, in Warwickshire. Nowhere near as far or as exotic as where you've come from," I said, suitably impressed with this individual's commitment and dedication to attend the festival.

I found out his name was Tony. I was dazzled by his expert hand at constructing my tent, with a small part played by me. I offered to help him erect his much larger tent, and this was gratefully received. The sun shined that late afternoon with a soft, warm light, which was very much unlike what had been forecast. I thought a little pessimistically that it would only be a matter of time before it worsened.

After supper had been and gone with two time slots – one at 6pm and one at 7pm – it was time for the evening singing at 8:30pm, and a brief talk by one of the leading nuns in the tradition. It was mandatory for informal festival participants to sit outside of the main hall under protective tent canopies, as we had not been formally inducted into the tradition. I entered the confines of the temporary structure. For a few moments I stopped and paused to take in all the many different people, who were mingling or seated. I noticed three large flat-screen TV monitors fronting the immediate collection of people, who would be seated under the closed tent canopies. I pondered that this tradition was not short of money, and they probably had some very wealthy donors, who had contributed large sums of cash.

I parked myself on the seat at the edge of an empty row just in case I needed to make a quick getaway. Most people came without their children, as couples. There were others who, like me, had arrived on their own. I was sitting in the chair, slightly apprehensive of what awaited me. I was wondering if they would play that sickly sweet tune, and then everyone would sing along. What grated was that, in my opinion, the music was far removed from the shades of dark in which reality could also manifest. The music displayed a definite one-sidedness to the light aspect of reality. To my refined ear, it seemed to filter out the deeper, darker underbelly that lurks in reality's union of opposites. I could now see why there were so many nuns in the tradition, as this sentimental music might well appeal to their seemingly sweet-natured temperaments.

During the start of the service, there was a video of the founding monk of the tradition. He was walking around a newly opened temple and commenting to the camera about the edifice. What struck me most about this individual was that, although he came across as a very kind and sweet man, he just appeared to lack depth and the quality of being rooted to the earth. It might have been his age that was tainting my view of him, but I had read somewhere about a very well-known Vietnamese monk, Thich Nhat Hanh. He was probably quite similar in age to him. He was described as the combination of a snail, a cloud and a heavy piece of machinery. I really got this description when I had subsequently seen him in a video clip giving a talk. The clip somehow seemed to confirm these attributes of the Vietnamese monk, but I just did not feel completely inspired by this founding monk of the Kadampa tradition. However, I was impressed by his dedication and tireless effort to disseminate the teachings of the Buddha to a much wider audience. I also thought that his writings, especially on the nature of emptiness, were exemplary, after I had read part of one of his books before embarking on the festival.

After about 45 minutes of singing interspersed with videos of the founder, the most senior nun of the order, who was already sitting cross-legged on the central podium at the far end of the hall, began to deliver an address. I was impressed by her confident demeanour – she held the stage. A third of the way through, I started to get restless on my chair as she was talking about empowerments. This was a concept with which I was unfamiliar, and of which, at that time, I was a little wary. After a little internal tussle, I rose from my chair and made a measured but determined route for the exit. I smiled graciously at the young woman, who was marking the exit of the tents. She warmly reciprocated.

After an unexpectedly good night of sleep on my first night, I unzipped the tent. I spied, with slightly bleary eyes, sunlight streaming and hitting the Priory building. I also observed the trees on one side were basking in the warm, rich early-morning glow. They were defining the edge of the main lawn to the building. My tent was deliberately set under tree canopies, so I would not experience the full force of the sun's morning rays. I could, therefore, extend my sleep that little longer. I glanced at my watch. It read 6:25am. I thought I could go and wash myself early, hopefully beating out the rest of the retreatants, who would descend on the single-sex communal bathrooms. No such luck was had. I patiently had to wait my turn in the queue.

Once I had my shower and got dressed in the slightly awkward shape of the two-person tent, I decided to venture into the Priory building while the service in the huge shrine hall was being conducted. There was a particularly friendly security guard sitting at the entrance area. Immediately, I engaged him in convivial conversation. I said to him,

"Are you okay?"

"Yes, fine thanks. How are you?" The conversation continued briefly with light-hearted small talk, until I felt compelled to ask him whereabouts in Liverpool he came from, as I had noticed his Liverpudlian accent. His name was Mick. He said he came from an area that I was not familiar with. In fact, I was not acquainted with most areas of Liverpool, except for where my grandparents and uncle had lived by Sefton Park. I knew Lark Lane quite well, as when I had visited my uncle in the past, we would gravitate in the morning and evening to that road with its lively bars, pubs and coffee houses.

"So, your grandparents and uncle lived off Sefton Park, hey. That must've been a pleasant experience for them. Sefton Park is a lovely park – very green and lush. There're the big, impressive houses at the edge of the park. Did they happen to live in one of those properties?" he asked with benign curiosity.

"No, they actually lived on one of the side streets that came off the big road, which was Aigberth Drive."

"That's right Aigberth Drive. I was trying to recall what that road was called."

I found from his exchange that he came across as kind. He did not want to labour any of the humour aspect in our chat. He might have suggested from my accent that my grandparents would have been the perfect candidates for one of those houses, along Aigberth Drive –

with a retinue of servants. If he had posed that humorous response to me, I would have taken it in jest. However, I believed that through his practice as a Buddhist, he did not want to conform to any of the usual stereotypes that so often were used to label and categorize people.

As I left him to continue with his duties, I saw that, just behind where he was sitting, there was a very large Buddha in a seated position with a purple halo around his head. I had noticed this statue on my arrival, the previous evening. After spending a few moments appreciating the aesthetic aspects of this seated Buddha, I went back to Mick. I asked him, "Mick, which Buddha is that statue meant to represent?"

"It is depicting Maitreya, the future Buddha," he said matter-of-factly.

I took one more look at the seated figure and thought that it was ironic that it wore a purple halo, as that was one of my favourite colours. Something in me felt it was significant. Also, the statue was a seated Buddha and not one in a full lotus posture on the ground, as was how the historical Buddha was so often depicted. *Could it be that this future Buddha would emerge from the West, as opposed to the East, as he was more accustomed to sitting on chairs than sitting on the floor, due to a particularly Western upbringing and conditioning?* Over the following days, I mulled over this thought from time to time when I was in more quiet and reflective moods.

Amongst the throng of people on the retreat, I spotted a particularly grounded yet effervescent and attractive blonde. Having consumed my lunch, I made my way to the light and airy tea shop set in a conservatory adjacent to the main lawn. As I strolled there, my eyes met with hers. She was waiting in the queue for the second lunchtime slot. We both gave each other warm, beaming smiles. I felt a frisson of delight in this pure and innocent non-verbal exchange. Ordering an Earl Grey tea from the shop, I sat on some outdoor furniture, which was conveniently provided. The sun was wonderfully strong, warming me to an optimum temperature.

After quietly sipping my tea, I watched various characters walk past and a few who were sitting amongst me. I decided I was going to have a brief lie-down in my tent for an afternoon nap.

Once I had rested for about 45 minutes, I went out of the tent, zipped it up, and strolled slowly from my tent to the main building. On my way, the blonde woman happened to be just coming out of her tent. I felt impelled to speak to her. "Aren't we lucky with the weather? It's so gorgeous today."

"I know!" she responded with verve. "It's wonderful, and to think they'd forecast bad weather for much of the country. It seems amazing that this is what we're getting."

"What are you planning to do now?" I enquired innocently, but with a sneaking hope that she would join me in conversation.

"I was just going to have some tea, go indoors and read this book. Would you like to join me?" she said expectantly, inadvertently flashing one of the Kadampa tradition books.

"That'd be lovely. I suggest we could go upstairs into the main Priory building, where it's quieter and cooler. I'd earlier noticed that there's some comfortable, soft seating up on the landing. Does that sound good?"

"Sounds perfect to me," she said with visible delight.

We both ordered tea in takeaway cups and made our way to the upstairs landing, slumping ourselves on opposing sofas that had a thin, old oak table in between.

"By the way, what's your name?" I asked.

"Sarah, what's yours?"

"Alastair. How long have you been engaged with this tradition?"

"Not long, probably only about a year and a half. I'm not always able to manage the weekly group study meetings, as I live in Essex and work in London. I normally don't get back home until quite late," she said with a forced smile, betraying a hint of weariness with her predicament. I sensed that she was probably contemplating, in a sudden flash of memory, all those early morning rises and thousands of hours of commuting she had to endure. This was the downside of her job in London. After talking about what we thought the festival was like, I asked, "What's your job in London?"

"My current job is as a marketing manager for an environmental waste-management company. I tend to work as a contractor rather than being PAYE. I like the freedom of working for a couple of years with a company for a decent salary, and then taking three to six months off to go travelling," she said with obvious joy welling up. I was reluctant to continue with the discussion on her job for the moment. Instead, I focussed on her travels, which would hopefully brighten her already buoyant mood.

"Where was the last place you visited on your travels?"

"It was Malawi. I spent six months out there. For three months, I taught in a primary school. Then, for two months, I travelled the country with a friend I had made at the school. Then in the last month I went around parts of the country on my own." Her face glowed.

"That sounds so thrilling and adventurous. What you're telling me does make being a contractor, with those benefits, an exciting prospect. I guess it helps to be also working in London, where jobs are plentiful. I think employers jump at the chance to recruit people like you. I'm sure it would impress any future employer that, when you have had a six-month break, you can show that you've been doing something worthwhile with your time," I said with a great deal of interest in her situation.

"You're right, employers do love that. I've been told I'm good at my job, which makes me even more marketable. I've started thinking recently though that I don't just want to take any job that presents itself. With my limited Buddhist practice, I'm looking for jobs that have an ethical standpoint, and so I'm a little more discerning than before. That's why I am so chuffed with myself in finding this job, as I sifted through quite a few adverts. I held out until this post came along. The company's got very good credentials towards their staff and the environment," she said with a healthy pride.

"Impressive! That sounds commendable! I hope I would do the same thing if I was in your position. Do you have many friends in Essex that you keep in touch with?" I changed the subject to learn more about her.

"It's funny you ask. I've quite a few male friends, either exes that have stayed in touch and remained friends, or else male friends with whom I've shared accommodations and kept in touch with. Where do you live?"

"I live in Leamington Spa, in a basement flat near the river. When entering the flat on a wet day, I normally wear a mask and snorkel to get around," I quipped.

"Don't forget your flippers," she said with a faint upturn at the side of her mouth.

"No, don't worry, the flat is perfectly fine. Issues to do with surface water run-off have been dealt with by an extra drainage system that was installed after a flood occurred a few years back," I added sensibly.

"I've been really enjoying my time off work over the last three months, as I've managed to inherit some money," I went on. "Since my time off, I've ploughed myself into my Buddhist practice and studies, and developed friendships with people I can have meaningful and soulful chats with."

"You mean like the one we're having now?"

"Except I'm still getting to know you, so we are still only skirting around fairly superficial topics, except for my basement flat, which is deadly serious!" I said trying to keep a mock stern expression.

"You mean your quasi-water pressure chamber. Do you keep exotic fish in your giant tank?" she playfully teased.

"Only the best kind from warmer climes with beautiful iridescent colours."

"I expect you've given them all names?" the edges of her mouth started to creep further outwards.

"Yes, I have. There's Harry, Jane and Peter, amongst others."

"You mean to say you can tell which sex they are?" By this point, she was positively beside herself with laughter.

"I'm on familiar terms with all my fishes, since we're all couped up in such a confined wet space," I was also now grinning like a Cheshire cat.

During our conversation, I noticed her cheeky sense of humour would surface every now and again. I was attracted to women who were in touch with a darker side of their personality, but also complemented by a lighter and more carefree stance.

I launched myself into explaining my version of the Triratna movement and their fundamental philosophical standpoints. I talked to her about the act of "Going for Refuge" to the three jewels – namely the Buddha, the Dharma and the Sangha – as the central and definitive act of being a Buddhist. I also shared the importance placed on spiritual friendship in the movement. I explained how my teacher, Sangharakshita, an Englishman, looked to the Pali scriptures for guidance, and pulled from the wealth of knowledge he had gained from many teachers whilst living in India for 20 years. These ranged from Theravadin monks to Tibetan lamas. There was another interesting angle to this incredible man. He had read very widely indeed, especially the classics in literature, philosophy and religious texts while he was growing up. He had an extremely retentive memory. I had witnessed a hint of this when I went to meet him briefly about 4 or 5 years ago, while he was in his late 80s. I happened to mention William Blake – in particular, his poem about a world in a grain of sand. Even I struggled to remember it word for word, but he dazzled me with a recital of that poem without any pauses. It could have been that he remembered especially well because it was close to his heart, but I was sceptical of this notion.

We both went downstairs. Immediately after I had set foot on the ground floor and said goodbye to Sarah, I was verbally accosted, but in a kind and good-humoured way, by a seated blonde Russian woman and a tall, sweet-natured man by her side. They were assigned to try and recruit as many volunteers as possible in helping with the multitude of tasks that were required around the building.

"Hello there! I'm sure you'd love to get involved. Just think how much merit you'll accrue by giving your time to some worthwhile activities. You'll also help to expend your energy in healthy channels," she said with bubbliness, which I found hard to resist.

"Sure! I'll sign myself up for some duties." I found that I was not attracted to her like I was to Sarah, but she had a palpable charm and appeal through the sheer force of her personality. Her name was Nastasia, which I found out during our brief chat.

Sarah had left for the late afternoon singing in the main shrine hall. I decided to go to the north wing in the Priory building, once I had figured out what my cleaning and helping duties were. There, I sat on a cushioned chair and meditated in the silent, medium-sized shrine room. This would become the place where I would meditate throughout this festival, due to its consistently quiet and peaceful setting. I had earlier been made aware of this room in my conversation with Mick, the security guard.

I had decided that I was going to see this festival more as a holiday. I, therefore, had planned to mostly do my own thing, while still undertaking my cleaning and preparation duties. Over the span of the festival, I spent quite a lot of time savouring teas in the tea shop conservatory or sitting outside in the sunshine. In these spots, I would read or merely observe people and nature. The weather was unexpectedly good. When I returned home, I found out that much of the country had rain rather than sun, which I saw as mysterious and magical.

The following day had some more superb weather in the early afternoon. At that time, I came past Mick sat at his desk by the entrance. I asked him how things were going. Mick replied with a seriousness tempered by a modicum of positivity, "Things are quite good, but we had a little incident arise last night. There were some intruders on the grounds. Obviously, we weren't sure what they were up to, but we've been instructed not to allow anyone onto the grounds. The safety of the people taking part in this festival is paramount. My security men who were on patrol rallied round. They got a few more of us from our beds, to help with the commotion. It was a little disturbing, to say the least, but I guess all part of the job."

"That sounds a little scary. It's good that you have such a disciplined and willing workforce. I suppose that's all your collective Buddhist practice coming into play."

"I think you're right!" said Mick. Just then, he got a radio call on his walkie-talkie, which buzzed with a crackling reception. Fortunately, Mick could make out what was being said, even though to me it was barely intelligible. He then answered the call with,

"We're not supposed to let anyone who hasn't paid onto the grounds, and you're saying that even though we started the festival on Thursday, he'd like to pay the full sum for the rest of the festival and retreat."

From what I could make out from the poor reception on the walkie-talkie, this person was insistent. He was in a fancy car, which seemed to suggest he had money and probably felt that, with cash and worldly influence, he could be much more persuasive.

"I really don't care if he's a famous dignitary – he hasn't paid and registered in time. My orders are not to allow anyone who hasn't met those conditions to come to the festival."

"He says he would like to speak to you. He does have a very fancy car," were the garbled words that came back through the receiver.

"Go on. Send him up to me. I'll tell him categorically that he cannot attend," replied Mick forcefully, yet with a degree of composure.

He signed off with the member of his team. He swivelled his head towards me, as I stood patiently by his side.

"Some people really don't understand. They somehow feel they can pay their way into events with their bulging wallets, and with what they feel is their degree of power and position," Mick said, clearly starting to get a little angry. He was speaking with a little more vehemence. Although, he spoke to the other security guard in a relatively composed fashion, his raw and visceral emotions were now bubbling their way to the surface. He was finding it a little difficult to contain his frustration.

About five minutes had elapsed before a middle-aged man came through the main entrance. He was well-built and tall, dressed in conservative summer clothes. He had some designer sunglasses perched on the front of his quite fulsome shock of light-brown hair. I guessed he was in his mid-40s. I did not know what car he drove, but as soon as I clapped eyes on him, I imagined he drove a very fast and aggressive-looking sports car. I had subconsciously linked the person with that type of car, as though they were synonymous. I noticed an immediate twinge of dislike towards this individual. Much of the man's overt values and attributes, which I was registering, were mostly what I was trying to move away from in my life, or, at the very least, lessen my attachment to. He spoke with a cut-glass English accent. He said to Mick, "Hello, you must be Mick, the chief security guard. I've been trying to persuade your personnel that I should be allowed to attend this event, as I'm willing to pay the full price."

"Well, I've been given strict instructions from the organizers that once the retreat has started, I should not let anyone else attend," Mick replied assertively but courteously.

"But I've driven all this way from Surrey. I thought you would show compassion for my plight. Isn't that what you, as Buddhists, promote?"

"We might preach compassion to all beings, but we are not pushovers by any means. We're also not doormats to be walked all over. I'm sorry you had to drive all this way to be told that you can't attend, but I'm under strict orders, and so my answer to you is still no." Mick was still managing not to lose his temper and remained admirably calm.

"How can I try and convince you? Perhaps if I pay you more than the going rate?"

"I'm sorry, but my answer is still categorically no, and I will also not be bribed." I detected the faintest hint of anger in Mick's voice.

"Where do I stay for the night, then?" said the gentleman with rising indignation.

"You'll have to work that one out for yourself. There are plenty of B&Bs around this area or even hotels. You could also drive back home now and perhaps make it back before the end of the evening," he responded, knowing that his resistance was rock solid.

"I thought you Buddhists were better than that!" he retorted and then stormed out of the building. The last trace of him was the sound of his loud, gravelly turbo engine receding into the distance.

I thought that Mick handled it beautifully. He was direct and assertive, yet kind in his delivery and manner. For a brief instance, I felt a sense of schadenfreude towards this well-heeled individual, but it quickly fizzled away when I thought he might have found himself in a pickle – for the night at least. I did, however, think that as the man seemed to have money, he would not be in too much of a scrape. If all else failed, he could drive back home that evening in his fast sports car. I did think it rather odd, though, that he would have come all this way and try it on with the staff to end up being turned away, which seemed to me to be the inevitable outcome. At the time, I did not ruminate on this incident, but later in the year, I felt that the previous night's commotion with the security team and the rich man's boldness were in some way connected to me being there on the grounds.

The following day in the afternoon, I happened to meet up with Sarah again. We both went for a long walk in the direction of the small town of Ulverston.

"Have you had many boyfriends in the past?"

"Yeah, I've had quite a few, and I nearly always stay in touch with them after we break up. I'd say that one of my exes who I had a long relationship with is probably one of my best friends now."

"I wonder why that is?" I queried.

"I guess it's possibly because I'm so relaxed around men, and that I'm accepting of their foibles. We all have dark spots and things that irritate us about someone else, but I remain open to those blemishes as well as their more favourable aspects. It's probably also due to having a brother who is schizophrenic. He's been holed up in a psychiatric ward for years. It makes me more understanding and empathetic towards people. I'm sure that's partly why I was drawn to Buddhism, because of its emphasis on compassion to all beings, and seeing that all our actions are determined by the myriad conditions from this and previous lives."

"You're so right! I couldn't agree more! I'm sorry to hear that about your brother. Do you get to see him much?" I asked tactfully.

"I usually try and see him every other weekend, normally for an afternoon visit."

"How is he these days?"

"He can get very angry at times and sometimes says nasty or hurtful stuff to me. I know he's suffering, and that this is his way of coping with his condition," she replied.

"I thought I would let you know that I suffer from schizophrenia myself. I've had it since I was 19, but I've been predominantly well and healthy for about the last 17 or so years, as I've been receiving a regular course of medication," I stated matter-of-factly.

"I don't think any one of us are actually 'normal'. We all have the potential to manifest mental disorders given the right conditions. Who wants to be normal anyway?"

"You're so right! I think so many people are living their lives trying to conform to one another's expectations of what we consider to be normal. We're all a mixture of the sublime and the ridiculous. When the Buddha cast his spiritual eye over the limitless beings throughout the infinite universe, he said that most beings were mad – chasing after transient pleasures and repelling or pushing away things that caused them emotional pain. People did not rest in an open way to their mixed, bittersweet experience. Beings need to turn towards their pain and bring kindness to themselves and others. Acknowledging their suffering, they then need to let go of the anger or hurt inside. Peace and bliss come from within and not outside of oneself," I remarked.

"I'm sure most people are so worried about what other people would think if they appeared in any way different to the so-called behavioural norm. I love getting to know more interesting and eccentric people. They make the world so much more radiant and colourful. Life seems to burst from their seams," she declared.

"I aim to be different and walk a fine line between madness and genius," I replied.

"Is that how you see yourself then, as a possible genius?" she asked, cocking her head to one side and narrowing her eyes.

"Well, I do feel that I might be a genius of the spiritual kind, without trying to sound conceited. I am continually trying to transform my negative emotions into one of calmness and stillness. I'm sure it will take a very long time though to reach my goal of supreme enlightenment."

"Well, good luck to you if you think that's possible, but to my mind it feels like an impossible task."

"As a wise man once said, and I think it might have been the Buddha who said it, although I'm not sure, but a walk of a thousand miles starts with a single step," I said.

"I like that – pithy and profound!"

I found my attraction to her growing through our honest and intimate exchange, analysing the differences between the sexes and how it did not have to be that way. We stopped to have tea at the first pub we saw on the fringes of the town. The weather still was uncharacteristically warm and sunny for that part of England. This just amplified my strong, passionate emotions towards her.

I had initially come down to stay at the festival and later the retreat until Wednesday, but I decided on Monday that I would make my way home, rather than wait another couple of days. The weather had become overcast on this last day of mine. I had exchanged numbers with Sarah, yet she was scheduled to stay on until the end of the retreat. So, she said her goodbyes to me before breakfast. She was happy to see me wearing my purple trousers on this last day, as I had mentioned my fondness for them in passing. I ate breakfast with a group that included Nastasia, who generously and very kindly bought me a book written by her founder and teacher to take home with me. She was a woman with a lot of energy and drive, complemented by a sense of fun. She urged me to stay in contact and said that if ever I was near Chester, I should pop in to see her.

After I had said my farewells to nearly all those I had encountered on the retreat, I set off for home, leaving a little before lunch.

The following morning, I sent a text message to Sarah, which said:

Hi Sarah, it was good to meet you at the festival. You are so easy and interesting to talk to. I can see why you have so many guy friends. You have an inner and outer beauty. Speak soon and enjoy the rest of the now retreat. Alastair x

She responded later that evening with,

Ah, such a lovely thing to say – wow! Ditto, lovely chatting to you and getting to know you. Hope you got back safely. Much love x

Her text message was the last time I heard anything from Sarah. I tried phoning her on several occasions, but she did not respond. I initially thought this was peculiar, as she did not have a boyfriend. I thought that she had been interested in me. Later in the year and beyond, her silence would feed into my burgeoning imagination, and act as evidence that things were not what it seemed in my world.

CHAPTER 20

THE ARCHITECT

By the end of June that year, I had found a new architectural post in a company that predominantly designed car showrooms for the likes of BMW, Citroen and Peugeot. The location of the office was in an easily commutable distance, nestled in the countryside. The offices were in a converted barn, and it was of a high architectural specification.

As soon as I started my first day, I was given the assignment of bringing together a working drawings package, or in layman's terms, a detailed construction set of drawings. This was for the refurbishment of a BMW car showroom in Yorkshire. I was tasked to single-handedly bring it together, and to have the bulk of the drawings and a building specification completed by the end of July, so I could show at a design team progress meeting.

There were about 13 members of staff. There was quite a relaxed atmosphere, although lately the work pressure had mounted greater than at any other time in the firm's history. Occasionally, tempers would fray, as the pressure escalated for most of us.

Not all pulled their weight. Behind where I sat there was an athletic man called Joe, who always left at 5:30pm on the dot. In the morning, he would often turn up at about 9:15am, a good quarter of an hour after work was officially meant to start. His attitude was very relaxed and *laissez-faire*, even though he had recently joined and was still working through his probationary period. What I found bizarre was that he had a family to feed and a mortgage to pay, yet his attitude – not only to timeliness, but also his application to the work –

was questionable. *Did he not worry that everyone could see he was not putting in the hours for specific deadlines?*

The managing director, George, was getting very twitchy with the possibility that I would not complete the body of work by the prescribed date. One sunny morning he came upstairs to where I and some of the others were sitting at our desks. He beckoned me with a jerk of the head, to follow him downstairs and outside the building.

"Alastair, I'm getting really concerned that you aren't going to have the majority of the work finished for that design team meeting."

"George, I'm working as fast as I possibly can on this project. Firstly, I'm working late into the evenings, and I've also come into the office on the past two weekends. I know you're getting restless, but I do believe that it will come together by the end of July, when the meeting's scheduled for."

"As I've explained to you before, there is so much riding on this! The drawings must be correct and in perfect shape, as the work will be tendered to a very problematic contracting firm. If the drawings are not flawless, then the contractor will have ammunition against us. I don't want that happening at all," he said severely.

"I'll try my hardest to get it right, but I can only do my best at the end of the day," I said, trying to keep a fabricated upbeat persona, but feeling a little weary inside from this brief and unwarranted attack.

"As long as there are no mistakes, I'll be happy," said George emphatically. I thought to myself that a drawing without any mistakes at all was impossible. That is why a contract will always have a contingency sum, to soak up any oversights and discrepancies, which get spotted by the eagle-eye contractor.

Fortunately, in the last week of the looming deadline, I pushed myself that little bit harder to prove to the boss that I could manage the work in a tight timeframe. For the first three nights in the last week before the submission, I worked until about 10pm. On the Thursday, I stayed in the office until midnight before going home. The following day was crunch time. After having had little sleep and starting to live off the power of adrenaline, I was back at my desk by 7am. I was working methodically but manically.

That day, by lunchtime, I had successfully finished the remainder of the drawings and the building specification. I had begun to develop a headache from all my mental exertion over the past few days. Seeing that I had finished after putting in a considerable amount of overtime, I went to George and asked if I could take the afternoon off. He was reluctant to give me time off in lieu, but he gave in on this occasion.

He insisted that he would not allow time off again in this manner unless it was part of my holiday entitlement. As I was driving home that early afternoon, I thought about what a hard taskmaster George was. I felt, in work, there needed to be a little give and take, and giving me the afternoon off was the least George could do in return for the many extra hours of hard mental exertion.

The following Tuesday at the end of July, he took me in his modest car up to Yorkshire, where the BMW showroom was based. Although he was speeding on the motorway to our destination, I was not fazed by his frantic driving. On the odd occasion, I would worry about the pressure he was putting on other drivers by his intermittent tailgating, but I mostly just acquiesced to this driving experience.

At the meeting in the main boardroom of the BMW offices, I felt emboldened in my discussion with the client, project manager and my boss. Although I was not in charge, the ability to create many of the drawings in such a restricted timescale made me feel an indispensable and vital member of the team. Jim, who was the project manager, had an especially commanding and domineering presence, to the point of steering the meeting to his own personal agenda, even though I had prepared one that we as a group should probably have followed. Inwardly, I thought that these business and boardroom meetings could sometimes be a clash of egos, with little opportunity of harmony. However, I tried my best to be a catalyst for concord. After a long, extended meeting, I felt elated that a positive outcome had been achieved. I was sure that the client and project manager held me in higher regard for the quantity and precision of the drawings, which I had so arduously produced. I also listened attentively and took on board their feedback.

CHAPTER 21

FAWSLEY HALL

My parents had booked a night's stay and an evening meal at a historic and captivating hotel in the Northamptonshire countryside for my 40th birthday. There would only be my parents, sister, her husband David and Theodore, their son, joining the muted celebrations. My brother, James, was living in Australia, so was too far away to make a visit for the occasion.

Before I had my main episode that year, I had planned to have a much larger event to take place at my parent's home, set up in a marquee. At the time, I felt that my parents and I would spare no expense, indulging our guests with fine food and a reputable DJ for the night. I had even contacted a band that I had seen at a friend's 40th, as I thoroughly enjoyed their playlist and acoustic set. As things transpired, this large birthday bash did not materialize. A sedate but nonetheless sumptuous affair was organized instead.

I arrived before the rest of the family and went straight to reception with my overnight bag, where I met a well-spoken woman in her early twenties. I was convinced, after listening to her talk, that she had had a public school or boarding school education, due to her posh accent, and at times, elaborate use of language. She asked me,

"How can I help, sir?"

"I've booked into a room for the night. The name's Gamble, Alastair Gamble."

"I like the name Gamble. It makes me think of a character in one of those British gangster films, like the hero," she said self-assuredly.

"I can offer you a choice of three rooms, which your parents have booked. If you like I could take you up to the rooms and show you all three of them, and then you can decide."

"That'd be marvellous, if you could do that." I was not disappointed by the degree of courtesy and efficiency that she displayed – honed from her solid upbringing and education. She gave a summary of the three rooms, before taking me up to them. I had been to the hotel before – never to stay the night, but just for evening meals. I had been made aware of Elizabeth I's sojourn in this historic edifice. I then asked her,

"Are any of the bedrooms that you're taking me to the one that Elizabeth 1 stayed in?"

"No. That one's a bridal suite for a couple, who have their wedding day today. Sorry, if you were keen to take that one."

"Don't worry. I'm not in the slightest bit fussed – just curious, that's all."

The first room seemed too dark and moody for my refined tastes. There was a lot of heavy mahogany, which gave it a mournful feel. The second room was brighter and airier, with natural light coming in from two sides, but it still had a four-poster bed with dark, heavy wood and bulky furniture. I was then shown the third room. This one was called the Jane Seymour room. All of the bedrooms in the hotel, at least those of a grander nature, appeared to have names. This room felt right. The furnishings were unfussy and light, there was no four-poster bed and it had a lovely view of the rolling countryside.

"This is the one I'll go for. It's lighter and less heavy than any of the other two," I said with conviction.

"This is the one I would've gone for too, if I was choosing between them," she agreed, with what sounded like sincerity. "Here are the keys for the room. I hope you have a lovely stay. If you have any problems with your room, just dial zero and that'll take you through to reception, and I'm sure we will be able to help you."

"Thank you. It's the best room out of the three," I said.

"I know, I do like it the most. I think the room has an air of majesty and pomp, but not in an overly done way," she said. With that she left and let me sort myself out.

I needed to do a number two. Once finished, it took two attempts to flush the toilet. I got a text from my sister, saying she was held up in traffic. She said she would be arriving at around 4:30pm and asked me if I would like to join her in the hotel spa. I told her I would wait, but after a few minutes of exchanging a volley of texts, I changed my mind and walked down to the spa on my own. Unfortunately, I did not let my sister know of this surprise U-turn.

On entering the spa building, I felt awkward and unsure as to how it operated. I also felt a little intimidated by the attractive looking clientele, assembled in their white dressing gowns. I asked at reception, with a shade of hesitancy, where the changing rooms to the swimming pool were situated. The young black-haired woman, who was covered in discreet make-up and had her hair tied back in a ponytail, gave me helpful directions. I sensed she was sympathetic to my slight ungainliness.

I felt under the spotlight, and a bit out of place in these alien, upmarket surroundings. This was partly due to being on my own, which made me stand out, and partly due to not knowing the appropriate etiquette.

I placed my clothes in one of the allocated lockers. The interior of the changing room was of a very high standard. I made my way through a narrow passage, and then entered the swimming pool area.

As I approached the stainless-steel ladder, a burly, middle-aged man with a shaved head stared at me from the pool. I slowly descended, rung by rung, into the shallow end.

I had no intention of making this a glaring contest and looked away when our eyes on occasion met. By his demeanour and general physique, I wondered if he would be the individual who would carry out the evil-intentioned crime against me that night. *Had he come with an accomplice,* I thought to myself, *or would he be acting as a solitary assassin? Or would there instead be a less obvious candidate residing in the hotel?*

I propelled myself through the water, predominantly swimming breaststroke in a vigorous fashion, interspersed with a bit of front crawl. I noticed a group of women in their thirties, who, I imagined, were part of the wedding ceremony. They had joined the swimming pool area but had then quickly retreated to the steam room, perhaps to chat more privately. *Had their sight of me sparked feverish interest that they felt they needed to vocalize, hence the shelter of the steam room being the perfect gossip refuge?*

After a good 15 minutes of vigorous exercise in the pool, I observed the shaved headed man go outside to the Jacuzzi, where other guests were mingling. I waited a few minutes before following him.

As I lowered myself gently into the whirling, foamy water of the outdoor Jacuzzi, the muscular man was chatting to a stunning blonde woman. They were whispering and laughing discreetly at sporadic intervals. The woman had given me a warm smile at the beginning, while I was gradually lowering myself in, but then chose not to look my way again. *Could this be the man's partner-in-crime?* I wondered if they were only acting like a couple for the sake of this covert operation.

They struck me as being an incongruous match. Whatever could be said about them, I found the pair to be deeply suspicious, especially the man's earlier confrontational stare in the pool. I did not buy that they were an item. I was convinced that they must indeed be MI5 operatives.

In the Jacuzzi, I alternated between resting my head on the top edge of the tub and gazing upwards at the circling rooks and the billowing, white clouds gliding across the fading blue sky, while continuing to pay special interest to this odd-looking couple. Not at any time could I make out what they were saying, as their voices were just out of earshot.

After 15 minutes of feeling especially awkward and a little lonesome, I walked back to the changing rooms. Finding the hot power shower invigorating and enlivening, I put on my clothes again. I then made my way back to my room.

On entering, I made a beeline for the bathroom. Suddenly, a deep convulsive dread gripped me. Someone had been in my bathroom. They had planted a number two, amongst a wash of discoloured urine. I knew I had tried to flush the toilet twice, but I was sure I had seen my urine and faeces flushed away on the second attempt. I was convinced that my earlier leavings had been replaced by clear water. To see not only faeces, but also urine in the mix, without any toilet paper in the bowl, convinced me that this was intended as an ominous message. This incident suggested that the assassin or assassins would be back later.

What was interesting to note was that the couple, who I saw at the spa building, had been nearby for most of the time that I was out of my room. They were probably genuine after all. Whoever was staying here, intent on killing me, was not apparent yet. As my dad had mentioned before, the spies were never the ones you expected them to be. They would just be the people who would melt away into a hazy, mysterious backdrop.

I steadied and collected myself. I could not mention this to my parents, or my sister, who I had a close relationship with, as they would consider my conviction to be fabrications of a lunatic. I probably could not mention this even to my closest Buddhist friends. They would view me with caution and mistrust. I felt vulnerable. *What magic could the gods exercise for my death not to occur tonight?* If the assassin and their accomplice were given a key, it would be very difficult for them to be stopped. Genuine doubt started seeping into my fragile state of mind. I just needed to try to let go and relax into the moment.

Having dressed for the evening, in my signature attire, I lounged in the chair in my bedroom with the latest issue of a popular women's magazine and read a piece on meditation and mindfulness. Its interest with the public had exploded in the last few years. The article was saying how everyone seemed to be talking about meditation and yoga now, with a specific focus on mindfulness. I was a little concerned how big businesses were jumping on the bandwagon, to promote greater productivity in the workplace. It somehow did not seem to align itself with the Buddha's original message of kindly awareness and ethical actions. On the other hand, this interest could be seen as a genuinely good development in society's further engagement with Buddhism and its fundamental principles – *Buddhism by stealth*, I mused.

My sister had still not arrived with her husband and son. After reading a few more exciting articles in the women's magazine, which I found much more entertaining than any of the men's magazines, I made my way downstairs to the great hall. It had a lofty, ornate ceiling, almost competing with the fine ceilings of some inspirational chapels. The ceiling was barrel-vaulted with historic beams and stone. The hall was built in the Tudor era and was hung with medieval paintings of the nobility. I ordered a soft drink at the bar and made my way back to the great hall, to wait for my sister. There were only three older women in the corner of the large space, speaking in soft tones. Occasionally, they would steal a look in my direction, averting their gaze when I looked inquisitively back at them. It had just turned five o'clock. I was sitting by the main route through the space, so I could easily clock any passer-by, especially from the reception end, where my sister would be arriving.

After drinking the cold, refreshing, sweet liquid for about ten minutes, my sister arrived at reception. She caught a glimpse of me and came over, holding Theo, who was just over a year old. With a big grin on her face, she said,

"Are you waiting for me so we can go to the spa together?"

"I'm so sorry, Chriz, but I've already been. I should've really let you know – I'm so sorry. It was starting to get dark."

"That's a real shame. I was really looking forward to having quality time with you in the spa. I was looking forward to it while I was stuck in traffic," she replied with a mixture of wistfulness and annoyance.

"I'm sorry. I was starting to get restless, and then I acted on impulse. I'm sorry – I know I should've let you know. You've still got David you can go with," I said.

"Well, technically, he's not allowed to go, as he's not staying the night here. He's taking Theo back home with him, after the meal tonight. I think it's a little unfair of you," she said, with rising indignation.

"Look, let's leave it there. I probably should've waited, but you were taking a long time, and I was becoming more and more restless. Next time we can do it." I was starting to get irritable myself. I had not been feeling well with all the events that had been happening in my life that year. At the same time, I could not share my experiences with anyone. This made me feel especially frustrated and isolated, like a forlorn stray dog, yet one with a great deal of strength and courage.

My sister let it lie, but I observed her picking up her bag quite abruptly and letting out a sigh.

"Well, I'll see you at dinner then?" she said with a petulant tone. She turned her head towards her husband, who was approaching. He greeted me with a firm handshake and then they headed for their room, with Theo now nestled in David's strong, protective arms. I could see that as a pair they were perfectly suited to each other. David was a thoughtful and courteous individual, not without a humorously playful streak.

It was 7:25pm and I was just preparing to go downstairs. My parents had said that everyone should meet at 7:30pm in the great hall to toast my 40th with champagne. While we all gathered round one of the seating islands with glasses in our hands, dad made a toast. The upright armchairs and body enveloping sofas were upholstered with a bold mix of eccentric colours. The surrounding windows were tall and narrow, with a tall, deep bay window on one side, overlooking the grounds and the countryside beyond. Admittedly, at this time of year, it was too dark to see anything outside the windows, although the courtyard on the other side of the hall was elegantly lit with washes of warm yellowish light.

After our drinks, we were ushered into one of the many dining spaces by the maître d'. I felt especially uncomfortable and anxious, being unable to share with my parents the bathroom incident. I also believed another attempt on my life would be made, with the cooks trying to poison my food at dinner under the auspices of the government authorities. The atmosphere in the dining space felt like a heavy weight on my shoulders. It was, as if a dense, pungent smog had enveloped my aura. Although my parents and sister did not comment that evening, I could sense that they were acutely aware of my solemn mood. Having prepared a speech earlier in the week, I was deliberating when would be the opportune time to present it. There was not a single point during the meal where it felt right to do so.

I ordered a starter of goat's cheese on a bed of rocket salad with dressing, and then a fillet of sole for the main course. My father asked for two bottles of vintage claret, balanced with a couple of large bottles of sparkling mineral water.

Throughout the first course, I pondered whether the chefs had mixed the salad dressing with a liquid poison. I also questioned what looked like black leaves slipped within the filleted fish for my mains, wondering if they could be a wafer-thin poisonous substance. Despite this, I did not refuse to eat any of it, gobbling everything up obediently. If I happened to die, then it had been a good life for me, but another softer voice, like on previous occasions, reassured me that I would live.

I was sure that my role on this planet and in the universe was much too important for me to die so suddenly. I vacillated in mood between thinking that the gods were able to perform magic feats over vast inter-galactic distances, and then, with the mind of a cynic, that magic was ultimately an illusion.

After the evening meal, we were all sitting in the great hall with our coffees. I decided to give my speech with a mild degree of nerves, worried that my loud, booming voice would be overheard by the other guests. I retrieved the slip of paper from the top pocket of my waistcoat and unfurled it, then began,

"I would like to just say a few words to all of you here, as a token of my appreciation. I'm so thankful of how wonderfully you have brought me up. This has been primarily down to the wise counsel and guidance you have imparted to me. What with mum's strong family ethics, and Dad maintaining an untiring patience and perseverance in helping me to realize my full potential in most aspects of my life. He has been primarily a mentor, guiding me through the tricky paths of work life, and helping me to become a more rounded individual. Overall, what I love about my parents is their fostering in me a broad interest in all areas of life's rich tapestry. Then there is Christina, my big siss, no, my darling siss. Since University, she has grown to become a very good, close and loyal friend. I really enjoy her company, and, in the last year or so, becoming more acquainted with my little nephew, Theo, who is such a delight and joy to behold. This praise would not be complete if I didn't mention David. I'm very fortunate to have a great brother-in-law, who is an able and caring father. His enthusiasm and gift for cooking is exceptional and allows Christina to relax a bit more. It's a way of shifting those traditional gender roles towards a more equal partnership. I might've said this before, but I'm so glad to have you in our family circle. It's a shame that James and Holly cannot be here to celebrate my birthday, but I'm sure they are here in spirit, without being present in physical form. I do hope that they still love Australia, but it would be nice to see them return at some stage in the not-too-distant future. Without further ado, I would ask you to raise your cups and toast to the Gambles and the Russells."

Both my parents and my sister were touched by these simple yet refined sentiments. Just after 10:30pm, we all went to our rooms, except for David, who took Theo back home with him.

For the first part of the night, I could not sleep. I moved restlessly in my Queen-sized bed. From about 4am onwards, I managed to sleep for the remainder of the night. There would be occasions, between one and two in the morning, when I would hear someone's feet outside my room. I would be on tenterhooks. Then a door would open. I would be lying totally still with bated breath until I realized that it was not my door. For a good hour in the middle of the night, I got out of bed and read the women's magazine again, hoping to pick up some fresh insights into a woman's mind. I often suffered from sleeplessness in new beds, but this night was more extreme than most, in such strange and foreboding surroundings.

The following morning, the curtains were brightly glowing. I needed to get out in the fresh air to clear my head and take some deep breaths before breakfast. After a hot power shower and the necessary ablutions, I dressed in my blue suede waistcoat, purple trousers and a grey Superdry T-shirt. I felt confident in this look. It was the sort of ensemble that I could see a rock star wearing. For all intents and purposes, I might already be famous or infamous, depending on one's point of view.

There was hardly anyone up and about, except for one dutiful receptionist behind the counter – a different one from yesterday. She had frizzled blonde hair and a charming disposition. She smiled and said "hello, how are you?" in an Eastern European accent. I responded with, "I'm well, thanks," in an equally engaging manner, and proceeded to ask her how she was. I found this short exchange immensely satisfying, savouring the warm feeling it engendered.

While wandering the grounds, I wondered if I could tell which window corresponded to my parent's room, and for that matter, which window was the room that Elizabeth I had stayed in. This sense of history and royal lineage tickled my fascination. Before he became the Buddha, Siddhartha Gautama was a prince, destined to either become a universal monarch or a great sage. Thankfully, for all our sakes, he chose the latter route. He taught the way to Enlightenment, as a path to liberation and freedom from the reactive mind.

I dwelt on the various similarities between my life and Siddhartha's. He was known to be extremely friendly with everyone he met. He was commonly known as the "Happy One" once he became the Buddha. This was a characteristic that I shared with the Buddha, albeit as a paler imitation. I did, at times, still find myself getting wound up by certain people, where patience needed to be nurtured and the quality of metta practised. I knew that the art of "letting go" was the fundamental principle to be adopted, by a truth-faring practitioner, who the Buddha and all his disciples were. I was also blessed with strength, good health, handsome features and enough wealth, which he enjoyed in a more extreme and pronounced way, before renouncing his worldly ties. Moreover, we shared an idealistic streak, in our pursuit of the goal of nirvana. There were, overall, a lot more similarities than differences between our respective lives.

Once I had taken some fresh air, I reflected on the previous evening's events, while observing the landscape and the trees around me, before returning to my room. After some quiet reflection, I made my way to my parents' room and knocked on the door.

"Come in!" my mother said in a loud, strident voice.

"Hi mum. Morning," I said. My dad was in the bathroom.

"What's wrong with you, Alastair? You were so solemn last night at the table," my mother said.

"It's nothing, really, just that I feel I'm being spied upon," I replied, unwilling to give too much away.

"Not this again. You aren't being spied on. This is just a problem with your mind, and the thoughts you're fabricating. Can't you see the truth of your situation?" she said, almost pleading with me to delve deep into the chasm of my saner mind. I was tired of the knockbacks from my parents, who I knew would not understand my predicament. They were too immersed in their ordinary worldly existence to see the truth of the matter.

"You're probably right," I acquiesced for the sake of keeping some semblance of stability.

"We know we're right. Trust us. We only have your best interests at heart."

"I was thinking I might write a book. I've got sufficient funds to live for a good year and a half. I'd like to use it wisely. I just want to do creative writing, as I believe that's what my heart wants to do!" I said, raising my voice.

"Don't give up the job you're in, like you did at that other office. Don't you think this might be another one of your pipe dreams?" she said mockingly.

"No, I really want to give it a go!"

"Well, if that's what you want to do then I can't do anything about your decision," she said with beleaguered resignation.

"Thank you for respecting my decision, mum. I'll see you at breakfast. How long will you be?"

"Probably about ten minutes or so…See you down there," she mumbled the remaining few words, as I left their bedroom. I shut the door a little louder than intended.

At breakfast, I could have sworn that I overheard the waiter, who was on duty the previous evening, saying to his colleague,

"Didn't he have the fish last night?" I inferred by this statement that although they had tried to poison me, the dish had been magically intercepted by the gods, and transformed into a harmless substance.

I planned to leave directly after breakfast. After making this decision, it felt like an enormous weight had been lifted from my frame. The weather was glorious, which helped relieve my discomfort. Although I was very grateful for the expense my parents went to in booking me into this wonderful hotel, I hoped I did not have to return for some time to come. On the solitary car journey home, I drove without the radio on, reflecting upon the events of the morning and the previous day. I could not be 100 percent certain that the chefs had tried to poison me, or if there was someone trying to kill me in my bedroom. One thing I could be sure of was that someone had entered my bathroom, while I was at the spa complex. They had defecated and urinated in my toilet, in what seemed like a message to say that they would be back later. This specific detail led me to believe that everything else I surmised was inescapably true and correct.

CHAPTER 22

WILDES

I was coming up to the end of my probationary period at the Architects practice, after almost three months of being an employee there. I had taken my medication myself that day, as the nurse was on holiday. The Crick surgery had established a long-standing agreement that I was responsible enough to administer the drug myself, in times when it was not possible for the surgery to carry out the procedure. I kept it safely stored in my kitchen cupboard. On that day I self-medicated.

That evening, my parents were coming round to see me for a meal out. We had decided upon Wildes on the Parade in Leamington. My mother relayed to me over the phone that on the Wednesday, when she had booked the table, the woman on the other end of the line apparently knew exactly who I was.

"Yes, I know Gamble," as if to say the name was familiar to her, almost to the point of being a famous icon. This made me think back to my earlier views on me being a Big Brother reality figure. *How could the woman possibly know who I was when I so rarely frequented the restaurant? She would surely be inundated with calls for bookings from so many different people. What was it about my surname that was so recognizable?* I initially considered the vague possibility of a Truman show conspiracy, but the implications steadily mounted in my mind. This was especially true during work that Thursday.

As the thoughts proliferated, I pondered my hypothesis from earlier in the year that the secret services were attempting to eliminate me.

This evening would be another opportunity for the chefs to slip some poison into my food, at the behest of MI5. This pernicious thought started to worm its way into my consciousness. It disturbed me. I was not sure I could completely trust that I would be protected by unseen forces, who could again exercise their magical powers and transform the poison into a harmless and benign substance.

At work there was a certain individual, named Luke, who displayed a high degree of frivolity and tomfoolery during work. He was an ardent Christian. While he took his religion rather seriously, he would act inanely in the office. I was suspicious of him. Like most Christians, I was convinced that he believed in a distorted and unhelpful idea of the way Satan would manifest. Not one that accorded with reality or reason.

That evening, my parents arrived around 7pm. I served them nuts, crisps and drinks and we sat on my small garden patio, talking about work, and how I was getting on. I expressed my frustration with one of the projects, and how I had been set the impossible task of getting the drawings perfect without any loopholes or errors. I brought up how the company would be working with a very contractual building firm. The building contractors were unreliable in finishing projects on time. This filled me with more anxiety. My father enquired,

"Did you take your medication today?"

"Yes Dad, I did!" I preferred not to be too honest with my father on this occasion and omitted to mention that my heartbeat was slightly accelerating. This seemed a little unusual. How could my heartbeat be starting to gradually increase, when I had administered the correct drug myself only that morning? I tried to push this slightly worrying idea from my mind. As the minutes ticked by, we were approaching the time to head out. I was experiencing heaviness in my mood, morbidly turning over the thought that I might not see the light of the following day.

The restaurant and wine bar were in a basement. It was well known in that area, for serving top quality wines. The main section was lined with exposed brickwork, and because of the lighting it had a soft, mellow ambience.

My parents and I arrived at the back entrance. We were greeted by a young woman with quite a stern expression. Immediately, she opened with the words,

"Table for Gamble?

"Yes, that's correct," said my mother with a polite demeanour.

Once we had all sat down, the waitress told us of the specials that evening. The main special she brought to our attention was a ricotta and spinach tart, accompanied by mixed vegetables. Normally, my parents would suggest that I have fish when we dined out. I was a vegetarian. My parents believed my diet did not give me the necessary health benefits. I tried to reason with them, but often it was futile as they were so entrenched in their views. They always seemed to have an answer for everything. Over the years, they became less persuasive in trying to change my positive habit, but they also saw that I accepted my mother's cooking, even when it contained meat or fish. I behaved in a flexible way to people whose cooking I shared, trying not to impose my vegetarian habits too rigidly. I believed in being a pragmatist, not a purist. This less obstinate approach my mother warmed to. She generally felt that, although she could not win in trying to change my vegetarianism, she knew that I would always partake in the eating of meat or fish that she served at their home.

On this occasion, my mother said,

"Alastair, that tart sounds good. You could have that for your main course."

I replied to my mother with a serious,

"That does sound like a good choice."

While my parents were still deciding what food they would have, I mulled over the reasons why the restaurant should highlight a vegetarian dish as a special. Vegetarian meals were still not the norm. Unless the staff knew of my eating habits, they would not ordinarily draw a vegetarian dish to people's attention, especially as a special. It made me think that the staff could have produced a tart, laced with poison, specifically for my consumption. Therefore, they made a point of drawing our attention to it.

The waiter, who had lines of tattoos along both arms and a black, bushy beard, brought the two bottles over. He already had the top of the sparkling water unscrewed before arriving at the table. He then skilfully placed them in the middle of our round table. His expression was earnest. I sensed the faintest degree of anxiety in him, while being in our presence. This triggered internal alarm bells. I thought whether my parents might be targets as well for the use of poison, in not only the food, but the water as well. The last thing, I felt, I should be doing is expressing my anxious thoughts to my parents. Firstly, they would think that I had lost it again. Secondly, they would not believe it to be credible, thinking instead that it was a preposterous accusation.

"Why on earth would we be a target for being poisoned?" They would think. I also thought that I would have to properly explain myself to them. In no way did I feel inclined to do so, at this juncture.

Once the main course arrived, we all proceeded to eat. My father, like always, seemed to be lost in a food trance, while my mother was more attentive to people and things around her, periodically looking up between delicately cutting her lamb and vegetables. I felt like I had a lump of coal in my heart, as if I was like a martyr. If I were to die, I could say to myself that I had had a good life. I had total belief in the concept of rebirth, and so silently consoled myself with the notion that I would be reborn again, if I were to die that night. A quieter voice whispered to me saying everything would be alright.

I harked back to a couple of memories of magical experiences in the past that I had witnessed: the first being in Yosemite National Park in the States back in 1998, where black bears would roam the park. The second was a driving incident in my car, which happened less than half-a-year ago.

The first incident happened when I was on a trekking tour with a large group of people – about 26 in total. We were camping in Yosemite National Park. I had not paid attention to the warning from the group leader that we should put all sweet-smelling products into the van we were travelling in. This was to stop any possibility of the black bears getting at the scented products, by ripping open the tents with their claws and seriously maiming the people inside, or even killing them. That night, after I had brushed my teeth, and placed my toothbrush and toothpaste back into the sponge bag with a bar of soap inside, I absent-mindedly placed the bag and its contents directly next to my head in the tent I was sharing with a large man from Holland.

That night I was out for the count. I slept like a log. In the morning, I awoke to find out that there had been utter mayhem in the camp that night. The Dutch man had told me that the bear had come by our tent, prowling by on multiple occasions. The female group leader, who was sleeping on top of the van, was awoken by the noise of violent rocking movements to the van, by the turbulent rage of the bear. I was mystified at the time, why it was the one and only time in the tent, where I slept right through, from when I touched the pillow to when I awoke in the morning. Even though the night was filled with noisy and brutal commotion. Years later I had realized and believed that the gods had been acting as guardians for me. This now hinted, once again, that my continued survival on this planet was paramount.

The other story transpired more recently, and I recalled it for comfort and strength. This was when I visited my sister in Oxfordshire on a Sunday. On my return, I was driving recklessly, testing the mettle of my small, fast car, while listening to guttural rock music. I seemed to be evincing a feeling of invincibility. As I came to the Leamington junction, off the M40 motorway, I approached the intersection. I gave a cursory glance to my left then my right and discerned no visible oncoming traffic in sight. I then propelled the car forwards. The vehicle suddenly juddered to a complete stop. It straddled the road I was trying to cross over, and the middle of the chevron marked central section. Almost that same instant I had violently come to a halt, a car sped by in the lane I was trying to turn into. At the time it was a sobering and humbling experience. It jolted my subsequent behaviour behind the wheel into a much safer and slower speed.

Later, it dawned on me how my engine had seemed to collapse at exactly the right time, when it was desperately needed. This was one further example to suggest my life was being monitored by cosmic forces. They were looking after my overall welfare wherever I went.

Once we finished our mains, and we decided against a pudding, as we had commenced with a starter, I could feel myself noticeably relaxing. These two personal stories softened my heavy demeanour.

My parents came back to my flat. We all had coffee together, outside on the garden patio. After a pleasant chat about the royal family, I felt a little more at ease in my current state. I said goodbye to my parents just after 10pm. They both commented on leaving my flat, as they normally would, how lovely and inviting my place was. That evening I wondered if the poison would take hold at any point during my sleep. I found it very difficult to get any beneficial shuteye, thinking about the incidents that evening and their ramifications.

I ruminated on the belief that had reemerged only on that Thursday, after about a five-month hiatus, that I was on display to millions if not billions of people around the world. Everything that was spoken about would be digitally captured and transmitted. During our discussion on that uncharacteristically balmy Thursday evening, I felt aware of the public's scrutiny. At times it made me feel silly and awkward.

The following morning, after arriving at work, and having settled down at my desk, I began to vigorously attend to my work responsibilities. Luke was hidden from view by the two monitors at his desk, while I tapped away at my keyboard. Once everyone had appeared in the office, I was aware of him passing by my side. My attention was suddenly seized by the sheer moodiness of his expression. He was looking straight at me. This brooding look stood out even more because I was so used to seeing him play the office clown. *Why was he so serious? Why was he now glowering in my direction? What had occurred to him that previous evening for this complete turnaround in mood?* I wondered whether this could be another sign that I was on show.

Could it be that he was noticeably disappointed that the poison had no effect on me, from my meal at the restaurant the previous evening? I was sure that he considered me to be the devil incarnate. I mused that most people were not aware of the truth around them. The fact that humans, the animal kingdom, birds, insects, fish, the whole natural environment and all other beings in the universe, possessed a consciousness that was mysteriously linked to each other, and each one had the potential for Buddhahood lying dormant within.

There was an architect, named Alfie, in the office, who had been exhibiting poor performance. He had been given a disciplinary on a couple of occasions. Once the end of the working day on Friday had come about, I slung my navy-blue jacket over my shoulder and made my way to the back exit of the offices, to drive back home. Just as I was opening the glass door, I spotted three of the most senior staff huddled together and whispering. I immediately thought they were talking about Alfie. On registering me with heads swivelling in my direction, they immediately, but as naturally as possible, disbanded and said their farewells to each other. I was positive that they were talking about me and not Alfie. I internally commented on this being another suspicious incident. *Was this further proof, for my now not so seemingly outlandish idea, of constant surveillance into every aspect of my life?* The idea began to take on ever more credulity. Over time, through visual evidence, it seemed to ossify and harden into a palpable reality.

I got very little sleep over the weekend. I seriously wondered whether the medication I gave myself was faulty. One notion that crossed my mind, and over the coming days was fast becoming a more and more distinct possibility, was the thought that the gods had miraculously transformed the liquid medication into water, to wake me up from my mental dream-like slumber. I had distinctly noticed that when I administered the injection, the syringe drained easily and quickly, even though it is meant to be a viscous liquid. This was unusual. I was convinced that this occurrence was helping me realize that I needed to make a stand in leading a more creative and fulfilling life, centred primarily on my writing and my spiritual development.

On the following Monday, I mulled over the possibility that the work I was undertaking was not reaping the emotional and imaginative rewards that I had hoped for. I observed how when I was tackling the tasks at hand, I could not help but fixate on the minutiae and specific details of the work without seeing the bigger picture. This was unexpected, and normally a sign that there was something not right with the medication. I had, however, injected myself. I had witnessed that it was the drug "Depixol". This then fed back into my belief of the gods' intervention.

Just before lunch that Monday, George came to me, and asked with deceptive calmness,

"How's it going with the drawings?"

"Well, I'm nearly there with them, but I still need to make a few alterations and tweaks," I said, feeling the inability to keep it emotionally together. He responded to me, saying,

"I'm getting very twitchy with your attitude! We need to finish the drawings straight away, and not dither at all!" He said this with a contained vehemence and obvious worry. His legs were in a slightly open stance and his arms were crossed defiantly. He said he was going out and he would be back soon. He hinted that by the time he returned, I should be able to say to him that I had finished the drawings.

This rattled me, like I was some unruly teenager having just been taken off by the scruff of the neck. I realized now that I needed to get out of this office, but I would do it as surreptitiously as possible. I also felt that, like a dutiful employee, I would finish the drawings, and hand them into the secretary before departing. I planned to leave at lunchtime.

What had worried me earlier in the day was I had been told that the firm would be interviewing an experienced senior Architect, who had been working in China. He wanted to settle back in Warwickshire. I thought this peculiar. I believed I smelled a rat. Could this prospective employee be an MI6 agent being reassigned to George's office, in the security services' ongoing quest?

Just after one o'clock, I calmly shut down my machine, slipped on my jacket, and made my way downstairs to the secretary. I passed her the drawings. I told her to send them to the client with a compliment slip enclosed. I had done my duty as best as I could muster. On walking to my car, I noticed Luke was in his car with the associate director, Patrick, in the passenger seat. They waited for me to pass. Instead of me letting them through, I extended a hand towards Luke in a gesture of gratitude and crossed his car's path. I thought that he would love to run me over and see personally to my death. Unbeknown to him, this would be the one and only chance he would get, as this would be my last day at George's office. I imagined that he would be kicking himself afterwards for this error of judgement. Ultimately, I believed that he would never have the bottle to carry out such a heinous and evil act.

As I got into my car, and pressed the ignition button, I was greeted on the radio with the start of "The Montagues and Capulets", of *Romeo and Juliet* by Sergei Prokofiev. This was truly uplifting and resounding music, befitting of my current situation – one of drama and intrigue.

I got home. After eating some sandwiches, I wrote a short but precise resignation email to the firm. Within about a quarter of an hour of it being sent, I received two calls: one from Patrick, and one from George. My phone was on silent. They had both left messages for me to call back. On seeing the missed calls on my phone, I decided to ring Patrick. I tried to explain myself. I also decided to be honest about having a mental condition. I did think after the conversation that Patrick was the wrong person to speak to. I probably should have divulged this piece of information to George instead, although I was sure that it would spread like wildfire around the office anyway.

Once I had spoken to Patrick, I decided to see if I could get any sleep, which at this point was utterly necessary. I got into my bed and closed my eyes. Suddenly, during my attempted snooze, I received a knock on the door. *Who could this possibly be*, I wondered? Opening my bedroom curtains, I saw it was George, standing patiently outside my flat. I hurriedly put on my clothes, not quite buttoning up my jeans, to make sure I answered the door in time. I opened my front door and observed George already making his way back to his car.

"George!" I said in a loud voice. George did an about-turn and walked purposefully back to my flat.

"Hi, Alastair. Thanks for being able to see me. How are you doing?" said George warmly and with what seemed to be genuine sympathy. His mood was such a turnaround from the morning's encounter that I regarded it with a degree of wariness and caution.

"Hi George, I'm alright, thanks."

"Can I come in and have a small chat about life and work?" I allowed him to go first into the flat. I offered him my red leather armchair to sit on. He wryly observed,

"You're making me sit in the hot seat then?"

I uttered a slightly unnatural and hollow laugh in response.

"Patrick tells me you have a bipolar condition," said George. I was more inclined to tell them that I had bipolar, rather than schizophrenia, as my condition was still being evaluated. It was a more palatable mental condition.

"That's right. I thought it didn't need to be mentioned, as I've been well and healthy on a continuous course of medication for over seventeen years." I decided to omit telling him about the incident with my last office. I continued,

"I get an injection every fortnight, and if I've received the medication, I'm well. Last Thursday, I administered it myself, and for some reason the drug had no effect on me whatsoever. I can't explain why – I suppose it was a dodgy ampoule." I was reluctant to explain my idea that the gods were involved. This would just cause unnecessary confusion. I would probably have to try and justify myself, which I in no way wanted to do. I continued,

"The symptom I show when I haven't had the medication is primarily a heart that speeds up in rhythm and pace." Again, I knew that I was being a little sparing with the truth. I did not want to mention that my internal body temperature had also escalated. This was probably a natural side effect of my increased heart rate, but it was a fact that might raise additional concern. Fundamentally, I did not want to share my most secret and innermost beliefs with George.

"Generally, I think you get on well with people in the office. You're a happy and smiley face. You do a lot of extra work, plus you always come in on time, and leave later than the allotted hours. Why don't you take the rest of the week off, and then give me a ring on Monday to let me know how you are, and whether you'd want to return?" he responded agreeably.

"Thank you. That sounds like a good plan," George saw himself out with me trailing. I confirmed that I would ring on the following Monday with whatever I had decided upon.

CHAPTER 23

MAITREYA

That Tuesday I was scheduled to meet my psychiatrist. I went by myself to the hospital. Once I had parked the car and registered at reception, I waited patiently for the appointment with Doctor Goodyear. There was a middle-aged woman struggling to operate the new-fangled tea and coffee machine. I offered to help, as I had seen it done once before. Wondering what this patient was in for, I felt a little embarrassed that I might still be being judged by the secretaries as unwell and insane, like this woman who I was trying to help. The woman by the machine struck me as being remarkably normal. I asked her a little tactlessly, or what I presumed was thoughtless just after I enunciated the words, what she was in for,

"I'm trying to join the army. They want me to have a test with a psychiatrist, seeing as I had a mental breakdown about thirteen years ago. This certification of being healthy is the last thing the army are after, for my acceptance. I've passed everything else that they've given me," she confided. I thought, *why would she want to go into the army with a mental condition, albeit one that occurred in the distant past?* I hoped that she would be well and happy, if she was given a clean bill of mental health by the hospital's doctor. I hoped she would not suffer prejudice, especially in an environment as unforgiving as that of the army.

After a brief chat, Doctor Goodyear came striding into the waiting area.

"Hi Mr. Gamble. Would you like to come through, please?" he said, smiling warmly.

"Hi, Doctor Goodyear," I replied, as I proceeded to his office. The doctor had a full head of black hair, unlike mine whose fringe was steadily receding with the slow march of time. This little physical fact did not disturb me. I was more concerned with my imagination and sharpening and educating my mind, than the more superficial ageing bodily characteristics that we all must endure at some point in our lives. As Franz Kafka once said, *"Anyone who keeps the ability to see beauty never grows old."* I resonated with this statement. I kept it locked away in my memory bank. I liked trying to memorize pithy and wise sayings or quotes, either from the Buddha, or from distinguished Western philosophers, writers or scholars.

I asked the doctor if I could help myself to the water from the jug parked on the side of his desk. My mouth was starting to get parched. I was not nervous, but the glass of water gave me not only liquid refreshment but also a sense of pleasant succour.

"Hi Alastair, what's been happening over the last five months, since I last saw you?"

"Well, I managed to get a job, with an architectural company, which was at the end of June. In the two or three months that I was working there, I completed a detailed drawing package for an important meeting, within a very tight timescale. There was real pressure from the boss on getting me to complete on time, so I managed to put in extra hours and worked occasional weekends as well. In the last week before the submission, I was in the office most nights until about 9:30pm. The night before the submission, I was working to midnight. Then, on the final morning, I was back at my desk by 7am. I achieved a completion and resolution by lunchtime. Unfortunately, last week my medication did not do the trick it was supposed to. In the last four or five days I've been labouring under very little sleep. I also quit my job yesterday," I said, matter-of-factly.

"That sounds a little drastic. How do you feel about having given up your job?" The doctor enquired with sensitivity but a degree of surprise.

"A relief, actually! I have started to write about the events over this last year, as a way of keeping me occupied, and giving me something to do, but also because I feel inspired to do so," I said, lightening up to the conversation.

"What you're telling me about your major deadline, and how you successfully completed it, suggests to me that you don't have schizophrenia. It is almost unheard of for a schizophrenic to hold down a job, let alone be able to finish a difficult project, after they have had a few episodes. Their mental faculties deteriorate with every episode that they experience. In your case you seemed to have thrived under the pressure. You were able to perform your work duties unencumbered by your condition. Just as you're talking to me now, I would say your cognitive faculties are still very good. I would therefore categorically state that you have bipolar affective disorder, which is the mental condition I mentioned last time to you. From what you're telling me, it fits in with the evidence. With bipolar affective disorder, you can experience the manic episodes without any accompanying bouts of depression. That's totally possible," he illuminated.

"Why do you think I was diagnosed a schizophrenic when I had my first episode all those years ago?" I said, eager for a cogent reason.

"A lot of schizophrenics have breakdowns in their late teens or early twenties, as opposed to those who have bipolar, who suffer later in their lives. I am sure that will be the reason why you were labelled with schizophrenia, because your first breakdown happened when you were nineteen. As I said before, there are overlaps between the two conditions, especially to do with the element of psychosis," he said authoritatively. He proceeded to ask me,

"Why do you think some of your symptoms have been resurrecting themselves in the last few days?"

I paused for a moment, before I began to answer. I was deliberating over whether I should be candid with the doctor. *Should I divulge my views on the gods having a direct influence with their use of magical powers, and my views on my own personal situation?* I then chose to speak truthfully to him, responding,

"I'll be very honest with you now. I believe I'm destined for great things. I believe I'll become Maitreya, or the future Buddha. What I think that means is that I'll become a Buddha in many lifetimes to come, but in this lifetime that will be my Buddhist name. Just to put you in the picture: Buddhism speaks of beings rebecoming or being reborn, and so journeying from body to body over innumerable aeons. My personal belief is that evil is increasing in the world. The time's now right for a visionary figure to emerge. Although I see myself as growing into the figure Maitreya, it's not the classical portrayal of Buddhist mythology, but a new vision of what that figure represents. I don't hold the view that Maitreya will be a Buddha in this lifetime. The title, 'Buddha', which means 'one who is awake or one who knows', suggests an individual, who brings love, awareness and wisdom into a world where it has been completely lost. There are too many people in this world searching for spiritual truth and genuine meaning in their lives for Buddhism to fully disappear, and if anything, that urge for spirituality seems to be gaining ground, rather than diminishing in scope.

Maitreya means friendly, loving, and compassionate one. I think that suits my qualities and aspirations perfectly. In the Buddhist movement I'm affiliated to, when we join the order, we get given a Sanskrit name, which reflects our main overriding quality. I strongly feel that my strongest quality is my friendly, loving and above all compassionate nature, which can still be taken to ever greater heights, but which surpasses any other quality of mine. I also hold the view that this is the reason why the gods have been seeing to my ongoing protection and safety, whatever I've done, and will do throughout my life.

In Buddhism, we believe in gods, who are more spiritually developed beings than us. They've cultivated positive qualities in very favourable conditions on other planets, like how our earth probably was a million or so years ago. Their higher power comes in the form of magic or miracles, which can be performed over vast immeasurable distances, as opposed to ours, which would be that of technology, which is of limited value, and is positively puny in contrast.

I thought I should explain a bit of the background before telling you about my view on why the drug had no effect. As I might have mentioned to you before, I'd been keeping the ampoule safely stored in my kitchen cupboard before administering it myself. I think the gods magically transformed the medication into water. I strongly believe that they deliberately did this, to wake me up to the reality around me. They did this to help me see that it was in my best interests to extricate myself from that office environment. Yet again they were looking after my continued welfare and security." Doctor Goodyear was taking copious notes. I was helping him by pausing between sentences when I felt I had rushed too far ahead with my line of reasoning.

"So, you think you're going to become this Maitreya figure?" the doctor said, stony-faced.

"Yes, I do. Partly, what's shaped this view is that I share quite a few similarities with the historical Buddha. Like him, I'm a very determined individual. I face life, overcoming obstacles with immense courage. Also, in common with him, I'm gifted with quite an abundance of talents. I'm not only good at Architecture and the Arts, namely painting, music and writing, but I'm also interested and capable in the sciences, especially Maths. Both appeal to me. I'm not only creative but also practical at the same time. From another angle, I'm an able sportsman, with a good eye for the ball. Another fact about me is that I came to Buddhism when I was eighteen. It is extremely rare here in the West to get involved with something as radical as that so early on in one's life. I could list other notable areas of my life, which would be revealing," I shared.

I was keen to present as much of a justification as possible for my idea of my potential greatness without sounding big-headed or egotistical. I thought how many people in the Triratna movement and the population at large would be astounded by these grandiose claims. However, the more I churned ideas about my life and the universe, the more the notion of my becoming Maitreya seemed to crystallize into a scintillating, jewel-like reality. I felt I was somehow the epitome of cultural advancement. Although, for now, I had nothing much to show for it, but I was sure that, with time, my name would become familiar around the globe through being a particularly creative individual. This would manifest, above all, in spontaneous compassionate actions.

"I think in the first instance we need to prescribe you some sleeping tablets, to help you get some proper sleep. You should also get your injection this Thursday, rather than wait until the following Thursday. I suggest we raise the quantity you receive to 60 mg,"

"I really wouldn't be happy for my medication to go up to 60 mg. As I said to you before, I don't think this incident will happen again. Apart from this one event, I've always been very stable and well, being on 40mg," I said, with passionate defiance.

I had gone to see my parents before the meeting with the doctor. My mother had tried to persuade me that I should agree to an increase in dosage to 60mg. I had notionally agreed with my mother, but after speaking to her, I felt strongly while driving to the hospital that I was starting to be drugged up to my eyeballs. I did not wish to be cajoled or bullied by my mother, or anyone else, for that matter. I resolved to keep to 40mg, as I honestly felt it was the optimum measure of medication for me. I would stick steadfastly to this resolution.

"Okay. Shall we see how the next few months fare and make a decision then?" he said, with compassion.

"That'd be great! I really, passionately, believe that I can be well with my dosage. If, of course, I haven't improved or remained stable, then I would wholeheartedly agree with you that it should be upped, but let's see first how I fare in the next few months," I said.

"You'll say something, won't you, if you don't feel right?" he asked.

"Definitely, and if I don't then I'm sure my father will get in contact with you on my behalf." This made the doctor chuckle to himself. He averted his gaze and nodded in agreement, before seeing me to the waiting area and bidding me farewell. As I exited the building, I met the army woman, who was smoking a cigarette. I asked her,

"How did it go with your interview?"

"The doctor said I was perfectly well, and my mental faculties and resilience are totally intact and good," she said with barely suppressed elation.

"I'm glad for you," I replied.

"Thanks. Good to meet you and good luck,"

"Good to meet you as well, and also good luck in your onward journey," I said, as we parted company. I hoped she would enjoy her time in the army, but I could not imagine a job further from my interests and leanings. There would never be a place for me in such an institution, as it went against my fundamental belief in the principle of non-violence.

CHAPTER 24

THE JOKER

The following week, I called my former office. Before I lifted the phone from its charger, I could feel my heart pounding. My pulse quickened to a rapid-fire beat. This seemed like a big event that I was undertaking. There was another aspect that felt significant. I had decided I would explore another area of London. I had kept it very much to myself. I wanted to keep the secret service in suspense again. Calling the office, I waited for a few rings before the main secretary answered.

"Hello, MDG architects, Sarah speaking."

"Hi Sarah. It's Alastair here. Could I speak to George, please, if he's available," I said, with a mixture of precarious poise and jangled nerves.

"Sure. He's been waiting for your call. I'll put you through," she seemed decidedly chirpy, which felt spurious. Before I had left the office, there were times in my last remaining days when she would not be so guarded with her emotions. Her body language and facial expressions had suggested a degree of hostility towards me. I had become finely attuned to gauging people's moods and temperaments through my regular meditation practice. I had a developed intuition.

"Hi Alastair, how are you?" George enquired.

"Hi George, I'm now a lot better. I've caught up on my lack of sleep. I've been thinking very carefully about my decision on whether I'll continue with working at your firm. I've therefore decided that I'd like to pursue the writing of a book, and so I would need space in which to write. With this in mind, I would like to follow through on my resignation e-mail. I would now like to discontinue my working relationship with you and your firm," I said, my heart stomping in time with every word I uttered.

"Are you sure about this?"

"Yes…positive. I want to make a fresh start, and make this a new chapter in my life," I said, seeing the irony of using the word "chapter", given the context of the previous sentences.

"Very well, I'm not sure I can realistically change your mind, but I wish you all the best in your subsequent endeavours. It would be good if you could stay in touch with us," he said.

"Sure, I will do."

I had no real intention of getting back to him in the future, but decided to agree with him, to keep up the harmony of pretence. Over the past week or so, I had become suspicious of the office's underlying motives. I was not sure if they were helping the authorities in my removal. On a couple of occasions, I wondered whether some of the employees had tried to slip poison into my tea.

On one occasion, Patrick, who normally never made the teas, had decided to make them near the end of my time at the office. I had asked for green tea and was brought a hot drink. It looked decidedly murky brown in colour, not normally what I would associate with the colour of green tea. When I had taken a sip, I found that it was unmistakably green tea. I thought it peculiar. Even Patrick had remarked on the colour, perhaps to indicate his presumed innocence in the affair, to not arouse suspicion. Although there was mistrust, I went ahead and drank it all with the heartfelt belief that the poison would not harm me. It was still common for me to oscillate in different situations between feeling self-assured and being sceptical and doubtful about the gods' influence. These two contrasting emotions would bounce back and forth in my fragile yet nonetheless courageous heart.

Another incident which made me think there was something going on was when I overheard Patrick talking with Luke in hushed tones. Patrick remarked that what was happening around them was very strange and mysterious. I had managed to eavesdrop on Patrick saying these words, even though Patrick thought that no one else was party to their discreet and soft-spoken conversation.

After I had finished my phone exchange, I got ready that morning to depart for London. I was particularly keen to hit one area of the city, which had once held significance for me. Again, I was dressed in my purple trousers, the light blue waistcoat and light brown shoes. This time, I decided to wear a black long-sleeved T-shirt, and not my customary white shirt. It was a warm day, being in the low twenties centigrade. If people were watching me on their TV screens, then another slightly modified image was important. One which subtly conveyed a darker aspect to my personality.

I had decided not to tell anyone where I was going that day. I imagined the secret service had a pretty good idea of where I might be headed, but I was reluctant to present it to them like *fait accompli*. I imagined they would bring snipers to that area of London immediately when they knew where I was. Stationed very discreetly on the tops of buildings, they would patiently wait, in radio contact with each other and their commander, until they sighted my whereabouts. They would then lock on for the kill.

After a pleasant journey on the train, during which I viewed the huge expanse of land that was only a tiny fraction of the vastness of Gaia, as well as the trees and buildings, which covered the area, I realized the enormous and unfathomably deep nature of supreme enlightenment, or Buddhahood, and what I was trying to aspire to. The goal was still so far out of reach. It required perhaps an aeon of time to be traversed before coming to its ultimate resolution.

After arriving at Marylebone station, I made my way to the Tube. I connected with a series of different underground lines, before disembarking at the required station. I had now arrived at the place in London with which I had quite a long-term connection. Angel was that place. There was the overt meaning in the name, which would not be lost on people.

As I ascended the long flight of escalators, I mulled over where I would venture. The thought occurred to me that I would first check out if there was a good movie on that afternoon at the main cinema complex. Scouring the movie display board there was nothing that stood out for me. There were a lot of action movies, but nothing that viscerally spoke to me.

I slowly sauntered along the high street, seeing a colourful assemblage of different stores, until I passed a Starbucks. I decided to continue walking, until I momentarily reassessed my decision. I retraced my steps and entered the coffee store. I was aware that while I was waiting to get served, there were a couple of girls seated at a table behind me. While I stood in the queue, they were furtively whispering to each other and giggling frequently. I also noticed that the staff seemed to be slightly amused by something. Could it be my appearance in the store that was igniting their collective mirth? They were being as diligent as possible, but I thought they were a little put off by someone famous, or even infamous, having just walked through their doors. It again dawned on me that there was probably a constant Big Brother surveillance into my life. A large proportion of those I encountered, either smirked, giggled, acted very inquisitively, occasionally ignored me, openly criticized, commented on me or gave me genuine and appreciative smiles.

On this specific morning, more than ever, it felt like the public really did know my life intimately, like some open book. I wondered for how long they had known about my actions. How much time had acquaintances and family friends been keeping it secret from me? I was not dismayed by this seemingly unpalatable truth. I had, in fact, wished and prayed for public exposure into my private life for so long. The chance to suffer humiliation, and grow in confidence from the experience, was an overpowering volition. I had come across "the secret", or the "law of attraction", on film. The film's premise was that if you truly wish for something to possess and own, or for something to happen to you, then the likelihood of it transpiring is almost guaranteed, as long as your heart is wholly intent on it. I did think that a little luck was also necessary, and that being in the right place at the right time were key ingredients, but I was drawn to the film's basic premise.

As I perched on a bar stool with a small, round, high table to plant my Americano on, I sat facing the entrance. I had total visibility of who entered and left the coffee shop. I was generally not conscious of the power behind my inquisitive gaze. A friend had once remarked that it bordered on a passive-aggressive look. I must have come across as quite intimidating, sitting directly opposite the door and eyeballing anyone who came in. The truth was that I was interested and curious with strangers – all of them containing complex inner worlds and universes. I would drink in their mannerisms, appearances and demeanours.

Suddenly, a person appeared who I had seen before. With not too much racking of my brain, I realized I had seen him at Marylebone station on my first momentous excursion after leaving the Architects firm in Knowle. He was a relatively young man, probably in his mid-thirties, if I was to hazard a guess. Like last time, when I noticed his presence, he was sporting a bushy, dark brown beard. He had a full head of hair. He reminded me a little of a Russian revolutionary figure. It was just too much of a coincidence that I should see him on both occasions, in two separate parts of London. I was sure he was unequivocally part of the secret service underworld. He directed a look at me. I sensed a slightly worried expression, as if to suggest he knew secrets that were mysterious and inexplicable, and therefore did not fall under the banner of rational logic.

I felt emboldened by this brief non-verbal exchange. I thought that however hard the authorities try, their attempts to rid me of my existence would always be foiled. I was not expecting this singular fellow to do anything other than keep tabs on me.

Once he had left the premises, I secretly imagined him making radio contact with snipers, nestled among the rooftops. He would tell them they needed to be on their guard and await my arrival along the streets of Angel.

After feeling thoroughly relaxed with my time spent viewing this wonderful assortment of individuals, I made my way outside. The weather was uncharacteristically warm for that time of year, but a little overcast, with brief spells of sunshine peeking through. It had been consistently good weather for most of the year, which we had not experienced for quite a long time.

I glided along the high street. I decided to cross the road and make a route for Waterstones, the main bookstore chain in the country. On crossing the threshold, I had a cursory glance at all the multifarious books on display. One book that caught my eye was *Bridget Jones Diary* by Helen Fielding. It was about a charming, hapless woman and all the heart-warming tales of success and failure in her love life. I decided that on this occasion, I would not purchase it, but that when I was back at home, I would buy a copy. There was a lovely quality about the female character. She was genuinely heartfelt and someone prone to mishaps, but always coming through scrapes stronger on the other side. This was not without a charming, self-deprecating humour. She was someone who was quintessentially English, in that most positive sense of the word – a loveable and endearing underdog. In some respects, I could see a lot of similarities between her life and my own.

As I placed a copy of the book back down amongst the others, I raised my head to see a pretty, young, blonde woman smiling affectionately at me. She appeared to be more interested in me than the books on show. I felt, if anything, a sense that she was a supporter of my life. Even though I would seem to get hostile reactions to how I conducted my life from a lot of people I passed on the streets, there would always be a sizeable proportion of the population who agreed with me and were perhaps even enthralled by the principles I lived by.

I ambled out of the store. I thought I would have a drink in All Bar One. The place was relatively empty, except for a few couples and some small groups of besuited businessmen and women. I ordered a sparkling mineral water from the blonde Eastern European waitress. She too smiled warmly. At a distance, every now and then, she would look expectantly in my direction, interspersed with quietly talking to her other male and female colleagues.

When I was settling the bill, I noticed on the back a note from her, which read, "Hope you have a great day," with a smiley face rounding off the message. When she came over to collect the money, I said to her,

"Thanks for the message. That was a lovely, sweet touch of yours. I really appreciated it."

"It's my pleasure. I really mean what I said." She said, sealing the brief conversation with a flirtatious wink. She looked gratified.

I left the establishment with a warm glow and a jaunty spring in my step. Along with the girl in the bookstore, this interaction had really buoyed my mood.

I was a little tired of going to restaurants and thinking that the owners might slip some poison or radioactive Polonium 210 – which the Russians used as their weapon of choice – into my food. I therefore opted for a sandwich shop on the high street. Here it would be nigh impossible for them to know what I would order, and therefore to have a deadly substance contained within. Instead of being predictable by ordering a vegetarian sandwich, I went for a tuna and mayonnaise baguette, to disarm the staff at the sandwich shop. The people working in the store were predominantly male. There was an atmosphere laden with testosterone clinging to the warm, stuffy air. They all wore stern faces from behind the counter. A couple of them appeared shifty. I wondered again whether it was my presence that caused them to be uptight and defensive. Although, they were very serious, I tried to be as courteous and amenable as possible, to try and defuse the thick tension that hung ominously in the store.

It had started spitting drops of rain. I took shelter just outside under the cover of an awning and sat myself down on a chair. I busily munched my way through the baguette, while taking the opportunity to survey the busy street life. Once I had finished, and the rain had died down a bit, I went for a meandering stroll. I knew not where. I let my instincts guide me. I first had a drink of sparkling water in a pub with "Angel" in its name.

It was relatively quiet, as it was a Monday. No one around me was alerting my suspicions. The few people in the bar seemed comparatively tame. The female bar staff shot me surreptitious glances. From time to time, they would titter amongst themselves. I was a little tickled by this presumed interest. Wherever I went I would be recognized, and I knew it.

Polishing off the last remaining mouthful of water, I left the pub. I ventured along a busy store-lined side street. I let the forces of fate, or destiny, lead me onwards. As I was a little over halfway down the street, I spied a lovely little store, selling all sorts of homewares and trinkets. I went inside and was immediately hit with a strong, positive and embracing energy. I made my way into the heart of the building when the shopkeeper emerged from a door next to the counter. He very affectionately asked me,

"Can I help you, sir?"

"No, I'm just browsing, thanks." After a momentary pause, I continued to speak, and said,

"I'm particularly noticing the positive energy emanating from this shop, though."

I was reluctant to express that I thought the same positive vibe was coming from the shopkeeper himself, being a little embarrassed that I might appear to be coming on too strong. The shopkeeper chuckled to himself. With a healthy glow he replied,

"Thanks. I try my best to make this as inviting a place as possible."

"All I can say is you're doing a good job. Keep it up!" I responded and raised my hand. I then left.

I carried on walking up the side street, the pavements of which were overwhelmed with a bewildering selection of people. At the end of the street on my right there was another pub, called The Joker. I thought it ironic that I was about to enter a pub, where my attire would suit that of the Joker's. Although I had come across the Joker as the archenemy of Batman, I thought that the true origins of the Joker had been tainted by the comic books, where he appeared in an evil and sinister guise. In my mind, the notion of the Joker in medieval times was someone who was much closer to reality. He was probably more upstanding than most people. He would wear a costume, and act as if he was the fool, but he was far from being one. He would often be the one to speak pithy words of wisdom and truth. The Joker would have the close ear of the king, while also being very brave, being the first to test the king's food for any sign of poison.

Ordering a coke, I sat down by the window and pondered the significance and meaning of the name of the pub, and how I had stumbled upon it. I had never been here before and had no way of knowing what was on that street. Names and numbers would normally speak to me as symbols, archetypes and myths, pregnant with meaning. As I sipped my coke, I wondered what the large group of foreign thirty-somethings were making of my presence. They were sitting at a table in the centre of the pub. I meant no harm to anyone, but I presumed that a large percentage of the population viewed me as a malign threat to their established beliefs and security. I felt a chill run down my spine at this disconcerting notion, which had entered the back door of my mind.

It was nearing 3pm and I had grown tired of my sojourn in Angel. I exited the pub and followed the route I had come down, popping into a local supermarket for a bar of chocolate. I then parked myself in a sheltered spot by the side, while slowly consuming my chocolate bar. After a good 15 minutes of watching people walk by, I saw in front of me a woman older than her years with dark straggly hair struggling to push her trolley. It was filled with plastic shopping bags, laden with produce. Seeing as she was getting no help from passers-by, I stepped in and pushed the trolley for her. I realized why she was faltering, as it was very stubborn in its motion. The wheels had become stiff and rigid. As I mustered my strength to push the dogged cart to the main entrance, I looked up and saw a fifty-something conservative gentleman with a tight beard, smiling appreciatively. I reciprocated and wondered how many other people were observing my spontaneously compassionate response. The woman was very respectful of my efforts. She repeated a couple of times that I was very kind to have helped her. I knew that I was in the right place at the right time. It just seemed the natural thing to do. After that I made tracks back home. I mused over the day's events during the train journey.

Over the subsequent week, with the aid of sleeping pills prescribed by the doctor, and a Depixol injection brought forward by a week, I settled down again into a stable state of mind. This time, I started to believe in a few aspects of the views I had formed after my episode in the early part of that year.

CHAPTER 25

THE WAKE

Having gone on a weekend retreat in October to the Herefordshire countryside, I suspected one of the retreatants, a man called Lee, was involved in planning my abrupt ending. What felt incongruous to me about this individual was his general obsequiousness and apologetic manner, coupled with the fact that he was a very muscly man, who presumably took an inordinate interest in his physique. He had a variety of tattoos festooned all over his exposed arms. There was also his inability to look me directly in the eye, as if to suggest he might be harbouring a wicked and uncomfortable truth. It was this juxtaposition of contributory factors, which alerted my finely tuned antennae. A sleepless night was had for both me and him, as we were both confined in a tight, claustrophobic four-person dormitory. He left the retreat before lunch on Saturday. This allowed me to settle into the remainder of the weekend.

On that Sunday, after all the retreatants had left, Saraha and I agreed that we would take a walk up one of the Malvern Hills close by the place. When we arrived at the car park that late afternoon, I donned some heavy mountain boots. We hiked vigorously up the designated path and passed by a middle-aged couple with their dog and later a family of four. The path then fizzled out into much steeper and more rugged terrain. The light was beginning to slowly fade. He suggested to me that we could attempt to climb the steep hill to the top. I was nowhere near as wild and adventurous as him. I baulked at this major ascent, especially at that time of day. It was dusk and the light was fading fast. "Let's go back to mine. I've got some soup and toast that we can have," I said.

I shuddered at the thought that he might be leading me to peril, but I immediately dismissed this idea as preposterous.

On the way back in the car, he said,

"Dave did my head in on the retreat, always trying to crack unnecessary jokes. There is also another thing about him…he likes to interrupt you when you're talking."

"I know it's a little disconcerting. It's almost as if he doesn't want to learn from his mistakes or undo his habits." I had the figure of Lee in my mind. I was reluctant to say too much, except by mentioning to Saraha,

"I thought Lee was a little weird. I didn't get a good vibe from him at all. He somehow seemed to squirm uncomfortably in my presence."

"That might be, because you are so intense," looking in my direction with a wry smile. Amused by what he said I responded,

"I know. I probably do come across as intimidating with my beady-eye stare." With that I looked at him, making a mock aggressive face. We immediately dissolved with laughter.

Since I had experienced this second very mild episode in the year, I had begun to regard a very small number of people in the Triratna movement with suspicion again. I was holding this view very lightly, but it still became an intermittent concern. Nonetheless, I trusted Saraha as a friend, not a foe. Despite this, I still could not banish a niggling deep-seated doubt that I was taking a bit of a risk by letting him sleep in my flat for the night. When I reflected on his life, there was no evidence at all to indicate that he was a charlatan. Instead, I was sure that he was the real deal. Still, I felt I was embarking on a leap of faith, letting him enter and stay in my abode.

While in the flat, I prepared some soup and toast, while Saraha made a call to his Kalyana Mitra, the Sanskrit word for a spiritual or beautiful friend. This was someone who was meant to primarily be more experienced and initially wiser than oneself.

Once the meal was ready, we both sat at my dining room table. We savoured the food with little accompanying discussion – just a nourishing stillness. After the meal, we washed up together. I then suggested we watch an old film, called *Withnail and I*, about two struggling actors and their adventures residing temporarily in the countryside. Saraha had not seen it. I suspected that he would enjoy it.

After the film, I asked him,

"How was the film for you?"

"It was a little frivolous and silly, I thought," he replied sagely, with a solemn expression.

"I particularly enjoyed the parts that the uncle spoke. His language was evocative, but I agree some of the other parts were a little silly," I said, weighing up in my own mind the implications of his words.

We chatted for a while, before we both decided to go to bed. My sofa adapted to a fold-out bed, which I unfurled. I then made up his bed with clean sheets.

I had a relatively good night's sleep, but I had awoken in the middle of the night to go to the bathroom. I subsequently spent a good hour moving restlessly in bed. I knew that this overnight stay was a test of his authenticity and fidelity. If I came through it, then it would be definite that he was a true ally and friend.

With relief and joy that I had made it to the following morning unscathed, I truly felt that I could now count him as a bona fide Buddhist practitioner.

Eating our breakfast, I experienced a profound feeling of joy and eager anticipation at the journey that lay ahead. It was as if a chink of bright light was breaking through from a dark cell in my mind.

I drove down to Saraha's uncle's funeral, on Solent-on-sea, at an agreeably measured speed, as I was now more accustomed to adopting. This was opposed to my more erratic driving near the beginning of the year. This earlier behaviour could well have been a symptom of my lack of medication. The car's steering was unresponsive though. I puzzled over whether the car garage had perhaps tampered with my vehicle, during its regular yearly service.

So many things around me seemed precarious, but were hanging delicately in the balance, due to benevolent forces at work.

We savoured some hard rock tunes, while also tuning into Radio 4. We relished a panel of distinguished and eminent guests involved in a heavy weight discussion about an aspect of philosophy.

We arrived with a little time to spare. We chose to get a coffee in a local supermarket café. I was tickled with amusement to see Saraha wearing some trousers, which I had lent him earlier. They were quite clearly too big for him, as he was a few inches shorter in height. We both chuckled to ourselves at the comicality of the situation. He was not the type to do things conventionally. He was renowned in the movement for going on solitary retreats for about two to three months in the wilds of the Pyrenees. There he would lead a simple and austere lifestyle, like some famous guru of old.

I was wearing my now trademark attire, that I had worn to London on previous occasions – this time with a white shirt. One aspect of my clothing, which was additional, was a red silk cravat, patterned with very small, dark blue paisley designs dotted all over the red silk fabric. Only very recently I had bought this romantic looking article of clothing, to complete my exuberant look, inspired by Dylan Thomas. Today was the first day I was trying this style out on inquisitive members of the public. I experienced an equal mixture of trepidation and joy.

Saraha had given me directions to the hotel where the wake would be situated the previous evening. Once I had dropped him off at the funeral, I made my way there. It was an old Victorian building with lots of distinctive features and a commanding view over the sea.

The weather was overcast, but this in no way dampened my spirits. This day would be a precious opportunity to deepen and strengthen my friendship with my wise companion. One's emotional mood depended on a lot of things, but more than ever it relied on human companionship and camaraderie – what Confucius called "jen" or "human-heartedness". This quality meant a sense of solidarity with all beings. I felt that this was, by far, the most important factor in one's health and wellbeing.

I made my way to the hotel bar, overlooking the bay and ordered myself an Earl Grey tea. The space had high, elaborate ceilings. It also had a bank of tall windows and a large bay window, within which I was seated.

I was contentedly reading that day's Guardian newspaper, while gradually taking in larger gulps of tea as it progressively cooled.

I engaged fleetingly in conversation with the waitress, who was wearing thick rimmed glasses. I commented on the weather and the hotel's idyllic setting. These were two familiar topics about which, I felt, I could realistically connect. I preferred entering into dialogue with strangers, who operated in a functional role in my life than being a cool, aloof and detached figure. I was forever curious about the diversity of human beings, but also the similarities we all shared.

I experienced a glimmer of the taste of freedom and formed a resolution that I would undertake more writing over the following year. I would immerse myself in the world of being an author. This would, above all, give me a purpose, and something to meaningfully do with my time off work. I thought that with the remotest of chances, it might even become a bestseller. I was therefore willing to live in hope, and not have my dreams smothered by others' cynicism or any crippling self-doubt.

While I was ensconced in the bar area, I became aware that the people attending Saraha's uncle's funeral were now descending on an adjoining room. He emerged at the entrance to my space. Walking over to me he said,

"You look as though you're thoroughly enjoying yourself sitting here. How long've you been waiting?"

"About the last three quarters of an hour to an hour. I'm really enjoying the space and peace being sat here, thanks."

"If you want to come through and join us, feel free to do so, or else you could carry on sitting here. There's food over in our section… if nothing else you could get some free grub. It's entirely up to you, though," he commented, with his body language communicating a blend of sombreness and lightness.

"Don't worry, I'll come through in just a moment, once I've put this paper in the car," I said eagerly. This was not without a little apprehension stirred in the mix, due to being the flamboyantly attired stranger.

On entering the ornate room that had recently been given a contemporary make-over, I went up to Saraha. He had an awareness of people around him, while he was still chatting to his father, Terry. My initial impression of Saraha was that he was not particularly enthralled with what his father was saying to him.

He had mentioned before how he struggled to communicate with his father effectively and meaningfully. On seeing me approach, he said to his father,

"Dad, I'd like you to meet Alastair, who brought me here. He's an architect."

"An architect! That's an interesting profession. I've come across a lot of architects in my time, working as a quantity surveyor," he said, with his eyes lit up and sparkling. I was equally responsive and effusive.

I mentioned my time working as Project Manager and Architect in the Estates Office at the University of Warwick, particularly because it was a good learning experience on construction techniques. Saraha knew what topics his father was keen on. For the next half hour, he let both Terry and me be captivated by our discussion on the construction industry without being party to our conversation.

I proceeded to mention that I had embarked on a book of my life, encapsulating the events of this year. Terry responded, saying,

"That sounds like a worthwhile venture to be doing with your time off work. Do you think you'll return to the world of architecture?"

"I think I might have to when the money runs out. I guess the likelihood of making the book a financial success will be very slim indeed," I said, concealing a lightly held belief that literary success might be a real possibility, even though on the surface it seemed utterly remote, like the chances of winning the lottery.

I clocked a young, pretty woman, who was talking to a small group of elderly people at a four-person table. She would repeatedly turn her head in my direction. A little time later, she moved to a long, rustic looking oak table with a group of young adolescents and one thirty-something man around her. I parked myself on a seat with one chair between us. I then took my moment and asked the obvious question.

"How did you know John?" I said tactfully, thinking she would reply with saying she was a relative. I was pleasantly surprised by her response.

"I used to know him when I was working at a bar not far from here. He used to be a regular. We got to know each other there, and then later, once I'd left that bar, I kept in touch and quite regularly went for coffee with him. Sometimes we would even come here, so I'm quite familiar with this setting…How do you know John?" she enquired.

"Funnily enough, I don't know him at all. I'm just acting as a friendly taxi service for my friend Saraha, who was his nephew." This comment brought a brief expression of mirth to her, and the afterglow of a lovely, rich smile.

"Have you come far?"

"I've only come from Leamington Spa. It wasn't a difficult journey – quite straightforward, really," I said. She replied by saying,

"John would've loved your dress sense, as he would also dress up colourfully. I really appreciated that quality of his."

I interpreted from this comment that it was an indirect way of saying she liked the way I dressed on this mournful day.

The more we spoke, the more I found myself attracted to her personality, physique and features. At one point I asked her if she had come on her own, to which she replied that her boyfriend had brought her here. She jerked her head in the direction of the embarrassed looking man sitting opposite her at the table. I was curious to think what she saw in him. I also secretly thought that I would love to be the one taking her for coffee in place of Saraha's late uncle, had I happened to live in that part of the world.

I became conscious that her boyfriend was beginning to move restlessly in his seat, as I was patently flirting. He suggested to her that they should make steps to leave. At this juncture, I also thought it right to suggest to Saraha that we make our way onwards from the assembled gathering.

Leaving the hotel, we said our farewells. I thought it would be more appropriate to give the pretty woman a handshake, due to her boyfriend's beady eyes boring into me.

Saraha and I both made our way along a few different roads, lined with big, substantial Victorian houses, along a coastal path and then onto a pebbly beach. On one side of the small bay, a series of big boulders were huddled together. It was as though they were united in seeking protection from the elements. The weather was still overcast. I climbed on one of the large boulders and began to look out to sea.

I started contemplating, like I would repeatedly do throughout my life, when I was confronted with large open views, conveying a tiny glimpse of the immense size of this planet. The vista I saw was only the tiniest fraction of the overall vastness of this globe. I was fascinated by whether the difference in size between humans and the globe was like that of the smallest creature in the world, namely the amoeba, a single-celled organism, to that of a fully grown human being.

In the words of my teacher, Sangharakshita: "man stands halfway between amoeba and the goal of enlightenment. Man has a choice to make a direct conscious effort to grow and spiritually develop, or else languish in a collective group dynamic and conditioning, which ultimately is regressive and reactive, not progressive, forward looking and creative."

As I was sitting entranced by the view before me, Saraha, on the other hand, had taken off his shoes and socks and was clambering over smaller rocks on the other side of the bay. He was being playful in a wonderfully spontaneous and childlike way. I imagined that he was probably relishing the feeling of aliveness that this contact with the icy cold water was bringing.

While he was being adventurous, I suddenly felt impelled to stand up on my feet on the big boulder and enunciate in a big booming voice,

"I'm an actor!" I said this with an inflection placed on the word, "actor".

It later dawned on me the implications of this statement. I wondered whether the viewing public would think that my words simply confirmed to them that the way I acted was only a charade, and I was thereby very artfully concealing my true intentions. I knew that this idea could not be further from the truth. I was sure that my action would only plant seeds of doubt and suspicion into the minds of the watching public.

After our time in the small rocky bay, we made our way back past the hotel and towards the town, still aligned with the coastal road. Eventually, after a good ten to fifteen-minute stroll, we got to a sturdy and well-maintained pier that jutted out into the estuary. It had a white two storey building at the end. Saraha and I ambled past anglers, who were mostly on their own, directing their view out to sea with their fishing lines. We passed a couple of fishermen huddled together and talking discreetly. They eyed us up with keen curiosity. Apart from the anglers, the area around the two-storey building at the end of the pier was almost deserted, except for a young couple walking arm in arm.

Once the couple had departed, we messed about by the building, acting playfully like a couple of mischievous school children. I took a few photos of him, with his head in the gap of a timber panel that had a painted sailor's body on it, minus the face. The photos later revealed him displaying a delightfully impish grin.

We then made our way back to the main road on the shoreline. There were quite a few bars and coffee houses overlooking the expanse of water. I pointed to the one which had the most life in it. It looked the smartest.

Entering the establishment, we caused nearly all heads to turn in our direction. We found a suitable spot by the large, white, timber-framed glass windows. The interior was of a tempered down funky design, with the bar counter made from a brushed stainless-steel finish. There were quirky touches, like a low, horizontally accented opening between ours and an adjoining room. I had a view of the bar area, while behind me was a traditional looking fireplace. The waitress, who was in her early twenties, smiled in our direction, while Saraha and I were sitting at the table, deciding what to choose. Like a hawk, as soon as we had put down the menus, she swooped in to take our order.

"Could we have a pot of Earl Grey tea and some scones, please?" I said.

"Sure – anything else?"

"No, that will be all, thanks," I cheerily responded.

"Your order will be with you soon," she said with a big grin on her face.

I then spoke to Saraha.

"I really enjoyed listening to your talk about the Honey Ball sutta that the Buddha had famously discoursed on. So, as you said, the mind creates stories about its experiences – especially the uncomfortable and pleasant ones. The mind then can suffer from a proliferation of narratives, where it can sometimes spiral outwards and get out of hand, being all-consuming for the individual."

"And yes, as I mentioned to all of you in the group, to prevent the mind from billowing outwards with increasing momentum, you must bring awareness to your mind, and realize that you need to stop habitually reacting. Instead, one needs to respond to any given situation creatively. The key is then, once either the painful or pleasant event has taken place, to try and stop the thoughts from mushrooming, without however blocking, or denying your experience. The most successful method is to let go of the negative stories, while nevertheless engaged in the process of experiencing and observing the unpleasant or pleasant emotionally loaded thinking. It's not a good idea to forcefully suppress your negative emotions, as that just leads to bottling them up, and ultimately repression. The way I see it, it's like witnessing clouds coming and going in the sky, yet not fixing your attention on them. As you and I know, it's much harder than it sounds. It requires a great deal of patience, time and possibly aptitude as well," he remarked wisely.

"Although it's a skill, I think some people have a much greater aptitude than others. I feel that I'm particularly able to transform unskilful emotions. Although I guess I probably haven't had many overwhelming negative or positive experiences to challenge me recently," I responded.

"We're always presented with situations that can cause a mental proliferation of sorts, but, as you rightly say, there are degrees of experience. Do you believe that you have more of an aptitude than others?" he asked inquisitively, but straightforwardly.

"Well, yes, I really do believe that I've got a greater propensity than most. It comes firstly from an innate ability, a definite perseverance in practising patience, also from the fact that I've been working on myself for the last 21 years as a practising Buddhist. Lastly, it comes from my own understanding of the law of conditionality or dependent origination, and how it affects our lives," I uttered forcefully.

"You might be right. I'm sure you know your wonderful mind better than anyone else does," he replied affectionately.

After settling the bill, we made tracks back to the car. I then took him back to his community in Birmingham.

When we arrived back at his place, I went briefly inside to go to the toilet. I came back out, and embraced him with a big, friendly hug. Reaching into his rucksack, he produced an object wrapped in paper napkins to give to me. Delicately un-wrapping the paper, he revealed a large scone that he had kept from our visit to the coffee house. He had concealed it, unbeknown to me, while I went to the toilet in the coffee shop. I thought this was a lovely touch from him, as a mark of gratitude for my generosity. Although it was a very simple material item, it was the surprise sentiment that I was really taken by. I had not seen it coming and was a little moved by my friend's solicitousness.

I drove back home, experiencing a warm fuzzy feeling stemming from the depth and intensity of our blossoming friendship. For the remainder of the week, I savoured the journey I had embarked on. I now had no doubt in my mind of his wholesome intentions. I felt I could now rest easy with this unmistakable knowledge about my wise companion.

CHAPTER 26

BRICK LANE

I had resolved to venture into London again. This time, I would try exploring a different location. I remembered how with a couple of university friends, I used to frequent the area around Brick Lane, with its fashionable bars, independent coffee houses and quirky shops. My choice of location was very much determined by how familiar I was with the area. This provided me a degree of comfort and certainty.

Setting off quite early from Leamington to London Marylebone, I arrived at around ten, and proceeded to Liverpool Street Station.

Again, like the occasion before, when I took Saraha to the funeral, I was dressed in my signature attire. This did not come easy but kept me alive and awake to my moment-to-moment experience.

I ascended the escalator at the entrance to Liverpool Street Station, onto the paved milling area outside. I stopped for a moment, panning my head round in a panoramic movement, witnessing the bustling scene with a colourful array of people and a multitude of vehicles. I was conscious that I was very visible to the public. I began to stride purposefully towards the crossing. Taking a trip through the new architecture of Spitalfields Market, I stopped in a smart coffee house, full of sharp lines of steel, glass, and mirrors. It loudly announced its trendy appeal. I chose a bottle of water for my purchase, as this would be safe ground for me. I had still not quite adjusted to a more relaxed and positive approach with the continued threat to my life.

The weather was glorious. The coffee house had outdoor furniture for customers, and I parked myself on one of the seats with my back to the store. I had a view out onto the other customers, the large extended pavement and the backdrop of tall traditional buildings.

As I was sitting, taking small mouthfuls of still water, I observed a couple of odd-looking gentlemen. It was not the fact that they looked odd individually, but that the two of them together were, to my mind, a little bizarre. The man, with his back to me, was probably in his mid-thirties. He was wearing a suit, a smart shirt and tie – pretty much what I would expect near the city of London. The other wore a black T-shirt with the logo of a heavy-metal band on the front. He also sported some mirrored glasses, so I had no way of telling who he was looking at. His hair was peroxide blond and was fashioned in a punkish hairdo. He was older than the other gentleman, by a good ten years if I were to hazard a guess.

While I continued to glug the water down, it seemed to me that this rock-and-roll looking bloke was taking a very keen interest in me. I could not be certain, but his face was very much angled directly at my head. Eventually, he shifted his mirrored glasses to the top of his face. I then became aware of his gaze meeting mine with a distinct inquisitiveness. I felt a twinge of anxiety, wondering why this bloke was inordinately fascinated with me. I knew that progressively, over time, the amygdala, the brain where the fear receptor resides, was probably diminishing in size. I was becoming more used to the idea of my life's constant surveillance, and forces trying to attack and silence me. I would continue to meet unsettling experiences with more and more calmness and patience. Every now and then my emotions would falter. I would then experience feelings of dread. I knew that if I kept up my meditation practice, and continued leading my life without obvious constraints, then the extent of the amygdala would further reduce.

I left the store and sauntered along the market stalls inside the huge modern building of Spitalfields atrium area. One stall caught my eye, manned by a sweet young woman with a fluorescent pink hairdo. She was trying to sell some of her arty photographs. They predominantly featured areas of London. These were scenes of streets, people and skies, but with a theatrical flourish and marks of bold colour set against black-and-white backdrops.

I spotted the pictures I really liked, and said to her,

"I love the way you've captured the bright red balloon floating away from the little girl, with the girl and the backdrop of the Houses of Parliament and bridge leading to it all being caught in black and white." She appeared very grateful and returned my compliments with a slightly embarrassed but nonetheless warm smile.

"Thanks, that's nice of you to say."

I discussed a few of the other pictures, and what specific qualities moved me. As I said my farewells to her, I moved away slowly, as if I was some stalking big cat. I decided I would get a coffee near Brick Lane.

Just before getting to Brick Lane itself, I spied a narrow-frontage coffee house, and decided to try it out. I saw that there were a couple of tables that were occupied with customers in the heart of the place. I ordered an espresso and was told that the coffee would be brought over to me when it was ready.

While sitting in one of the banquette seats at a two-person table at the back of the deep store, my view of the staff was shielded by a dividing wall between their area and mine. Even though there were few customers in the store, it took what felt like an age for my coffee to be brought over. The person who delivered it was a big, bearded bloke with ginger hair. He flourished a laddish grin when he laid down a jug of tap water and a glass along with the coffee.

I proceeded to taste the coffee. It was utterly revolting, and seemed to stick, like glue, to my mouth. Whatever they had put in the coffee was not what I had ordered. Even so, I polished off all its contents. Just before I made my exit, and without turning to look at them, they remarked,

"You've not wasted any time with drinking your coffee. You've just downed it in a flash." They then dissolved into raucous laughter.

"Yeah, it was quick wasn't it," I responded. Still not looking in their direction, I made an abrupt getaway. I decided I would never visit that specific coffee house again. I experienced a negative vibe from the store and all its staff.

I quickly glanced at my watch. Seeing that it was time for lunch, I decided to go to Pizza Express. Again, this was somewhere I was familiar with from my past excursions.

While walking to the restaurant, I noticed how I felt light-headed. I was not walking in a straight line but taking an uneven path in the direction of the restaurant. My immediate thought was, *They've done it! They've successfully managed to poison me.* This was tempered with a quieter and more soothing voice saying, *Don't worry, you'll be okay. Time will be the healer.* I then thought that if the poison at the coffee house does not affect me, then the poison at the Pizza Express might do the trick, as a double whammy. I truly felt that I was putting my life in the hands of the gods, yet I was continuing to develop greater trust and confidence towards those gentle and benign but spiritually powerful beings.

I stepped through the frameless glass doorway of the restaurant, which was situated on the corner. The restaurant was full of groups of businesspeople in smart suits, along with quite a few groups of young girls and some couples possibly finding a spot for lunchtime romance. A man in his late forties asked in an Italian accent,

"Table for one, sir?"

"Yes, please," I said with a subtle fear mingled in with the clarity of my voice. I was directed to a seat at the far corner next to the till and the entrance to the kitchen. The door to the kitchen was discreetly hidden away.

The staff seemed generally to give me a cold reception. I was not perturbed by this and continued to be as charming and polite to all of them as possible. They were only being given orders by the authorities. They had been influenced negatively towards me by unhelpful propaganda.

After ordering and consuming a pizza Fiorentina and washing it down with a large bottle of sparkling mineral water, I spotted a couple of waiters standing by the entrance door. They were talking quietly between themselves. Every now and then they looked in my direction with serious faces. Perhaps they were feeling the guilt and shame of their actions, or they could not quite believe what was happening, I speculated. I noticed that I was not feeling as woozy as earlier. I wondered whether with the time and space, the gods were magically nullifying the poison in my system. Settling the bill, I then left the restaurant.

The weather was still sunny with a few fluffy clouds scudding across the bright blue sky. Heading towards the big piazza, just by the entrance to the new Spitalfields development, I chose to get an americano from a Costa coffee to take away with me.

After my purchase, I took my coffee to a stone slab at the edge of the piazza, where other people were sitting. I parked myself next to a woman, who was in her twenties. Seeing as I had barely talked to anyone in the last couple of days, except for purely functional reasons, I decided to strike up a conversation with her.

"It's lovely the weather we're having this year."

"I wouldn't know, as I'm not from here," she responded with a pleasant smile.

"Oh, where are you from then?" I detected an unmistakably thick German accent in her voice but did not want to appear presumptuous.

"I'm from Austria. I've come to visit a friend of mine who works in London," she said, visibly buoyed by the random engagement in communication.

"I thought you might be German speaking, from the accent. Are you over here on your own then?" I enquired.

"Yes. Why are you here, if you don't mind me asking?"

"I've given up my job, as I've some inheritance money to fall back on. I've decided that I want to write a book about the events which have taken place this year, because they have been dramatic to say the least. I also love exploring London, which will feed into my writing material."

"What a bold move! I would love to do the same and quit my job. It's nice to meet someone who has taken that leap of faith and carried it through," she paused for a second, and then continued, "What have the dramatic events in your life been then, apart from leaving your job?"

I paused for a second, deliberating on whether I should take the plunge and reveal an enticing snapshot of my book that would also expose uncomfortable truths that I still found difficult to admit to the public.

"Well…it's about a person, who believes there's a conspiracy around his life and that he's under constant TV surveillance, as a kind of Big Brother figure. The authorities believe he's a threat to the established world order and are trying any way they can to eliminate him. The other aspect to him is that he has bipolar, which is a mental disorder."

"Yeah, I know of it," she remarked confidently.

"So, the question to the reader is: whatever he's thinking about the threat to his life, is it a symptom of his bipolar or is there in fact truth to everything he is experiencing? I will try and show that there is mounting evidence to support his claim."

"That sounds really interesting – maybe even a bestseller,"

"Well, I can continue to live in hope. The dream's still alive for me!"

"Do you know what you're going to call the book then?" I had a vague idea, but was reluctant to share it with her, as it had not been fully formed in my mind.

We continued chatting about what she was going to see while in London. She became ever more animated in her speech. I could sense with her wide eyes and intense focus on what I was speaking about that she was very interested in what I seemed to stand for.

After about 20 minutes of uplifting conversation, she said,

"As I mentioned to you, I've been meaning to tick a few of the sight-seeing destinations off on my map. I also need to be back for my friend early this evening, as we're going out later."

"Well, have a lovely time this evening, and try not to get overwhelmed by visiting too many sites. The fewer the better, I would say. Quality rather than quantity is the best strategy."

"Not to worry, I'm only intending to see a maximum of two sites, and if I feel tired after the first place, I'll go and get a coffee somewhere," she replied with a radiant healthy glow.

"That's the spirit!"

She jumped up from the seat in an exuberant manner. She turned her whole body to mine, shook hands, and said,

"It was lovely to meet you. You've given me food for thought, and even inspiration for the future course of my life."

"I wish you every success in your life, and by the way, enjoy the rest of your stay here in London and your night out tonight," I said, mixing the profound with the trivial.

With that she thanked me and walked briskly away from where I was sitting. For a moment, I delighted in the wonderfully arbitrary nature to our short exchange.

I remained in that spot a good ten minutes after she had left, basking in the sunlight. I was then emotionally stirred to venture into the heart of Brick Lane. I imagined that, as it was a Saturday, I would meet a lively throng of assorted people amusing themselves over drinks and perambulating through the street.

One place I wanted to visit was the Vibe bar, a popular place which I knew well from previous excursions. It had an outdoor area that on weekends with good weather would be invariably packed. On arriving, I was not wrong in my assumption. It was teeming with people. This aroused a degree of anxiety in me, being so flamboyantly dressed. I opted for the safer confines of the inside of the building, feeling slightly shaken by the sheer numbers.

Inside there were far fewer people to observe. I could also find a single seat arrangement more easily.

I ordered a lager shandy from the bar, my favourite alcoholic tipple. It was not the sweetness I necessarily enjoyed, but the quantity of alcohol was lower and would not be sufficient to cloud my judgement. Yet still, it would be enough to slightly quell my frayed nerves, which felt so outwardly visible.

Once I had been served, I parked myself on the raised platform, adjacent to some old industrial looking steel framed windows. With open shoulders and an open stance, I looked around the joint. I appreciated the interesting comic book style cartoons painted on the walls. They depicted both male and female figures for the respective toilet areas. The bar had a grungy feel about it, yet it was still well-maintained and looked after. Things inside the space were generally clean and ordered, but in a free and relaxed way.

There was a large party of girls and a couple of guys at a long table. It appeared that this was them just starting their day's revelry. They were talking quietly, with the occasional raised voice and sporadic, raucous laughter.

When I glanced in their direction, while they were sat to the side, and a little behind my chair, I saw one of them immediately look away. She then fixed her attention back to the group. On the periodic occasions I turned to them, I felt as if they were surreptitiously observing me when I was not looking. I just had a hunch that this was the reality. It caused me to feel a little on edge, but the effects of the alcohol were ever so slightly mellowing my demeanour. Just as they were beginning to depart, I had finally become comfortable in their presence.

I was becoming aware that the bar area was starting to fill up with Saturday revellers. There was recurring riotous laughter. When I felt that my ego was being wounded, through what I presumed was hilarity directed at me, I pondered that they were all entitled to their laughter and amusement about me. If nothing else, I was not getting physically injured. Fundamentally, I saw this as a learning experience, being buffeted by the worldly winds of praise and blame and fame and disgrace. There were also the worldly winds of gain and loss, pain and pleasure, but these characteristics were not as strident in the current circumstances.

After sitting awhile, having consumed two drinks, I had the sudden and surging desire to dance to the visceral, grungy music that was being played. I would therefore be making an even bigger spectacle of myself than I already was. Although the urge was powerful, I thought about the arguments against such a decision. Firstly, it was about half-three in the afternoon. Secondly, there was not even a dance floor to be had in that space. Although I was brave, even I could not venture into such choppy waters as these. I backed down, mulling over my decision and thinking it was probably for the best. It might have been a particularly foolhardy act that even I would find embarrassing.

I left the bar and was sauntering leisurely further down the main part of Brick Lane when I noticed a quirky, Moroccan looking tea shop with its sliding doors opened wide. This allowed an enticing Middle Eastern looking interior to be made apparent. Liking what I was seeing, I went inside.

Ordering a green tea, it came to me in a large, ornately decorated metallic pot, with accompanying refined crockery. Lounging on low, comfortable seating, I enjoyed listening to tracks from the Beatles. The choice of music, which was the psychedelic end of the band's musical spectrum, was another of the store's attributes that had drawn me in.

Directly opposite me, a middle-aged father was sitting with his two young children. He had a full head of hair and black, thick-rimmed glasses. Looking like the intellectual, bookish type, he was wearing a dark brown, corduroy sports jacket. His expression was one of world-weariness. He did not seem to be particularly engaged with what his children were asking him. His interest was more focussed on me, but in discreet intervals. I felt a pang of compassion for his predicament. I sensed that this life with children was thrust upon him by conventional mores. If he could do it differently next time, he probably would. I wondered if this gentleman felt a yearning to have the life I was leading – one of freedom and authentic happiness.

Slowly but surely, I was becoming accustomed to the notion that nothing would kill me off. However hard people tried, my life would be implicitly guarded by the gods. Throughout my time in the coffee house, the notion of poison in my tea was at the very fringes of my consciousness. It was not making any discernible dent in my faith and trust.

After spending a good hour slowly drinking the large pot of tea, I paid up. I then walked swiftly yet gracefully back to the station and headed home.

Ensconced in one of the two-person seats in the train carriage, bound for its end destination at Snow Hill in Birmingham, I churned over the day's events in my mind. I mused that overall, it had been an enlivening experience, one which was waking me up to a bigger reality around me. A reality that felt fresh and full of vigour and excitement.

CHAPTER 27

THE REFLECTIONS

It was a wet Friday morning in the early part of 2015. I had managed to book myself on a last-minute retreat to a former hotel, by Loch Voil, north of Stirling. The night before, I had packed my clothes and other miscellaneous items into my large travelling bag. I collected my vibrant blue waterproof coat, put on my sturdy waterproof shoes, and then, with my gear, proceeded to lock the flat. Making some final mental checks, I took the series of steps up from my flat to the pavement above.

As I opened my black metal gate, I spied a man in the driver's seat of a white Audi A3. It was parked a few vehicles away from where I was standing, with its engine on. He was holding back expectantly.

I had parked on another road adjacent to the one I lived on. I made my way to my parking spot. Opening the boot of my car, I took longer than expected to sort out and arrange its contents. Just as I reached for the boot door to close it, I was aware that the same vehicle that I had clocked on my street was passing at a slow speed.

Once it had passed, it sped up gradually to the end of the road. Instead of turning either left or right, it continued to the opposite road, and started making a three-point turn to come back in my direction. It then stopped by the side of the road, a fair distance away. It waited ominously.

I found this very suspicious. I wondered if I had been that bit quicker in closing my boot and taking the couple of paces to my driver's door whether this would have been the perfect opportunity for this lone figure to squeeze the side of his car to my vehicle, while I was about to get in. He would then squash my body and cause severe physical injury. I would probably double over in agony and fall to the ground. This would then give the spy a chance to run me over, and convincingly seal my fate. I felt that the chances of this being the reality were not remote, due to so many other events happening that year.

As I made the long journey up to the retreat, I started mulling over the other events that had occurred in the past four to five months.

The first episode that dealt me an emotional body blow transpired in the early part of October 2014. For a few days the temperature had plummeted to the low single figures. After I had meditated that morning, as per usual, my routine would be to open two of my windows – one to my bedroom and then the transom window to my living room. This was so I could get a good crossflow air circulation. I had meditated quite early that morning. At about 7:55am, I was reaching for the transom window when something unusual struck me. There was a wide dormer window at the roof of the terraced house directly opposite. What was alarming was that the middle window was wide open, and what appeared to me like the thin barrel of a sniper rifle was being aimed straight at me.

Although I experienced a sudden but brief pang of fear, I still opened the transom. With as much calm as I could muster, I carried on my duties without being too shaken. This was where I believed that a marksman would have the perfect opportunity for a direct shot at my head or heart.

As nothing happened, I could only conclude that this was just one more area to convince me of extra-terrestrial help, using their disabling magic to safeguard my passage through the world. I tried to doubt the veracity of this assumed marksman, but I thought what was also notable was that it was particularly cold that day. *Why would someone living in that flat have the window so wide open, when it looked a particularly cold and un-insulated space?*

Another experience cropped up in my mind. This time I had gone to the Buddhist centre in Birmingham. On returning home at about

10:45pm, I had parked my car a long way up one of the adjacent streets. As I walked past some of the warmly glowing curtained rooms on my left-hand side, I spied a house that had its curtains wide open with the owner's TV screen on full display. What I then noticed, which later became extraordinary and peculiar, was that the TV image showed a figure standing by some windows with a hedgerow in the background. It seemed like the identical stance and backdrop in which I was standing. I could not make out the appearance of the man. At the time, I did not take much notice of it, so I did not bother to compare the details of the clothes the figure was wearing to mine. I initially assumed that it was a detective programme that the householders were watching. Later, the near identical match of my position and surroundings with those television images gave me another shred of evidence that my life was on show across the country and possibly the world.

I curiously observed that whenever I subsequently walked past that house, the curtains were drawn shut, or at times at least partially drawn, so as not to allow any onlooker visual access to their TV screen.

There was another specific incident that happened to me near the beginning of November, when the nights were drawing in. It was a Saturday, and I was about to settle down on the sofa to watch a film I got from Lovefilm, a DVD rental place. Before reclining on my sofa, I had resolved to wash up my dishes. I found this mild exertion a worthwhile undertaking before my reward of a carefully selected movie.

While standing and leaning over the sink, going through my methodical system of washing up, I heard a low flying helicopter passing overhead. It then rotated and hovered just in front of my kitchen window, a good 30–40 meters from where I was standing. It was positioned directly opposite my flat. It had its front angled away from my kitchen window, at a 45-degree angle. I could not make out any figure inside, but I again imagined that there was probably a trained marksman resting his weapon on a fixed contraption, desperately trying to fire a bullet into my head.

This time I had a bit more faith in otherworldly figures and the spells that they could cast, so, with comparative calmness, I continued drying the remainder of the cutlery. By the time I finished the washing-up and drying, the helicopter was still hovering in the exact location it was before. It was only when I calmly settled down on the sofa and pressed play on my remote that the noise gradually disappeared. It left a wonderfully glistening trail of peace in its wake.

There seemed to me to be such overwhelming evidence to support my general hypotheses. I truly believed that there were a lot of people hoping for my removal from this planet, due to their deluded thinking. However, there was quite a huge section of society in the world who thoroughly endorsed the principles by which I lived my life and believed that I was completely genuine.

As I got past Birmingham, I turned my mind to the retreat I was embarking on. I knew there would be something waiting in store for me. GCHQ would have immediately clocked that I had booked myself on this Scottish retreat. They would have got MI5 to dispatch their most lethal double-0 agent to be a retreatant. I thought that this person would have had previous meditation experience. I believed that the secret service world knew the effectiveness that mindfulness and meditation could bring to their staff's productivity and lives. Ultimately, they knew that it would make their secret agents more effective killing machines, able to act methodically and with precision.

While these dark thoughts swilled around my head, the palms of my hands began to sweat, as I alternated between gripping the steering wheel tightly and opening my palms to allow them to breathe. My body temperature was also becoming warmer. The weather that day was overcast. On occasions, it was accompanied by drizzle. It almost felt more satisfying to me when the rain really poured down in torrents than a lukewarm and feeble rainfall. This sentiment might have been dependent on my being snugly cocooned in my car.

I got to the Tebay service station, near Kendall. In the past, I had stopped off here many a time with my father, while being taken to Dundee University. I remembered those times at my *alma mater* with fondness. I had spent a good deal of my twenties in that part of the world. In my first year of university, I had really discovered myself, slowly nurturing the trajectory that I was going to take throughout the rest of my life. This was one of combining my architecture with the practice of Buddhism and developing what later became a relatively stable marriage of the two. Although, in 2014, I had become disillusioned with working in architectural firms. I knew it took away from the space and time that I could devote to meditation and Buddhist study.

As I stood waiting to be served at the buffet counter, I acknowledged that I had come a very long way and had made considerable personal and spiritual progress. I was starting to find a path that really worked for me, not just in meditation and Buddhism, but also in my writing endeavours. I could feel the unbridled passion surging within me with all the possibilities that this could bring.

I sat down at the edge of a busy and lively space, cut across with oak beams that loosely defined the large open-plan area. Tucking heartily into my macaroni cheese and chips with baked beans, I savoured the stodgy nature of the meal.

Between mouthfuls, I stopped fixating on my plate of food and instead viewed the assorted clientele, who were collectively chatting and consuming their meals. One young guy with long brown hair, who was with his wife and child, was taking a particular interest in me. I met his intense gaze. This prompted a devilish grin from him. I could feel a sharp jolt in my guts. My ego felt affronted. Instead of reacting, either by trying to outstare him or looking away embarrassed and not meeting his glare again, I pursued the tack of glancing at him in intervals. I was tracking my own emotional response to the situation and applying wisdom and understanding. This man found me amusing. So be it. I was amusing in a foolish way. I had done many things in my life that would be considered humiliating. As had many other people, but, unlike my life, they had gone mostly unnoticed. They could be brushed underneath the carpet. We are all fools, but the ones who are wise know that they are fools.

Ryokan, a famous Zen monk, who was renowned for being a very wise man, described himself as a "Daigu", which literally means a "Great Fool". I could see how Ryokan's statement might come across as paradoxical. On the one hand, why was he saying that he was a great fool, if he was meant to be a wise individual? Was it not self-evident that a foolish person could not also be wise? The way I understood it was that Ryokan saw all his foolish tendencies very clearly, due to being extremely aware of the devil within his own spirit. This was accompanied by the devil's horde of demons, tempting, seducing and belittling him. Ryokan saw that these obstacles would always be in play until one gained enlightenment, or complete release and freedom from the reactive mind. In this respect, Ryokan was very wise to see himself as the great fool.

I tried to let go of the issue I was having with this certain individual. I just continued, as calmly as I could muster, with eating my lunch. After buying some chewing gum, I left the motorway services. I then continued with my journey up north of Stirling, to a place just outside Balquidder, where Dhanakosa, the retreat lodge, was situated.

CHAPTER 28

THE RETREATANT

With a slow and measured speed, I navigated the narrow, winding road leading up to the retreat lodge. To the left of me extended the beautiful loch with a hilly and partially wooded backdrop. There were various houses dotted around the idyllic vista. The weather was overcast, but with no droplets of rain in sight.

As I approached the gate of the lodge, I observed a non-descript, bespectacled man of relatively tall build getting out of his vehicle. He made a few attempts to keep the gate firmly open. The gentleman rolled his eyes at me. He gave the impression of wondering why a small thing like opening a gate would not work the first time around and questioning what on earth he was doing coming on a retreat like this. This was how I surmised his body language. He looked at me sharply. It seemed like there was an attitude of condescension in his demeanour.

An insidious thought crept into my mind. It suggested that this man – it seemed wrong to call him "gentleman", as this word seemed too refined for his look – might well be the secret service's deadly weapon in person removal.

My father once told me that when he was working for the MoD, that when interrogating spies in a Whitehall bunker, they struck him as having no discernible features. They were not the classic Bond character, of good looks and debonair charm. Instead, they appeared to my father to be very plain and somewhat boring looking. I noticed, as I parked my car and unloaded my belongings, that the lone figure, stationed at the opposite side of the car park, was making a call. He was sitting very serenely inside the comfort of his modest vehicle. He made me think that he was like a large deadly venomous viper. One that was cool and calculating. One which would move slowly and deliberately, waiting for the opportune moment to strike out with a killer blow to the neck, to sink its fangs deep into my flesh.

The house was white, with a large expanse of garden in the front grounds. It had a cottagey feel. As I entered the vestibule and took my shoes off, I was greeted by a young woman I had seen at a previous Buddhist festival over four years back.

I could think of better things than being cooped up in this retreat for a whole year. I enjoyed the freedom that was afforded to me, living in Leamington Spa. There was so much more room for manoeuvre there.

While I chatted to the woman, it felt like there was a thick, dark thunder cloud hanging over me. I could not help but be reminded of the ominous nature of the man I had seen on my arrival.

After sorting out the administrative procedures with her, I took my large travelling bag upstairs to my room. I dumped the bag on the floor adjacent to one of the lower bunk beds and quickly made my bed, so there would be no ambiguity as to which I had chosen. As soon as I had prepared the final touches, I walked back along the corridor and then downstairs to the living room. My mouth was feeling parched, so I went to get some tea from the dining room, which was connected to the long, narrow living room in an open-plan arrangement.

The solitary man, who I had seen on arrival, was sitting in one of the dining room chairs. He was looking right at me. I averted my gaze as I walked past. Immediately, as I passed him, he emitted a barely stifled expression of mirth. I could feel my ego inwardly tensing up with a mixture of fear and indignation. I wondered if the man was thinking that his mission would be straightforward and was finding that intensely amusing. Or was his barely contained hilarity due to all the embarrassing things I had done in my life that had been caught on film, to be discussed by everyone else ad nauseam? It could have been another reason, but I was not so convinced by any third option.

After supper, all the retreatants gathered in the shrine room. It was in a small rustic outbuilding with timber flooring, which could comfortably contain the eighteen people who were booked on the retreat. The theme was "Body, Earth, Breath". This appealed to my sensibilities, suggesting a groundedness with one's body and Mother Earth, to be all-encompassed by the breath. This intimated to me that a large slice of the activities would involve meditation.

We all sat in an oval arrangement with warm, glowing light radiating out from four big candles in the centre of the space. One-by-one, we went round sharing with the assembled group our names and reasons for taking part in the retreat. Over the years, I had become more at ease with large groups. I would now rarely get flustered. While I was waiting my turn, I could not help but try to formulate the key points of my justification for being part of this themed retreat. Once my turn had come, in which I expressed my fondness for the title, which really piqued my interest, I waited to hear what the lone figure had to say. It slowly moved round to the serene but suspect man. He slowly and deliberately spoke, almost as if he was imbuing the principles of mindfulness wholeheartedly. His words were,

"Hi, my name is Oliver. I've never done anything like this before, but I thought there's always a first time for everything." This was all he had to say. It was very concise and sparing in its disclosure.

I discovered the following day, while I was sitting diagonally opposite him at lunch, that he lived on a farm just outside of Norwich. He had come a great distance for something which, I felt, did not in any way appeal to him, but, as he stated, he was prepared to give it a go. This just confirmed that there was some Machiavellian plot that had been concocted by the authorities. Oliver was their main operative.

That Friday evening, I brushed my teeth and was the first in bed. I had not yet met my roommate, as our paths had not crossed. My head was screened by the towel draped over the rungs of the ladder to the top bunk. This gave me a discreet view of whomever entered, without them easily noticing my open, inquisitive eyes. The side light of the other person sleeping in my room was on. I had turned my side light off, to wait like some anxious hare in the undergrowth of the duvet.

About ten minutes passed before the door to the room opened. The person walked very methodically through the passageway and then stopped in between the two bunk beds by my head, pausing for what felt like a good 30 seconds. My heart immediately pumped faster. It was the lone man. My fight or flight instinct was kicking in, but I remained still with a queasy feeling, reassuring myself that I would not suffer. Slowly but surely, the doubt started to take hold, worming its way into my mind. *How could I survive a whole week of this retreat with a potential assassin sleeping at such close quarters?* It was a tall order, even for the gods.

For the entire duration of the night, I was having an inward tussle. On the one hand, there was doubt, while on the other there was a confidence and trust. This caused me to have a near sleepless night worrying about the implications, but also intermittently soothing my mind with sweet, whispering words of comfort.

The following morning, after getting up at about 6:30am and having a quick shower, I went to make tea before the early morning meditation. There would be about an hour and a half of meditation before breakfast. As I had a steady and quite lengthy daily meditation practice, I was genuinely looking forward to this quiet, peaceful time.

What troubled me during the meditation, which was broken up into two sittings, was that it was primarily guided. This was more for beginners than intermediates or advanced practitioners. The retreat leader's words got in the way of the clarity of my meditation. I was curious to know how I would get on with the body movement in the latter part of the morning. I seriously doubted whether this retreat's theme was appropriate for me. *Had I made a foolish mistake by choosing this retreat?* It was also particularly wet and cold that day, which compounded my bleakness.

From about 10:30am to 1pm, we all congregated in the shrine room for explorations into the body and its sensations. I threw myself into the exercises that were given. One of them was to act out an activity that you really enjoyed doing, perhaps something creative. After each person performed an imaginary activity, everyone else would repeat that same action in a process of mirroring. One of the guys, a sweet-natured man, with a genuinely friendly smile and soft demeanour, acted out, a little abashedly, the process of brushing his teeth. I acted out myself playing the piano, both gently and vigorously, which I, a little smugly, thought was more in keeping with something creative. The minute I thought this, I also believed I was being foolish for judging the sweet man harshly.

Oliver, on the other hand, acted out himself kneading dough. What gripped me quite forcibly was that he had his shirt sleeves rolled up. I was acutely aware of the strength in his arms and hands while he performed the actions. They were large and muscular, typifying a brute strength that could easily be deployed to potentially suffocate me with a pillow while I slept. Again, the idea occurred to me: *how long could I maintain my survival with the help of the gods?* There were so many conditions and factors working against me. Surely, there would be a time when the gods would slip up, and there would be an opening for the intelligence services to claim victory.

After eating lunch, I went out on a solitary walk. It was still cold and wet outside. My walk was bracing due to the light but steady rain pelting my face. I felt thoroughly invigorated on my return. After dropping my coat off in my room, I settled on a sofa in the lounge, next to an older woman.

I got talking to her. She was dressed plainly, but she was well-spoken with a cut-glass English accent. Her name was Daphne. After some introductions and pleasantries, I asked her,

"What do you do for a living?"

"Well, I've turned my hand to writing books. I've just completed an illustrated book on horses, both in cavalry and in dressage. I drew the horses in all sorts of poses. I must've created about 200 images of them for the book. I've long had a fascination with horses, and in my younger years I used to ride them a lot."

"What medium did you use to create the images of the horses?"

"Well, it was several different mediums. I did them in charcoal, pencil, watercolour, and acrylic," she replied with a very positive spirit. Before I could interject, she proceeded to say,

"I was very lucky to have been given a small advance for the book. It was a delight to receive, even though it was only a few thousand pounds."

"As advances go, that isn't bad at all, I'd say," I replied.

"Mind you, it was hard work. I had to complete it all within the space of a three-month window. By the end of it, I was completely shattered. The good news is that I did it within the timescale," she said, with an obvious joy and healthy pride welling up.

"How do you find living on your own? You did say that you live by yourself, didn't you?" I asked her. I saw vague similarities to my own life. I was experiencing a kindred spirit.

"Sometimes it can be tough being on your own. I don't always have people to come and see how I am. Although, while I'm occupied with work, I'm generally fine. It's when it dries up that I sometimes get despondent. I love tending to my garden, which nearly always lifts my mood, but the hard part is motivating myself to get started on it in the first place. But once I'm doing it, the positive energy levels flow through me. How do you find living on your own then?" she delicately enquired.

"I'm writing a book myself. If I have that as a project, I'll often be buoyant and content. There are some days when I literally feel that I'd rather be in bed doing nothing. It's on those days that the internal battle can be quite immense. There are some days when I manage to shrug off the boredom and occupy my time with writing, while on other days the inertia can be too strong. I then succumb to slumber," I said with resignation in my tone, as I reminded myself of the reality of my predicament.

By all accounts, I could see and feel that she lived by modest and humble principles. She was a grateful woman and expressed that she was not a Buddhist but was very keen on the body movement angle of the retreat, having done a lot of dancing in her time. I imagined her to have been a very glamorous woman in her heyday. Her charm and vivaciousness had not been lost. It still sought to exert its influence on the people she met.

After our entrancing conversation, in which I described more of my book and its subject matter, I took myself off to my room for a quick nap.

That afternoon at about 4:30pm, all the retreatants assembled again in the shrine room. We all did more acting and body exercises with half of the group performing, while the other half acted as witnesses. This would then be swapped around. The afternoon seemed to drag. I began to feel a sense of pointlessness during the exercises. There seemed to be no Buddhist teaching being expounded, or time for quiet meditation. I was starting to think that this retreat was a waste of my precious time.

I knew that it was my own fault for not carefully checking out the details of the week's programme. I should have enquired more with the retreat administrators before plunging headlong into payment. However, sometimes I acted on gut instincts and intuition rather than purely rational analysis. This time, at least, it had not paid off.

That evening, Oliver went off to bed early. When I entered the room, he had his side light switched on. His eyes were shut as he rested fully clothed on top of his duvet, lying on his side with both hands tucked under his head. I noticed he had a box of aspirin on his bedside table and a glass of water.

Getting undressed and into my pyjamas, I found myself wondering if Oliver was going to try something tonight. *Could the headache he had be a way of the gods disabling him for now and giving me the respite I desperately needed?*

After brushing my teeth, I slipped into bed and waited. My eyes were still concealed by my towel, hanging over the bed's ladder rungs. They were wide open. I remained poised and alert. After about ten minutes went by, Oliver raised himself from his side and slowly went to the bathroom. On his return, he lingered by the side of my headboard, like he had done on the first night. This time, the duration seemed to be that little bit longer. This potential looming threat hung menacingly in the confines of the room.

I felt decidedly tense and lay rigid in my bed. All the while, over these two nights, he had not spoken to me in the bedroom. I was, admittedly, unwilling to speak to him either. The feeling was mutual.

Oliver undressed and got into bed. He switched off his light. We were then plunged into darkness with just the very faintest illumination from one solitary light outside. I carried on waiting and ruminated obsessively. For most of the night, I got very little sleep, with a lurking fear coursing through me. This feeling manifested in restless tossing and turning under my duvet, accompanied by an incessant inner dialogue.

Gradually, over the course of the night, my mind eased off into a comparative stillness. Only in the last remaining hour or so, did I finally fall asleep. Oliver, on the other hand, remained totally silent. *Could this have been the same situation as the previous retreat, when that character Lee made very little movement? Lee had confessed to not getting any sleep, had he been biding his time too for the right moment to strike with a killer blow or suffocating move?*

The following morning, I engaged Oliver in a brief, "Good Morning." I asked him how he had slept. His reply was what I half-expected him to say, which was,

"I slept very well, thanks, considering I had a blistering headache." I was sure the gods had played a part in his deep sleep and pulsating headache the previous evening. This occurrence had not happened by chance. I also thought about how much longer I could bear this proximity to an assassin. I started to seriously think about an impromptu exit.

That Sunday after breakfast, we all gathered back in the shrine room for more movement exercises. It was only about ten minutes into the programme when I made the conscious decision to make a sharp and noticeably abrupt exit. I went to sit in the quiet room, which doubled as a library, inside the main house. It had a wonderful view over the loch. The waters were shimmering in the sunlight breaking through the big, greyish clouds. Everything looked fresh and alive. The hardy trees seemed to sparkle and glitter with a magical quality. Slumped in an armchair, I reflected on the previous two days.

I was set on leaving the retreat today. Nothing would veer me away from this hardened resolution.

After a good hour had passed, I heard the patter of steps making their way for toilet breaks or liquid refreshments. The main retreat leader, Akahana, a Mancunian woman, opened the door to the room. She came and sat next to me.

"How are you? Are you not enjoying it?" she eased in the question gently. She was a kind woman, with a lot of bubbly but at the same time settled energy. I could tell that her yoga and meditation practice gave her this embodied attribute.

"No, I'm really finding it difficult to persevere with. I know what you're probably thinking. Why did I book myself onto this retreat, when I knew there'd be a lot of attention placed on the body and its movements? I guess it was just my impulsive streak coming out," I replied sincerely.

After a brief exchange in which Akahana offered prudent advice on the merits of staying, I tried to persuade her that it was more than just natural resistance. I had very rarely experienced it this strongly. She concluded by saying,

"Don't you think you should just keep giving it a go? Don't you think that this is always the resistance that comes up for everyone. You probably need to break through this psychological barrier," she said, trying her best to appeal to my reason and understanding. I was reluctant to tell her the other reason why I was keen to leave – Oliver's foreboding presence in the bedroom, and what I thought he might be capable of.

"No, I think I'm now resolute. I can hear what you're saying, but I think my heart is telling me to listen to my resistance and acknowledge it. I've also been sleeping badly, what with one thing and another. Don't get me wrong, I feel alright now, but I know my lack of sleep will catch up with me," I said with gentle defiance.

"Well, it's up to you. If you do leave – for the sake of the group dynamic – it would be best for you to leave directly after lunch. Also, could you make an announcement, during lunch, of your intentions to leave. This will allow for a clean break in your parting," she said with benign and appropriate authority. I thanked Akahana for her time and confirmed that I would make an announcement during the lunch period.

I started to feel a little jittery due to the upcoming speech I would have to make. I knew that there were some people among the participants who would not take kindly to my decision, while others would genuinely sympathize. I realized again that these were the worldly winds of praise and blame, buffeting me in this upcoming ordeal, with the latter of the two being, of course, a little difficult to accept.

After Akahana had left, I collected my thoughts on what I would say. I then decided to retreat to my room. I had been lying on my bed for about ten minutes when the door opened. I was surprised and a little perturbed by this occurrence, as everyone, except me, should have been in the shrine room.

Oliver entered the space. He had brought with him two dining room chairs. He fumbled a little to decide how the two chairs should be arranged. He then positioned them parallel to the two bunk beds, facing each other. As I continued to lounge on my bed, he sat down on one of the chairs, and started talking.

"I hear you're leaving us today."

"Yes, that's right. I'm not getting anything out of the body movement exercises, and the mornings don't give me the chance to do a proper meditation."

"I'm sorry I couldn't get more of a chance to speak to you, as we're roommates. I'm not sure why I came on this retreat. It's so far away from where I live in Norfolk. I'm not sure, like you, I quite see any point in the movement exercises, but I guess I will continue to see it through to the end. It'll be a shame not to have someone to confide in about the retreat, but such is the notion of change and impermanence – a very Buddhist concept. I used to be part of this movement in Norfolk a long time ago, in the 70's and 80's. I was instrumental in shaping it in Norwich, but I lost interest. I then retreated to my farm."

As he was opening up to me, I pondered on the intelligence of the man. He made a lot of sense, speaking volubly and with a measure of worldly knowledge. His admission that he had been part of

Triratna in Norfolk in the 80's, where there had been alleged sexual shenanigans, just reinforced my belief that he was a spy working for the British government. I wondered whether he had played a pivotal role in the unscrupulous proceedings there, considering he described his role as being "instrumental". I believed this would be to undermine the movement's standing later in its history.

The thoughts that he was sharing with me touched darker aspects of his psyche. They seemed to me to be quite revealing of his deeper motivations. He then said, "Come and sit down in the opposite chair to me." The request made me uneasy. My breathing started to accelerate, becoming shallower and more audible. Was this a manipulative game that they taught at MI5 and MI6 to their special agents? Once I had sat down opposite him, he said,

"Let's sit here for a moment and close our eyes." Initially, I was hesitant in shutting my eyes, but rather than appearing nervous, I gave myself to the moment. My eyelids were quivering a little, and I tried desperately to control my breathing pattern, to hopefully appear more confident than I was. I presumed that the appearance of calmness in me would hopefully suppress whatever malicious motives he might be harbouring.

Five minutes elapsed before I opened my eyes to see Oliver looking intently at me. He extended a large, powerful hand out to me. I did the same. I grabbed his hand to shake it, in a strong forceful action. We then stood up. Oliver embraced me, which I reluctantly reciprocated. I was experiencing a chink of light emerging from my mind. I seriously believed that I would now come through this ordeal unaffected, while still feeling deeply suspicious about his underlying motives for this short and peculiar set up. He then uttered,

"I'm sure I'll see you again, and that our paths will cross in the not-too-distant future."

"Yes, I'm sure we will," I said, secretly hoping that I would never see him in this life again.

"It would be good to get your email address, so we could stay in contact." I could not be honest and reveal that I did not want anything to do with him, but politely yet insincerely replied,

"Yes, we could do that." I then left it at that. The sun continued to break through more grey clouds with wonderful crepuscular rays, which magically echoed the splinters of light emanating from my heart.

I made the announcement at lunch. I was surprised to find that I was more confident than I had expected myself to be. As I had already imagined, there were some who took my decision well and appreciated the bold move I was making, while others engaged with me as little as possible. Instead, they gave me the cold shoulder. Daphne pronounced to the group, directly after my speech saying,

"Good on you, Alastair! It was great to get to know you. I wish you all the best!" She was smiling radiantly. I was touched by her heartfelt sentiments of well-wishing. After saying my farewells, which always were a protracted business, I went to the retreat's administrative quarters and paid for the weekend.

Finally, as my car trundled along the narrow lane, with the loch to my right, I said goodbye to another close shave at an attempt on my life. I knew that they would keep on coming, but one way or another, I had faith that I would come through these ordeals unscathed.

CHAPTER 29

THE HELICOPTER

In the early part of May 2015, I had arranged to pick up Pawel, a Polish man, who I had been on retreat with a couple of months back. I had started to get to know him over the last few months. He showed me around his rented house, which he shared with three others, before we set off on our retreat.

During the car journey, Pawel continued to emphasise the idea of mindfulness to me. It seemed to be the only concept he wanted to acquaint himself with. I tried to argue or reason with him that, although the key to the spiritual life was mindfulness, there were still many more riches to be gained from a deeper exploration of Buddhism. I also felt that his approach to the concept of mindfulness was a little one-sided. I got the impression that he seemed to be only scratching the surface of what mindfulness entailed, and that his understanding of the subject was a little too dry and barren. He just listened and at times murmured while I made my case. I tried to understand where Pawel was coming from, but I considered his view of Buddhism a little too narrow and circumscribed. All I was trying to do was open his eyes a little to the greater and more wondrous truths of the Dharma, or the Buddha's teachings.

I let go of the subject when we got closer to the venue. We were both concentrated on how to get there, with him helping me navigate using the GPS on his phone. I looked out for signposts to the village. It had been a sunny day, but by the time we arrived it had descended into darkness, interspersed with bright dots of light scattered amongst the silhouettes. When we got out of the car, I noticed a palpable stillness in the countryside around us.

"Pawel, can you feel how quiet and peaceful it is around here? It's wonderful, don't you think?" I said convivially. I looked around at the twinkling lights from homes in the distance and at Pawel's soft glowing face.

"Yes, I feel it as well. There's a beautiful energy," he replied with a slight hint of emotion, which he did not normally show. I also viewed prominent bright stars and a crescent moon in the night sky.

We made our way to the small registration building, where Bedwyr, an order member, and an older member called Orla, greeted us.

"Welcome to the retreat! It's good to see you both," Bedwyr said effusively.

"Hi Bedwyr! Thanks for the welcome," I replied.

"Likewise," Pawel pitched in.

"You'll all have a room to yourself, you'll be pleased to know. Do you require bed linen, or have you brought your own?" Bedwyr enquired.

"No, I'll be fine, thanks. I've brought my own. What room number am I in?" I asked.

"You're in Room 9 on the first floor, just by the stair door." Bedwyr said confidently without looking at the roster.

"That's very perceptive of you. You've obviously got a good spatial awareness and memory," I said with a measure of astonishment.

"It goes with the Buddhist territory," he replied with the faintest hint of smugness on his face. Why not feel a little proud knowing the whereabouts of the bedrooms so instinctively, I pondered? It is an art remembering the details of one's environment – both immediate and distant. Having been assigned our respective sleeping quarters, Pawel and I went straight to our rooms.

I set about making up my bed. Quite a few familiar faces from the Buddhist centre were here. Daire, for one. I would enjoy chatting to him, and perhaps spending a little quality time together. There was of course Bedwyr, and Dharmada, who was a very warm and conscientious practitioner of Buddhism and a good friend.

That night, I slept surprisingly well. I felt thoroughly refreshed the following morning. The theme of the retreat was specifically directed towards intensive meditation with no guidance or study at all – only interspersed with periods of silence and free time to explore the countryside.

On Saturday, after a full day of meditating, walking in the countryside, forging new friendships, developing existing ones and eating tasty vegetarian meals, we all rounded off the evening with a seven-fold puja. I then took myself off to bed with a light and buoyant heart.

That night, I was awoken by the drone of the rotating blades of a helicopter, as if it were a giant moth buzzing around the room. It sounded like it was landing not far from the building. It was 3:30am when I glanced at my watch, just after I had awoken. My ears had pricked up with immense curiosity at the unexpected noise. I wondered if it was perhaps landing in the field, as quite a lot of land belonged to the retreat headquarters.

The site used to be owned by an oil company. They had owned a large swathe of land, as well as the cluster of new and old buildings that were tightly grouped together in the sprawling complex. I thought it extremely unusual for a helicopter to be landing so early in the morning, especially in this hitherto peaceful and quiet countryside. Could this potentially be a crack team of SAS commandos trying to noiselessly storm my sleeping quarters, to kill off, in their eyes, this most wanted of men? Unlike on other previous occasions, I felt more robust and confident in facing this specific ordeal. Each new threatening experience would in some way deepen my confidence and trust in the cosmic forces mapping out my safe passage through the world. Although, with the events of the last couple of months, I still felt burdened by restlessness and a modicum of fear.

Awake, I calmly rested in my bed. The noise of the helicopter reverberated for what seemed like an hour. I imagined that the gods had magically warped the distance from my sleeping quarters to where the helicopter was stationed. The hit squad would think that they had not very far to run before they arrived at their target destination, but their range would be increased a thousandfold by the gods' magic.

The last thing I remembered before falling asleep was the continued hum of the moth-like beast. The next thing I knew I had awoken just before 6:30am. I collected my sponge bag and towel and went to the bathroom for a quick shower. I returned to my room with the curtain closed and the light on in my room. I rifled through my suitcase, deciding on the most appropriate article of clothing to wear, when Daire opened my bedroom door. He did not just open it a little, realising he had got the wrong door, but pushed it wide open. I was naked and crouching down on my haunches. Daire's eyes clapped onto mine for a good four to five seconds. Then with an abashed face, he stepped back, mumbled a soft "sorry", and closed the door. I immediately thought that this must undoubtedly be an honest mistake on the part of my friend. I let the incident wash over me.

At the first early morning meditation that Sunday, I noticed that none of the resident Buddhists had come to the morning sit. This was unlike the Saturday morning, when all of them were present. I pondered on whether this absence could be due to their complicity in last night's helicopter operation. *Were some of the Triratna order members perhaps trying to help the authorities with their aim of removing me from the planet?*

Later that morning, after a couple of sessions of rigorous meditation, I took myself away from the shrine room. Feeling light-headed due to the intensive nature of the meditation, Bedwyr advised me to lie down. He suggested I bring my focus into my feet and the lower part of my body to compensate for the giddiness I was experiencing. I was glad that I had never gone to the retreat in North Wales, where one would do intensive periods of meditation. From this minor incident, I was sure that I could not sustain that amount of meditation practice over a weeklong period. Probably due to various biological and psychological factors, I believed that some people were just not gifted in sustained periods of meditation. We would therefore need to meditate for relatively moderate periods at a time.

While I lay on my bed, the other retreatants were still in the shrine room. As I was trying to get over my trippy head, I still heard, on the odd occasion, a helicopter flying overhead with its subtle roars receding into the distance. I thought this would again be an ideal opportunity for someone to take my life, yet I nonetheless maintained a dignified calm.

On that Sunday in the early afternoon, we all gathered outside in a tarmacked area between two buildings with a border of different coloured roses lining one side. We all arranged ourselves in a circle. Orla asked the assembled throng to collectively recite a verse, entitled, "Transference of Merit and Self-surrender", in call and response. She then suggested that we chant in unison the beautiful phrase, "Sabbe Satta Sukhi Hontu", which translates as "May all beings be happy". This continued for a few minutes before the chanting gradually petered out.

I noticed that when we were saying our farewells, a few of the people were a little unfriendly. One tall woman in her thirties had a very unconvincing smile. She weakly draped her arms around me. She left me feeling cold and a shade suspicious that she might be doubting my honesty and authenticity.

CHAPTER 30

THE MONK

A few days after the retreat, I arrived at the Birmingham Buddhist Centre for a study group session. While I was sitting by one of the many tables in the main café area, I was engrossed in conversation with a mild-mannered German man named Sven. We were discussing how his PhD, in a particular aspect of Psychology, was going. He was relating how he had needed to produce a lengthy document in record time. This had taken its toll on his stress levels. This was due to the tight time constraints, but also because it was a very important document that would be assessed by senior academics in his field.

After about 15 minutes rapt in intriguing dialogue with him, Ciaran, an order member, emerged from the corridor adjacent to the café area. As he came up the steps to the elevated seating area, I said, "Hello." This amicable gesture he completely ignored. Instead, he chose to talk directly with Sven in a friendly manner.

Ciaran was a softly spoken man in his seventies. He appeared gentle and humble, but in my opinion, appearances can be deceptive. He would now and then show a more harsh and critical side to his personality. I could not be sure, but I believed from our various encounters over the years that I knew him that he was not entirely genuine and sincere, at least to me. He was an intellectual and a Cambridge graduate. In some ways, I wondered if this fierce rational intelligence sometimes got in the way of a more heartfelt warmth.

He parked himself opposite, and rarely looked in my direction. He wore a very stern expression. The weather happened to have been sunny that day. I asked him gently,

"Did you sit out on your terrace this afternoon?"

"Terrazzo, please – not terrace! And no, I didn't sit out there, but just remained indoors." He said this with venom, which I distinctly registered. I felt he just wanted to be difficult. Whatever I had said, he would have responded with a harsh comment. I was sure of this.

Afterwards, on my drive home, I mulled things over in the car. Could Ciaran's unexpected hostility towards me be in any way connected with the events of that previous weekend retreat? It was a possibility. He had rarely been so unwelcoming in the past. It was not as though he responded to Sven like he had reacted to me. Therefore, one could assume this was not his general mood that evening. By all accounts, it was uncharacteristic of his normally mild-mannered demeanour.

Also, on the retreat, why did Daire open my bedroom door and stare at me for so long? He must have known that the door he was opening was not the exit to the staircase. *Surely!?!* I was still prepared to give them both the benefit of the doubt and tried not to jump to conclusions.

The following morning after I had showered, I came out of my bathroom with a towel draped around my waist. I checked my phone for messages or calls. There had been a missed call from Ciaran. He had left a voicemail. I thought he might be feeling he should be apologising for the previous evening's behaviour. Instead, he said in the message,

"Hello, Alastair. It's a lovely day today. I'm thinking I would like to go for a walk. It would be nice if you could join me. We could perhaps go to the woods. It would be good if you could get back to me, thanks."

In the message, his tone wavered. It sounded bogus. This made me exceedingly wary and distinctly anxious. He had never taken the trouble to get to know me outside the context of the Buddhist centre. *Why was he doing it now, and so soon after yesterday's antagonism towards me?* My first thought was he was working in collaboration with MI5, and they would engineer an allegedly innocent stroll. This would result in secret service agents trying to carry out a hit on my life again, while hiding in the bushes.

A mushrooming narrative was building in my mind about specific members of the order and my perception of their possible duplicitousness towards me. *Had what I experienced last weekend been kosher? Did I need not be suspicious? Or had it in fact resounded with deceitfulness and a sinister edge?* I could not be 100 percent sure, but I felt that I could not place my trust in some of them anymore. Again, I continued to reflect on all sorts of characters I had met on my retreats in Birmingham and in other centres I had gone to, both in England and in Scotland. This time I was well. I believed I was thinking with a heightened clarity of mind.

I was still getting my regular course of medication, and it was completely beneficial for me. I was eating healthily, and getting regular daily exercise, while also finding emotional nourishment in my relationship with family and friends, whom I visited often. With my friends especially I could be open and honest in my communication, which was a good substitute for talk therapy. Although I still thought that I might be a Truman show character, I was not fixating on the idea, which showed that I was in a much better mental space.

I was open to the fact that, on the one hand, my experience of the recent helicopter incident and its aftermath had been tainted with a scintilla of confusion, but I also felt that it was filled with a degree of lucidity. I could not be certain though.

I spent the whole of that Thursday and most of Friday reflecting on this topic. On the Friday evening I joined an evening's puja with a very small number participating. I appreciated this small, intimate gathering, given my slightly delicate mental state.

Throughout the evening, I mentioned nothing of my intent to leave to anyone. There was a woman at the puja, who I had total faith in. She had expressed to me some views that a lot in the movement would have found outlandish. To my more open mind, they were in sync with my own very personal takes on reality. I discreetly got her number before she left, saying I would contact her soon to discuss something that I could not divulge at this present juncture. She had a rather open energy, but as I found out later, she was extremely sensitive to the way some order members behaved towards her. This could sometimes be painful.

After the puja, Dharmada, who had been leading the evening's devotional ceremony, would often talk to people with sensitivity. He displayed a genuine quality of kindness, normally manifesting through calm and interested facial expressions and mannerisms. He spoke to me softly and slowly, saying,

"A taste of freedom tonight, don't you think?"

"You're right there! You know, Dharmada, I really value you as a good friend that I can trust. I hope we'll continue to have contact with each other." We then hugged, which felt nourishing. Inwardly, I thought that this was a wonderfully appreciative way to part from the movement, so unlike my poisonous email last year. I made sure that evening that no one would know that I was leaving, pretending to be fully engaged with it all.

Saraha, who I had got to know over the past six years, was someone who I could also profoundly trust. However, he was too deeply embedded in the structure of the Triratna Community to be able to clearly see the issues with certain order members. I would not hold that against him. I knew I had to act on my own impulses to leave behind the fellowship that I had been drawn to for so long.

The following morning, I wrote an e-mail to the ordination team in Norfolk. It read,

Dear All

Following certain events that happened last weekend in Herefordshire, and what I learned through my episode near the beginning of last year, plus how one order member acted towards me, leaving a very peculiar voice message on my phone this Thursday morning, I have decided not to be part of Triratna anymore, in any shape or form. Before you ask if I am experiencing another episode, I would say I have never felt better health-wise, mentally as well as physically. I have come to this conclusion from the evidence around me. As mentioned before from last weekend, I do not want

*to go into the reasons – suffice to say – I have been applying the principles
of reason and intuition to my experiential findings.*

*The other notable difference between this and the last time I announced
my resignation from the order is that I feel a lot of love and appreciation
for you all, and not the previous ill-will. A lot of you have been very
accomplished teachers. You have taught me so much useful and helpful
material. A lot of you have also been very friendly towards me, and this I
have also very much valued.*

*I will be, from today, withdrawing all contact from the movement, and I
wish you all well with whatever you do with your lives. However, it would
be futile to try and persuade me to come back to the movement, as I have
now made a firm resolve.*

With Metta,
Alastair

Once I had sent the email, I went to London on a day's cultural
excursion, which I had been planning for a month.

I had a great day out. One symbolic – one might say mythical –
event happened, while I was walking to the Tate Modern, just
underneath the Oxo Tower Wharf building. As I walked under
the arcade, a Far Eastern Buddhist monk in dark brown robes
magically appeared from behind the columns and outer wall. With
a distinct glow in his eyes and a beaming smile, he wanted me to
have a shining gold card and dark brown rosary beads. The card
read "Lifetime Peace" on one side, and on the reverse, it said, "Work
smoothly". It also had a picture of a Bodhisattva, a being dedicated
to enlightenment for the sake of all other sentient beings, or in other
words a Buddha-to-be, emblazoned on it. He then asked me for
donations, in return for the gift.

As I displayed my cash, which was tightly wedged inside a slim
metal case, the monk gesticulated vigorously. He pointed to my pound
notes, expressing what seemed to me like an urgent plea to part with
all my cash.

"Donations, donations!" the monk kept repeating in a jolly and exuberant way. I was a little reluctant in donating the rest of my cash to him, although admittedly, I could still use my credit card to pay for a meal at the Tate Modern. I did feel a little uncomfortable in letting go of all my physical money but felt this incident had acted as a spiritual test. I therefore went ahead and separated myself from all my remaining cash.

What seemed mysterious was how I had left the Triratna Buddhist community the previous evening, and now on the first day emerging into a new dawn, I had met what I felt was a truly spiritually developed being. What happened that specific Saturday morning was a wonderful exchange of positive energy. This chance encounter made me feel totally inspired and exhilarated. I realized then that as I was stepping out into a new horizon, the universe would forever be looking out for me.

ACKNOWLEDGEMENTS

This book emerged initially from the praise of two senior order members at the Birmingham Buddhist Centre, whose opinions I valued and respected. The two older gentlemen's encouragement really sowed the seeds of confidence that I could embark on the enormous challenge of completing my own book. Then, in 2014, the thought came to me that the events that had taken place in my life that year were momentous and could make for an exciting read for anyone interested in knowing more about psychosis, mania, the architectural field or my long-established path as a Buddhist.

This is where I would like to thank Sammacitta Muller, the chairperson of the Birmingham Buddhist Centre at the time, for helping me to edit and refine the text in the first four chapters of my book. I believe she played a large role in enlivening and sharpening the text where it was most crucial. Unfortunately, she had to attend to an unwell mother, so could not continue with the work on the book. Above all, she brought a freshness and joy to our exchanges.

There is also Sarah Bayliss, a wonderful woman and dedicated English teacher, who I met at a Buddhist class. She commented, after having read the book, that I should probably not pitch it as a psychological thriller. Another woman thought it would work better as a memoir. I was a little reluctant at first to change the genre, but once Paul Rose, a good friend, had read it, and concurred with Sarah's statement, saying that he felt in no way tense or frightened while reading the book; I decided to pitch it differently – as an enlightening memoir of mental health and spirituality.

Then there is Adam Ryan, a lover of books and writing, who helped me to edit and proofread my initial manuscript. He gave some very welcome feedback at the initial stages, as well as a thorough and meticulous examination of the text, which I very much welcomed. Unfortunately, his work commitments were onerous, and he had to attend to them. However, he was able to give me very helpful written feedback on the first seven chapters of my book.

At the very end of the editing process, I asked Sue Kenney, a woman who I had just got to know at the Buddhist group in Leamington Spa, whether she would like to give me a critique of my manuscript. I think it was the good vibe I got from her that persuaded me to enlist her support. With a very limited timescale, she really rose to the challenge, and gave me some invaluable advice, which has made the text that bit richer.

I would particularly like to thank Cherish Editions, the hybrid publishing house, who have been so supportive in bringing this book to life, with a special mention to Soraya Nair, Sean McLeod and Andrea Marchiano. They unfailingly replied to all my queries and held my hand throughout the publishing process with an attention to detail yet with a lightness of touch.

Finally, I want to thank my parents for being so loving and supportive throughout my time writing and for coming to the view that it was doing me a world of good, despite being unconvinced of the financial rewards that might come my way. I have poured my heart into this work with a searing honesty, and I hope you appreciate this illuminating account of the struggle I underwent during this eventful period of my life.

ABOUT CHERISH EDITIONS

Cherish Editions is a bespoke self-publishing service for authors of mental health, wellbeing and inspirational books.

As a division of Trigger Publishing, the UK's leading independent mental health and wellbeing publisher, we are experienced in creating and selling positive, responsible, important and inspirational books, which work to de-stigmatize the issues around mental health and improve the mental health and wellbeing of those who read our titles.

Founded by Adam Shaw, a mental health advocate, author and philanthropist, and leading psychologist Lauren Callaghan, Cherish Editions aims to publish books that provide advice, support and inspiration. We nurture our authors so that their stories can unfurl on the page, helping them to share their uplifting and moving stories.

Cherish Editions is unique in that a percentage of the profits from the sale of our books goes directly to leading mental health charity Shaw Mind, to deliver its vision to provide support for those experiencing mental ill health.

Find out more about Cherish Editions by visiting cherisheditions.com or by joining us on:
Twitter @cherisheditions
Facebook @cherisheditions
Instagram @cherisheditions

Cherish
EDITIONS

ABOUT SHAW MIND

A proportion of profits from the sale of all Trigger books go to their sister charity, Shawmind, also founded by Adam Shaw and Lauren Callaghan. The charity aims to ensure that everyone has access to mental health resources whenever they need them.

You can find out more about the work Shaw Mind do by visiting their website: shawmind.org or joining them on

Twitter @Shaw_Mind
Facebook @ShawmindUK
Instagram @Shaw_Mind

Your Local Mental Health & Wellbeing Charity